The Unofficial LEGO Color Guide

Christoph Bartneck, PhD

5th Edition

i

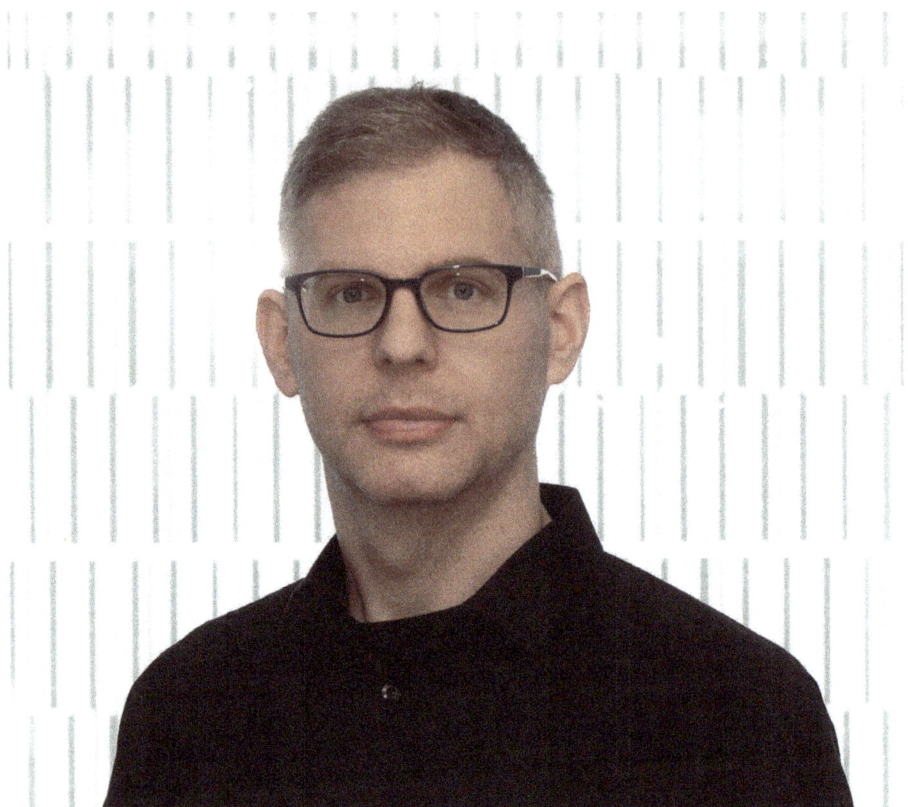

Dr. Christoph Bartneck is a professor at the University of Canterbury, New Zealand. He worked for the LEGO Group in Billund in the 90s, which reignited his passion for LEGO. Since then, he worked in the USA, Netherlands, Japan and now in New Zealand as a researcher and designer. His research focuses on anthropomorphism in robots and figures, and his research has been published in acknowledged scientific journals and books.

5th Edition, Version 1.0, printed in 2022 by IngramSpark
ISBN-13: 978-0473628550

National Library of New Zealand Cataloguing-in-Publication Data:
A catalogue record for this book is available from the National Library of New Zealand.

Table of contents

Also Available:

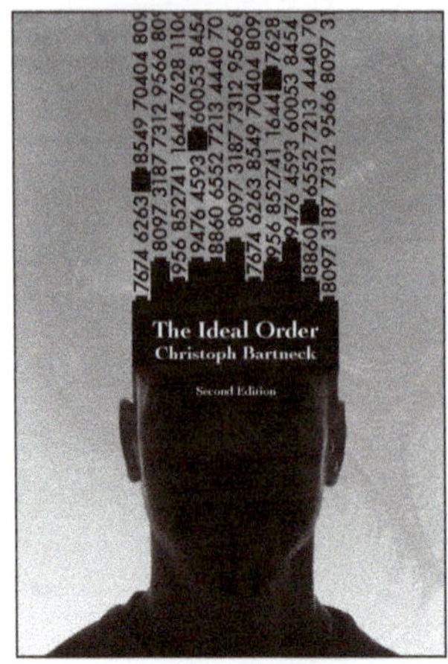

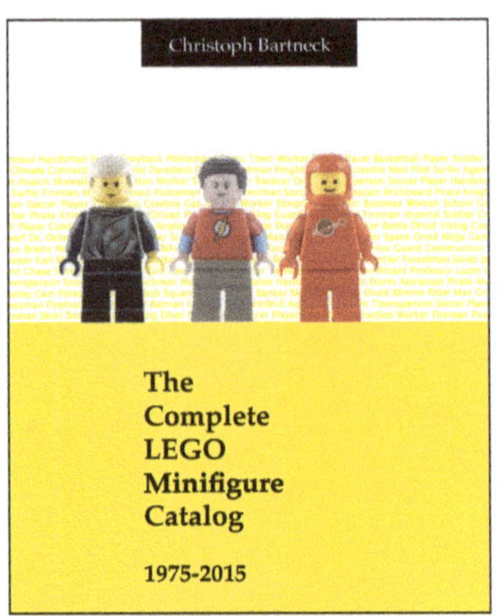

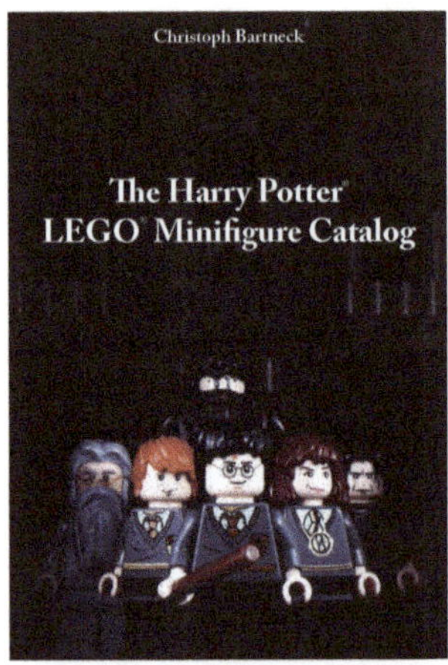

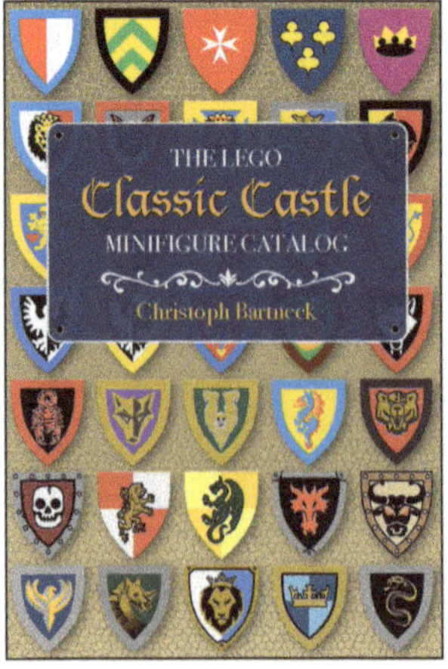

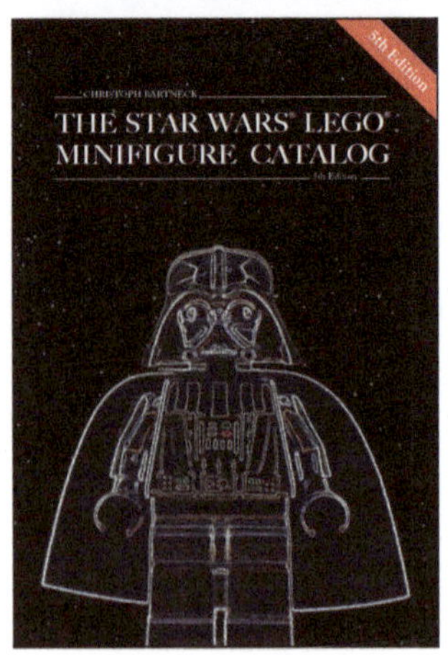

Introduction to the fifth edition

The LEGO company introduced several new colors in recent years and while most of them will remain exotic outliers, it is still worthwhile to include them in this catalog. A notable exception is the Medium Brown color, which is a welcomed addition to the spectrum of skin colors.

It is also important to notice that since the LEGO company took over Bricklink, some changes to the nomenclature have been made. Six colors were renamed. Most of these changes included the word "Flesh". For example, Medium Dark Flesh was renamed to Medium Nougat and Light Flesh was renamed to Light Nougat.

Around 26 colors that are in this catalog have now also been adopted by Bricklink and hence their meta information has been added, such as their rarity and their Bricklink ID. In addition, the color proximity scores between the different colors are now included. A low score indicates a similar color.

Another improvement to the book is the rarity indicator. It is now being calculated based on a decimal scale. Colors that occur in more than 1000 parts are labeled "Many", colors that occur more than 100 times "Several", more than 10 times "Some" and more than 1 time "Few". Colors that are not listed as an official brick are considered "rare".

An important update happened behind the scenes. In the past I exported the color database to Adobe InDesign and then create the catalog from there. This process was complicated, labour intensive and error prone. The database has now been changed to create the catalog pages directly. Unfortunately, not all the design tricks possible with InDesign can be replicated with the database. The visual design was therefore modernised and extended.

I would also like to address one of the major criticisms that have been voiced. The ink colors in the book do not match the plastic colors of LEGO bricks. Printing is typically done with four colors: cyan, magenta, yellow and key (black). The mixing of these pigments opens a certain color space and many of LEGO's colors are outside of this color space. Some LEGO colors cannot be printed on paper. You computer screen or your mobile phone screen, however, have a much bigger color space and they are capable of approximating the LEGO colors much better. For identifying colors I would therefore recommend the eBook PDF and for lexical use the books. I hope you enjoy this updated and extended fifth edition.

Introduction

The colors of LEGO bricks are one of their main attractions. The spectrum of choices empowers LEGO builders of all ages to express their creativity; the more sophisticated the models become, the more conscious choices the designer will make about what exact color to use for their forest, building or vehicle. Over more than fifty years of producing plastic bricks, the LEGO company has produced more than 250 different colored bricks. The exact number produced is difficult if not impossible to determine since the differences are at the edge of what humans can perceive, and also because the LEGO company experimented with far more colors than those that made it into an actual product. Further, some colors have only been available for a short period at some LEGOLAND parks, and still others only as part of a watch or other accessory.

Many LEGO fans try to keep track of the colors, and the LEGO company itself released its current color palettes in 2010 and 2016. One of the main problems is that in those lists of colors the names and values do not always agree with each other. If we consider the Brick Yellow/Tan color, for example, we can find the following color definitions:

Source	Red	Green	Blue	Color
LEGO Palette 2010	217	187	123	
LEGO Palette 2016	221	196	142	
LEGO LDD	176	160	111	
Peeron	215	197	153	
Ryan Horwerter	176	160	111	
Bricklink	222	198	156	
Ldraw	228	205	158	
Clark Stephen	215	197	153	
Brickowl	222	198	156	
Linus Bohman	176	160	111	
Pantone 467 C	211	188	141	

Table 1: Definitions of Brick Yellow / Tan

One of the few device-independent color spaces is the International Commission on Illumination's LAB color space (CIELAB). The three dimensions of CIELAB represent the lightness of the color (L), the position between red and green (a) and the position between yellow and blue (b). CIELAB vastly expands other device-independent color spaces such as sRGB or Adobe RGB. The colors that a CMYK printer can produce are far less than those of sRGB (see Figure 1).

To overcome the problem of defining and representing LEGO colors this book takes two approaches. First, I used an X-Rite colorimeter to measure the solid LEGO colors in the CIELAB color space (see Figure 2). I verified the colorimeter by measuring the 24 patches Datacolor's SpyderCheckr 24. The colorimeter deviated by only 0.684% from the calibrated patches, showing that its accuracy and reliability are well suited for this task.

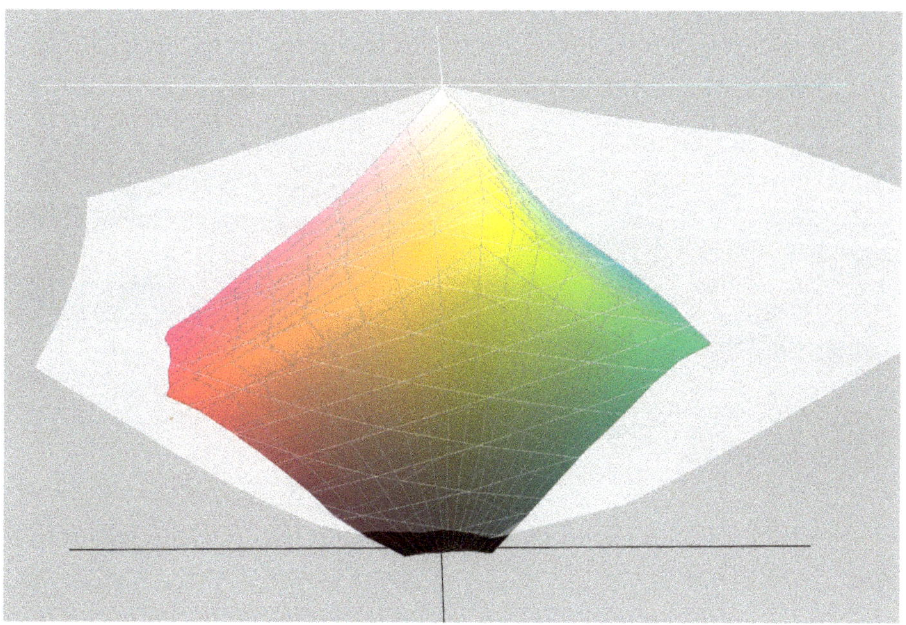

Figure 1: CMYK color space within the AdobeRGB color space.

Measuring sparkling, speckled or pearl surfaces makes little sense since the measurement will differ depending on the position of the colorimeter on the brick. Measuring the color of translucent plastics requires an expensive Transmission Densitometer. Needless to say, translucent materials cannot be accurately represented in a printed book. For non-solid materials it makes sense to fall back to the great work that fans have accomplished already and by using the information provided by the LEGO company. Second, I used a professional color management workflow to photograph sample bricks for each color. I calibrated my Nikon camera using Datacolor's SpyderCheckr 24 that includes 24 calibrated color patches. The accompanying software then calculates a camera and lightning specific profile. Moreover, I color calibrated my screen and worked with the publisher to include the color management information of their printers.

Once the colors have been defined they also require names and identification numbers. Again, we observe several competing and non-matching nomenclatures. If we use the example of the color Brick Yellow/Tan again, we notice that Bricklink gives it the ID 2 while the LEGO company gives it the name Brick Yellow and the ID 5. LDraw and Peeron give it different IDs and the color is also known as Sand. For the purpose of this book I gave preference to the original LEGO names and complemented them with Bricklink data when necessary. There were even a few cases in which I identified a mismatch between LEGO and Bricklink that required a new name and ID.

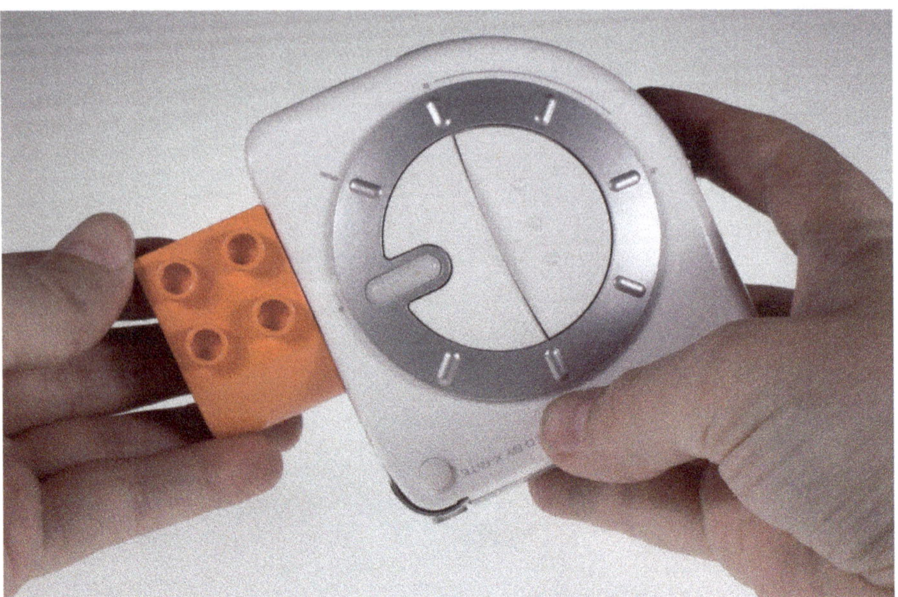

Figure 2: Measuring the color of LEGO brick with a colorimeter.

The remaining challenge is to order the colors in a meaningful sequence. The nature of a book is a one-dimensional representation. Each page shows a color and the sequence of pages is fixed. Reducing data points from the three dimensional CIELAB space to a one-dimensional sequence can only be achieved by dismissing information. One could, for example, sort all the colors along their lightness dimension, but this would result in a spectrum with many jumps in color. There is no good way of sorting the colors and hence I resorted to sorting the colors by their hue. For practical reasons I grouped them into four main categories with several subcategories as shown in the table of contents.

Finally, the company allowed itself at some time to produce colors that only ever appeared in one brick, with the brick itself also unique. Those are highly specialised and serve little purpose for builders. These bricks are labeled as "few" for their availability, while current colors are typically labled as "many".

I hope that this guide will help LEGO enthusiasts to identify colors and create amazing color palettes for their models.

Similarity

Some LEGO colors are very similar and it makes it hard to identify them. Below you find a comparison of popular color groups.

Pink/Purple

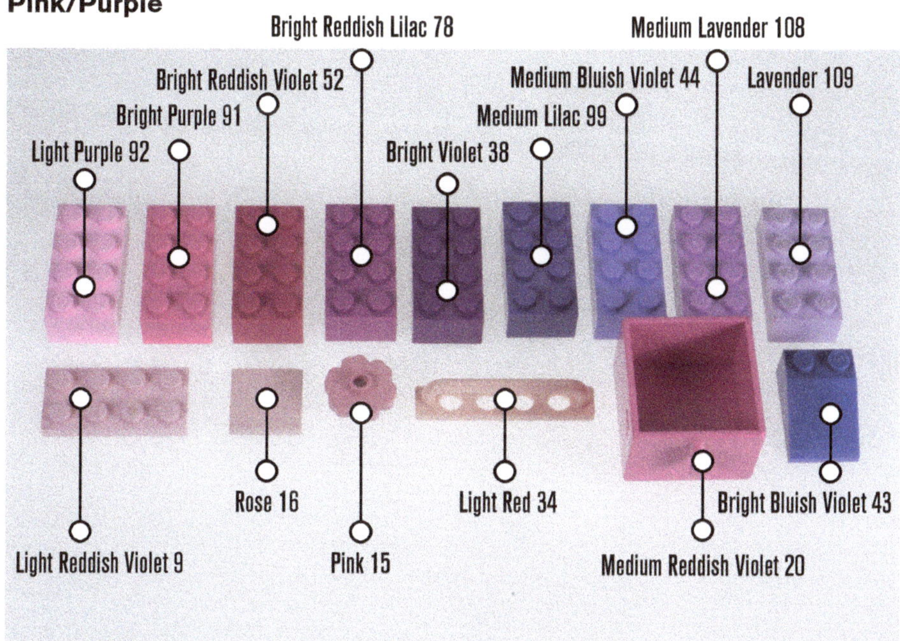

Blue

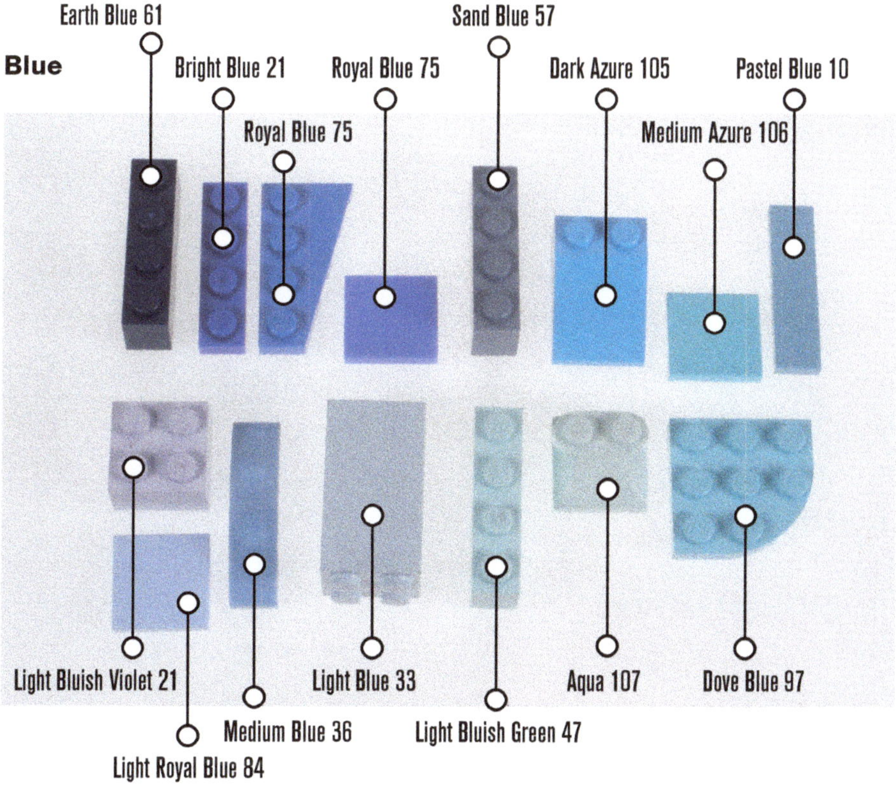

Brown

Brick Red 4
Light Orange Brown 11
Brown 87
Brick Yellow 5
Nougat 17
Medium Nougat 104
Sand Yellow 60
Dark Orange 31
Reddish Brown 72
Earth Orange 23
Dark Brown 103

Red

New Dark Red 66
Fabuland Red 113
Bright Red 19
Rust 112
Red Orange 12
Sand Red 65

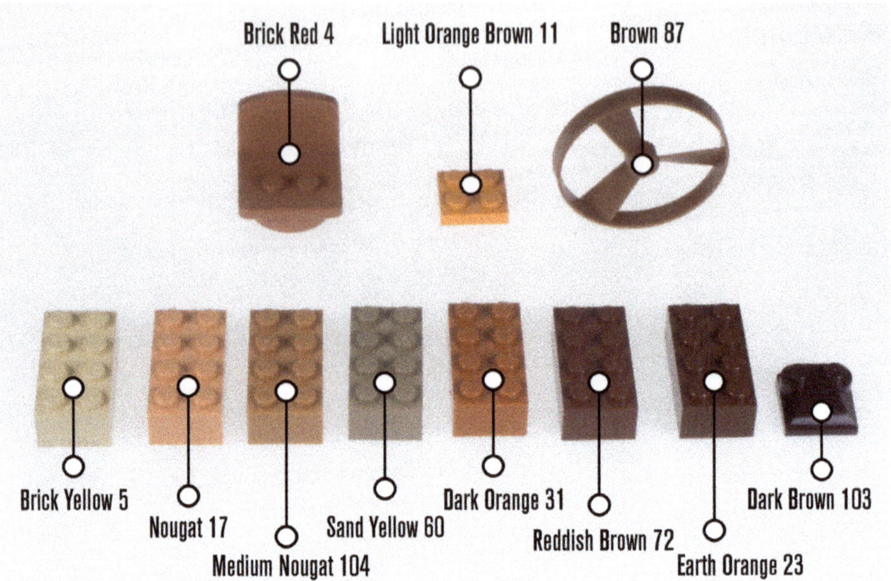

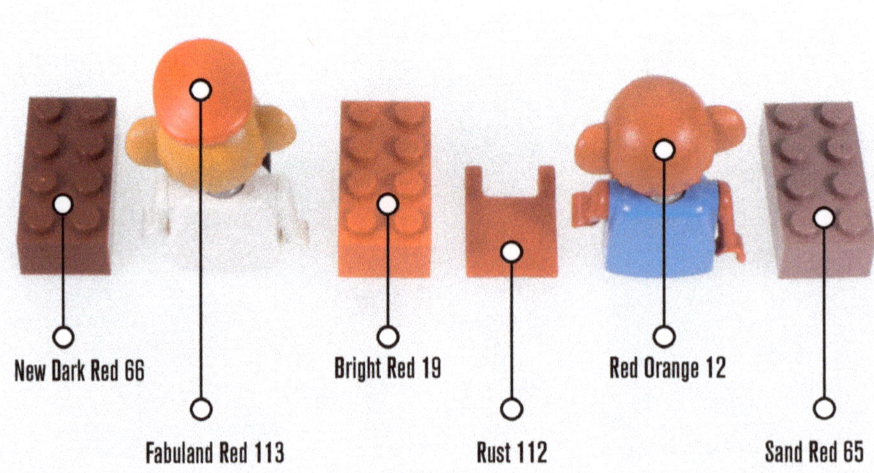

Orange/Yellow

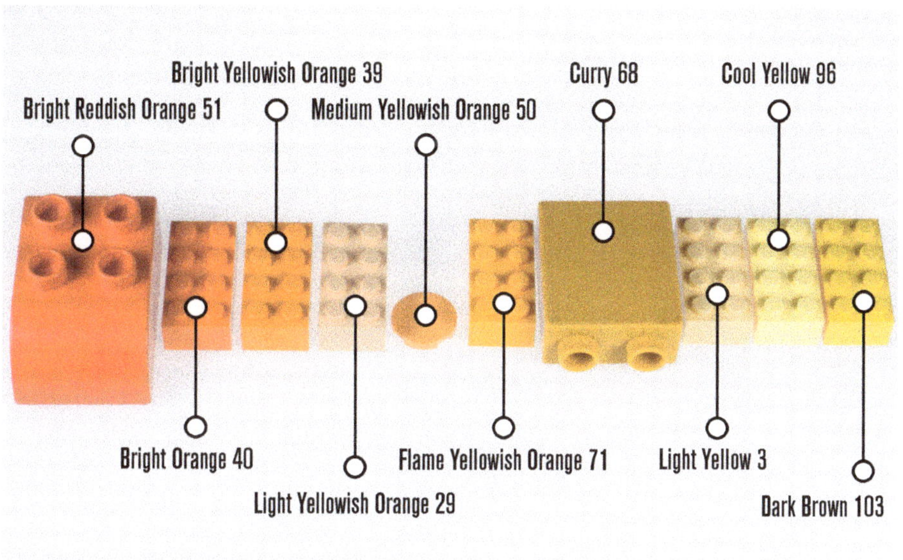

Green

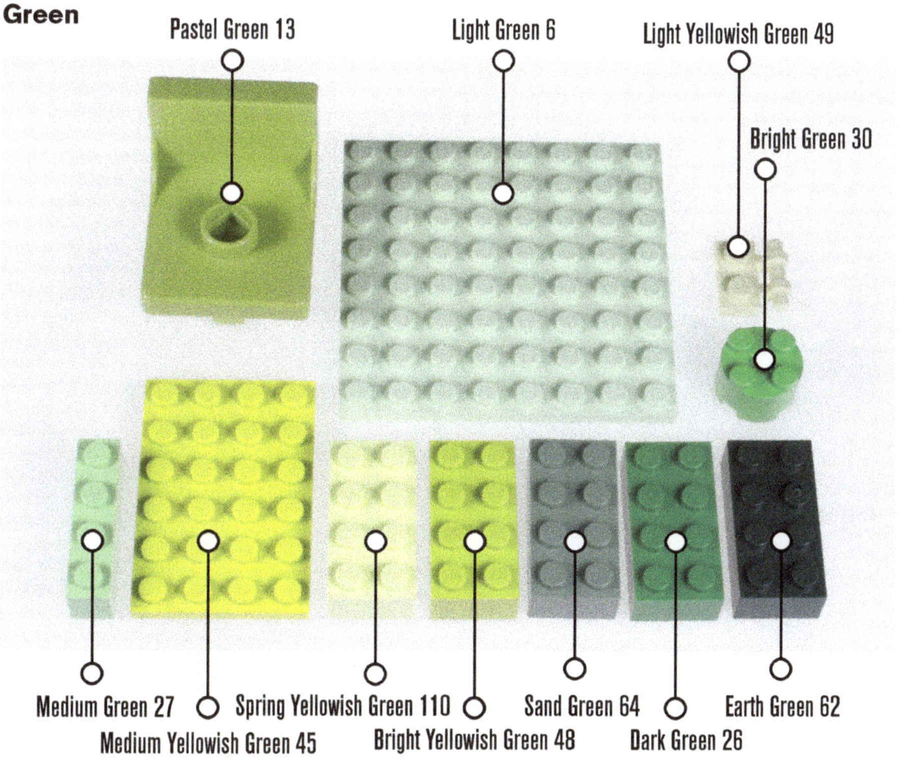

Grayscale

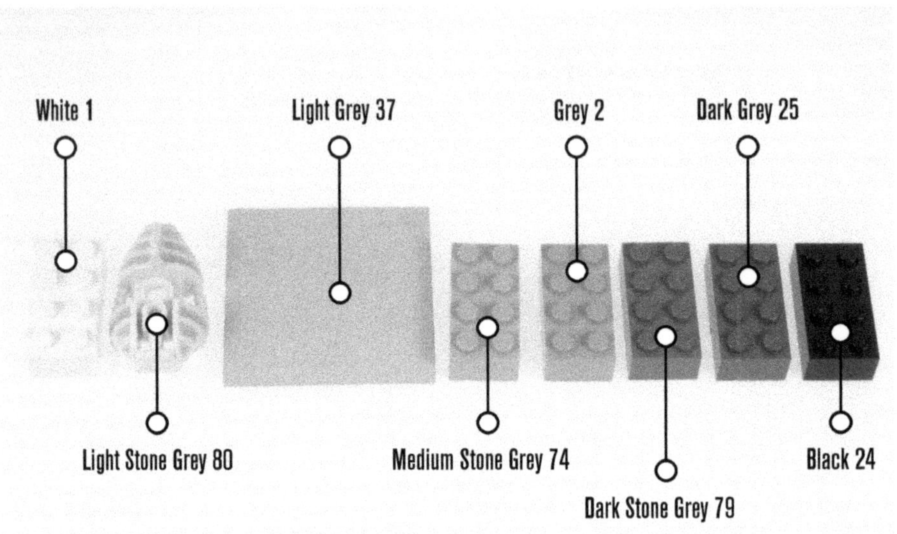

Silver

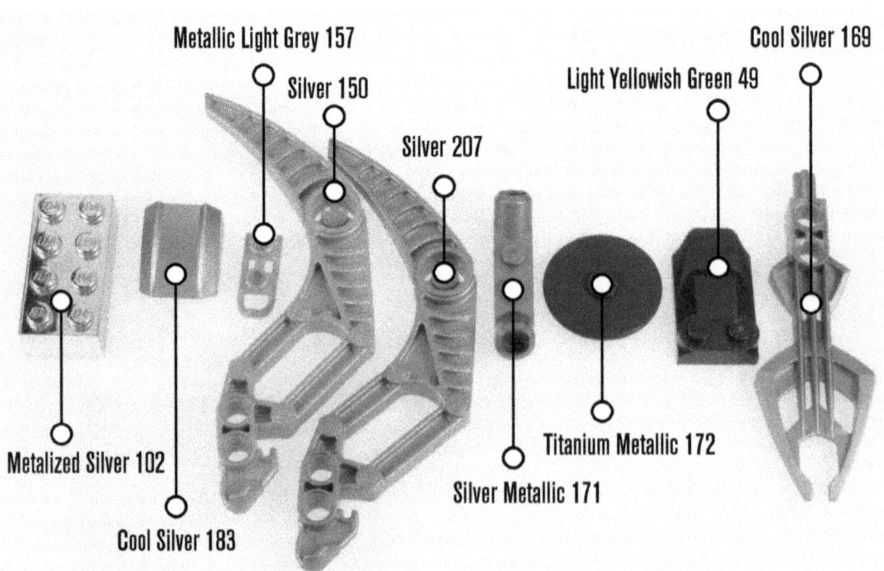

Gold

Metalized Gold 175
Warm Gold 184
Warm Gold 170
Gold 149
Reddish Gold 167

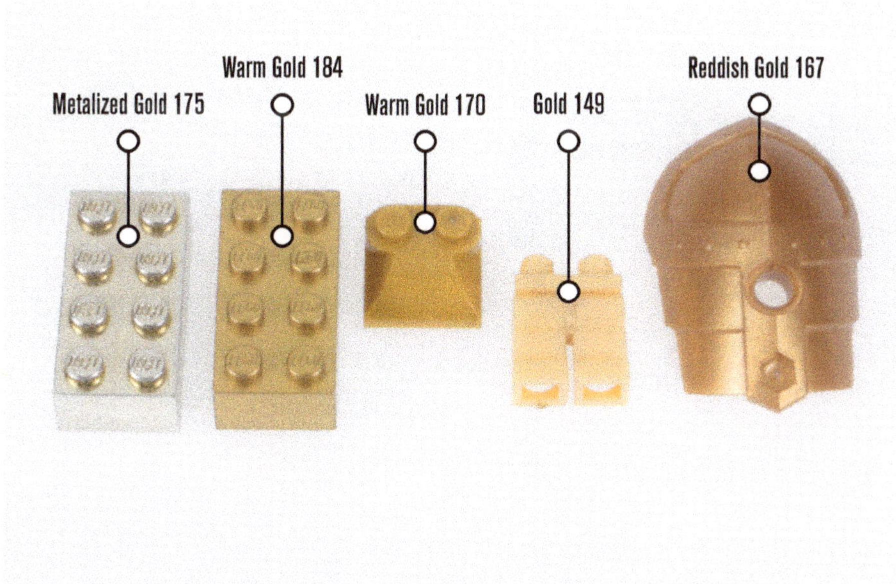

Color Index

The next pages show an index of all the colors in this book. Its information
is structured as:

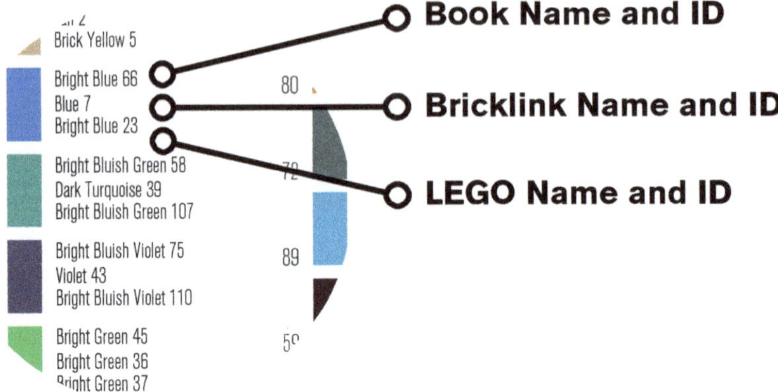

Solid Color

113 Solid Grayscale

Shiny Chrome

Transparent Glitter

Transparent Milky

183 Transparent Pearl

Mixed Glitter

Mixed Speckle

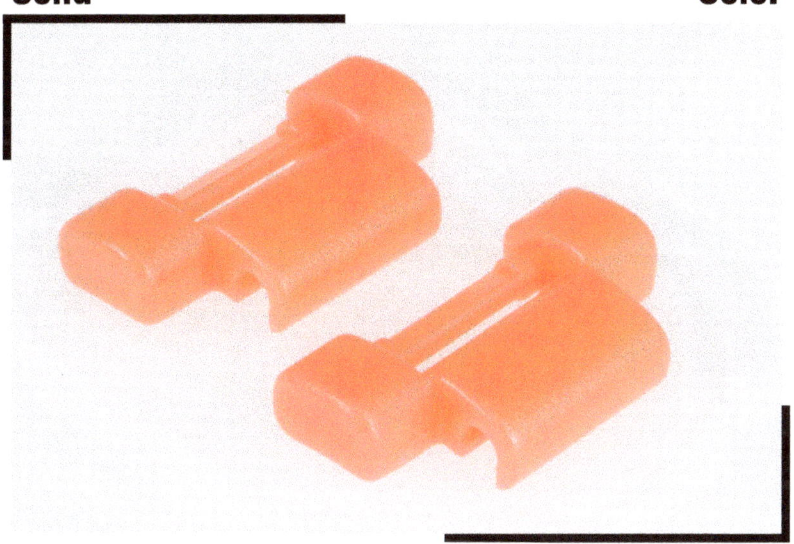

Neon Orange   1

Lego	Neon Orange	133
Bricklink	Neon Orange	165
UUID	8CFA91BD-3813-4251-8F24-FD6410EDB4BC	

Year	1997	**to**	2001	**Availability**	Rare

LAB	73	77	41	**Pantone**	805 C
sRGB	255	109	107		
CMYK	0	70	90	0	

Notes   Only used in Cyclone Master watch.

Proximity	Related Colors		Page
14.18	Vibrant Coral		114
28.79	Bright Reddish Orange		26
31.26	Medium Red		21
35.09	Fabuland Red		19
36.79	Bright Red		23
38.09	Red Orange		25

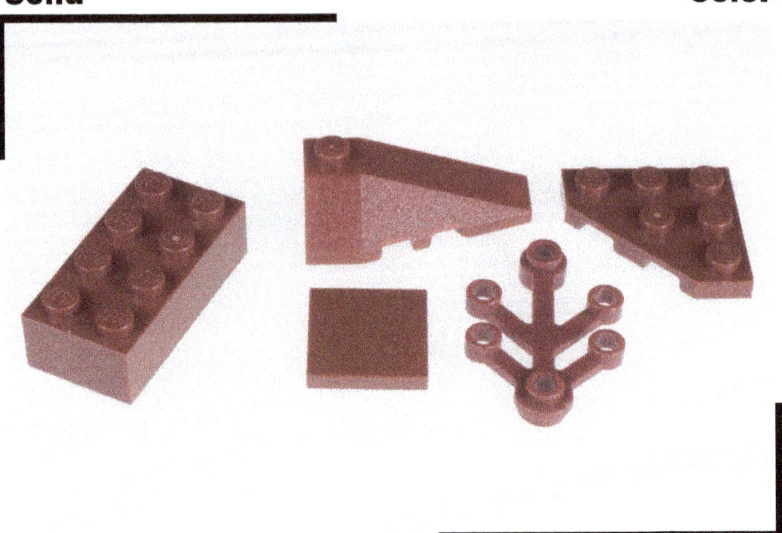

New Dark Red   2

Lego	New Dark Red				154
Bricklink	Dark Red				59
UUID	06A6F972-99A1-429C-8DC7-8554DE6F9E56				
Year	2001	to	current	Availability	Many

LAB	28	43	31	Pantone	181 C
sRGB	119	28	23		
CMYK	21	93	88	50	

Notes   In current color palette.

Proximity	Related Colors		Page
11.53	Rust		22
22.32	Reddish Brown		29
22.92	Rust		28
23.91	Red Orange		25
25.40	Earth Orange		36
26.88	Brick Red		31

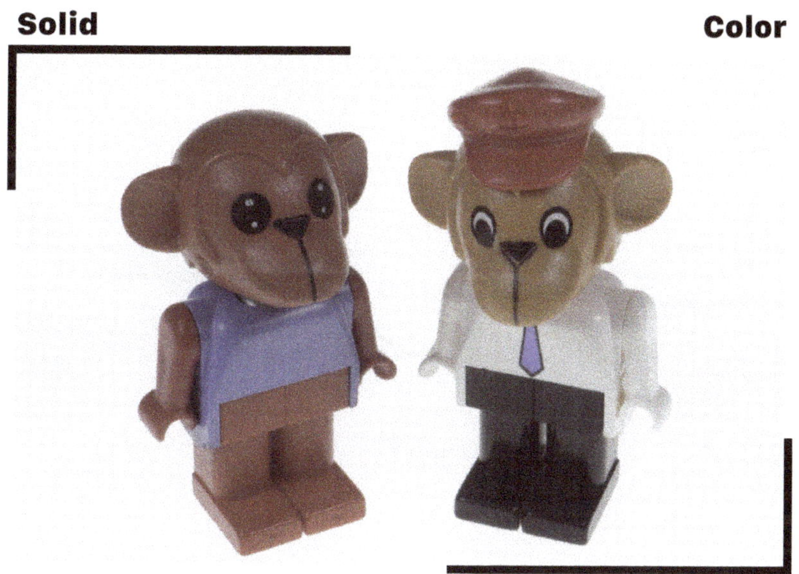

Fabuland Red   3

Lego	
Bricklink	
UUID	FD02333A-E187-41D5-A851-B5EB0266E233

Year	1979	**to**	1987	**Availability**	Rare

LAB	42	62	50	**Pantone**	1797 C
sRGB	180	36	22		
CMYK	2	97	85	7	

Notes   Red of the hat and the arms of the figures.

Proximity	Related Colors		Page
7.39	Bright Red		23
16.73	Red Orange		25
18.45	Bright Reddish Orange		26
20.54	Rust		22
27.49	Dark Orange		40
30.19	New Dark Red		18

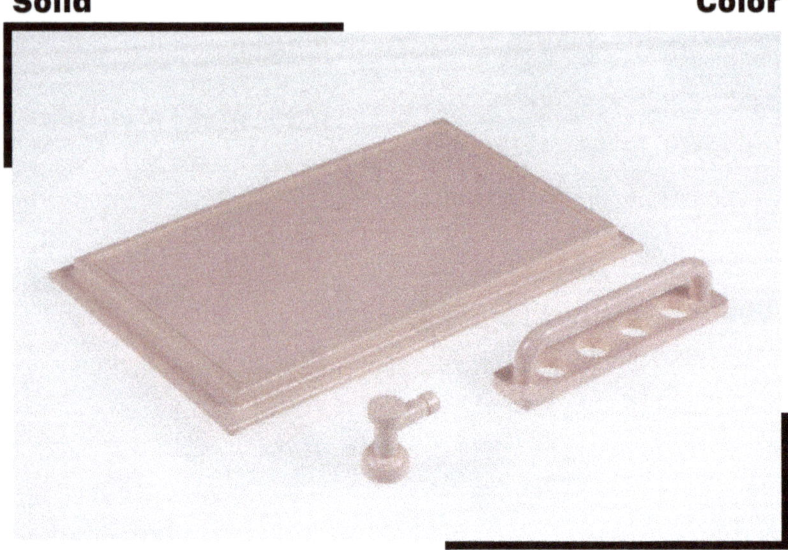

Light Red   4

Lego	Light Red				100
Bricklink	Light Salmon				26
UUID	648FDF75-697C-45E7-B138-08AE6C8CD306				
Year	1997	**to**	1999	**Availability**	Some

LAB	80	23	14	**Pantone**	169 C
sRGB	242	182	176		
CMYK	0	30	26	0	

Notes	Popular Scala color.

Proximity	Related Colors		Page
8.65	Rose		115
12.88	Light Nougat		37
16.31	Light Reddish Violet		112
22.76	Light Brick Yellow		48
23.75	Brick Yellow		49
27.02	Light Purple		107

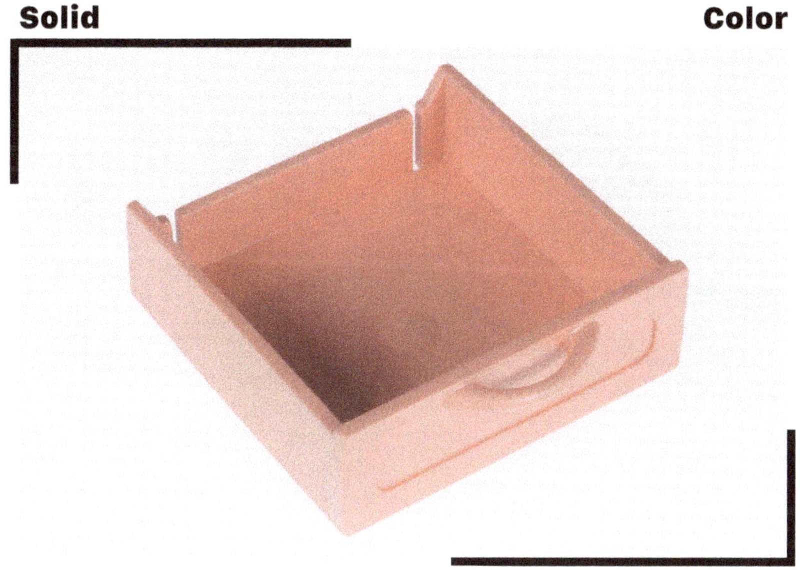

Medium Red   5

Lego	Medium Red				101
Bricklink	Salmon				25
UUID	BA2E3889-45C4-4961-9900-09963843E7AE				
Year	1997	**to**	1999	**Availability**	Some

				Pantone	
LAB	65	48	33	**Pantone**	178 C
sRGB	233	117	105		
CMYK	0	70	58	0	

Notes   A popular Scala color.

Proximity	Related Colors		Page
18.98	Nougat		35
19.21	Red Orange		25
23.51	Bright Reddish Orange		26
23.58	Vibrant Coral		114
25.51	Dark Nougat		33
27.60	Brick Red		31

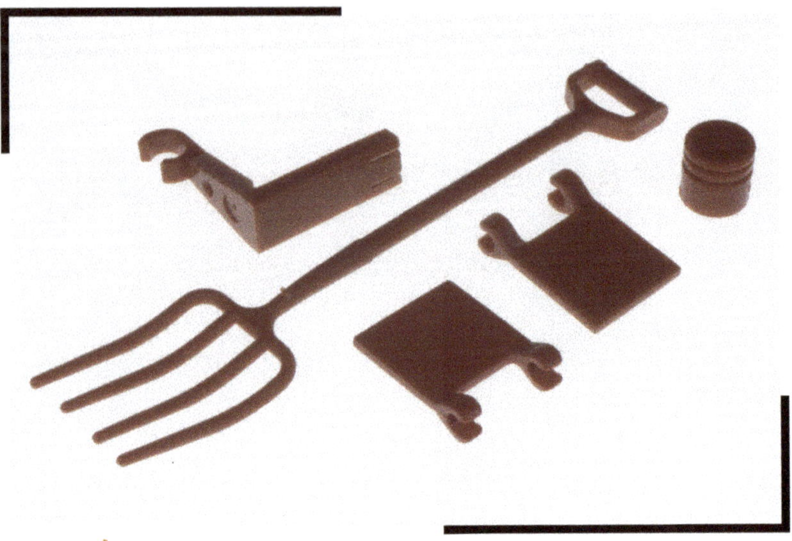

Rust   6

Lego					
Bricklink	Rust				27
UUID	B571E539-0878-4763-ABDA-314266DF96AB				
Year	1977	**to**	1999	**Availability**	Few

LAB	37	47	36	**Pantone**	484 C
sRGB	151	46	35		
CMYK	8	92	100	33	

Notes   One of the rust colors.

Proximity	Related Colors		Page
11.53	New Dark Red		18
12.72	Red Orange		25
20.54	Fabuland Red		19
23.91	Rust		28
24.01	Dark Orange		40
25.19	Brick Red		31

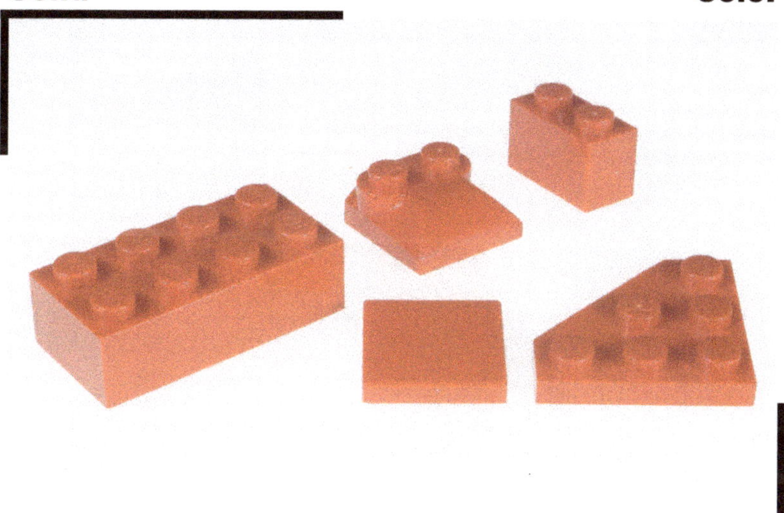

Bright Red   7

Lego	Bright Red	21
Bricklink	Red	5

UUID   58E11C64-2642-4FAA-BBAE-B049E34E65BF

Year	1950	**to**	current	**Availability**	Many

				Pantone	1797 C
LAB	41	65	56		
sRGB	180	23	5		
CMYK	2	97	85	7	

Notes   In current color palette.

Proximity	Related Colors		Page
7.39	Fabuland Red		19
20.12	Bright Reddish Orange		26
23.05	Red Orange		25
27.28	Rust		22
30.28	Dark Orange		40
36.08	Bright Orange		38

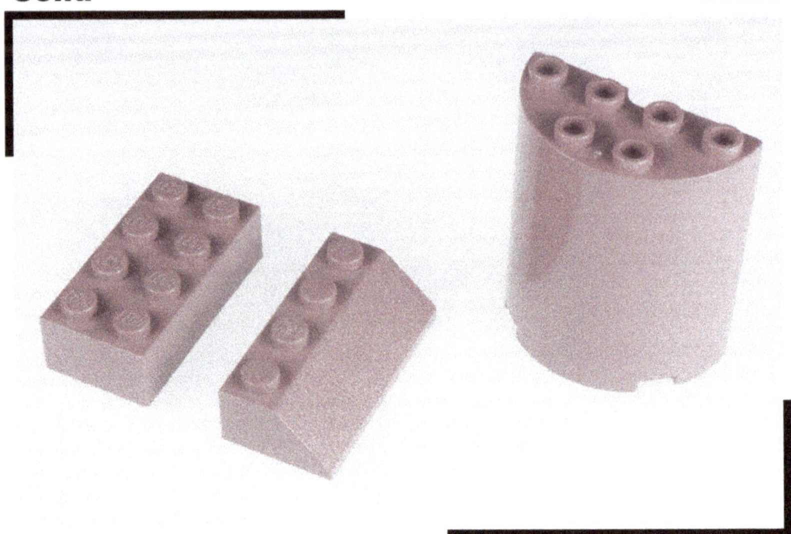

Sand Red   8

Lego	Sand Red	153
Bricklink	Sand Red	58

UUID	A085EA77-7AE9-4E4A-BA26-708A7283286D

Year	2001	to	2004	Availability	Some

				Pantone	4715 C
LAB	53	18	11		
sRGB	158	115	110		
CMYK	17	59	60	45	

Notes	Only lasted for four years.

Proximity	Related Colors		Page
15.17	Pink		113
16.42	Sand Yellow		47
17.51	Brown		34
18.98	Sand Violet		104
19.27	Rust		28
20.08	Brick Red		31

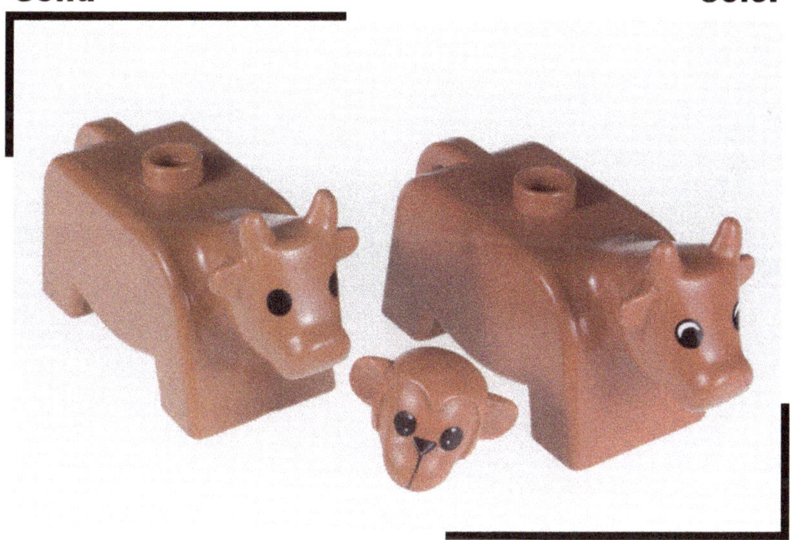

Red Orange   9

Lego	Red Orange				13
Bricklink					
UUID	08481AB0-5375-4621-A9ED-6E01BF580BB6				
Year	1979	**to** unspecifi		**Availability**	Rare

				Pantone	
LAB	48	48	43	**Pantone**	180 C
sRGB	185	72	48		
CMYK	3	91	86	12	

Notes   Another rust color used in only a few Fabuland parts.

Proximity	Related Colors		Page
12.72	Rust		22
16.73	Fabuland Red		19
17.80	Bright Reddish Orange		26
18.84	Dark Orange		40
19.21	Medium Red		21
23.05	Bright Red		23

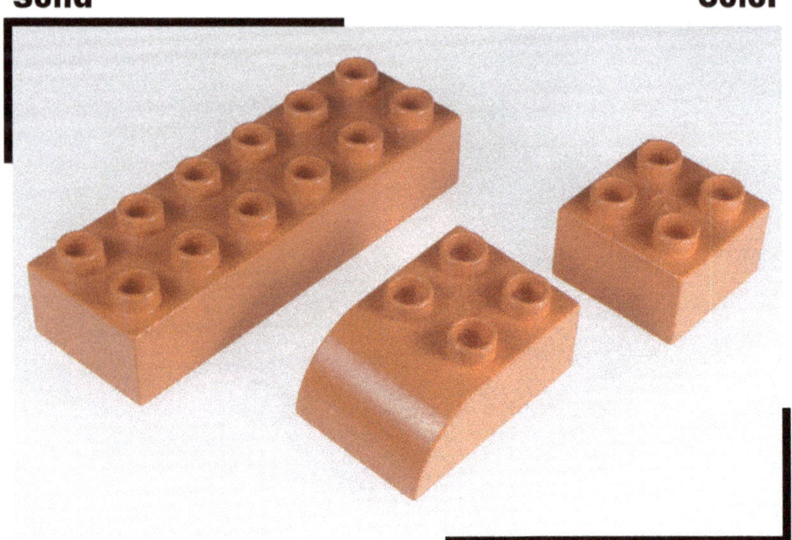

Bright Reddish Orange   10

Lego	Bright Reddish Orange			123
Bricklink	Dark Salmon			231
UUID	618C8401-96C3-4550-A05B-4A90CD3D7F82			
Year	2003	**to**	2004	**Availability** Few

LAB	59	56	54	**Pantone**	172 C
sRGB	227	90	52		
CMYK	0	73	87	0	

Notes   Only appeared in one DUPLO set (3513).

Proximity	Related Colors		Page
17.80	Red Orange		25
18.45	Fabuland Red		19
20.12	Bright Red		23
23.51	Medium Red		21
25.80	Bright Orange		38
25.81	Dark Orange		40

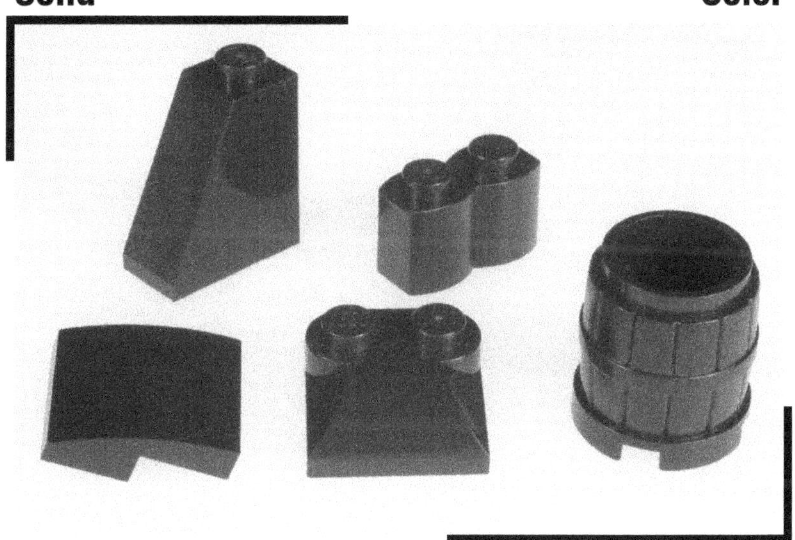

Dark Brown   11

Lego	Dark Brown	308
Bricklink	Dark Brown	120
UUID	CDD164EF-0837-4E37-B1FA-458222AD1CAA	

Year	2008	**to**	current	**Availability**	Several

					Pantone	476 C
LAB	21	10	10			
sRGB	67	44	37			
CMYK	30	71	75	81		

Notes   In current color palette.

Proximity	Related Colors		Page
16.24	Medium Brown		32
20.50	Earth Orange		36
21.07	Reddish Brown		29
21.53	Black		123
22.71	Dark Grey		118
22.96	Brown		34

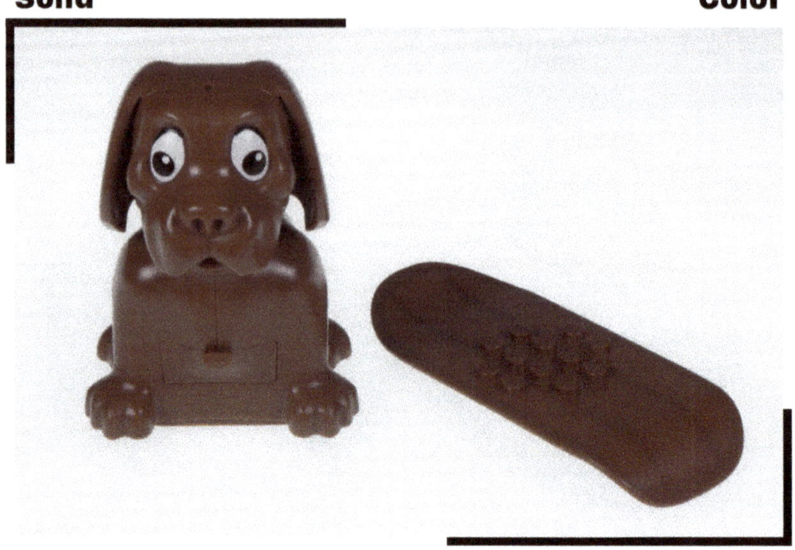

Rust   12

Lego	Rust						216

Bricklink

UUID   D3F71288-7012-485B-9612-96DE320030EF

Year	2004	**to**	2005	**Availability**		Rare

					Pantone	7524 C
LAB	43	27	25			
sRGB	144	82	63			
CMYK	12	78	62	25		

Notes   Another rare Rust color. Only appeared in very few sets.

Proximity	Related Colors		Page
6.87	Brick Red		31
10.86	Dark Nougat		33
12.66	Brown		34
12.77	Reddish Brown		29
16.57	Medium Brown		32
17.39	Medium Nougat		39

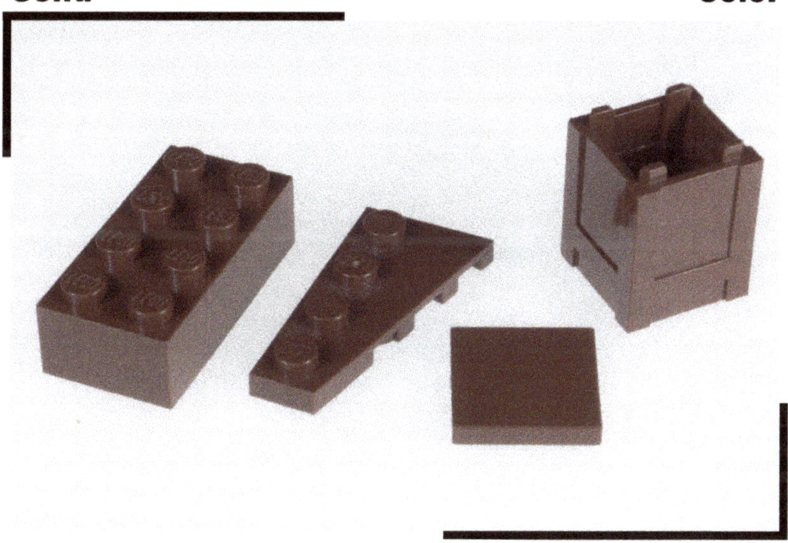

Reddish Brown   13

Lego	Reddish Brown	192
Bricklink	Reddish Brown	88
UUID	B2F7D162-6914-497B-80E7-8B78E309BB63	

Year	2003	**to**	current	**Availability**	Many

LAB	31	22	24		**Pantone**	478 C
sRGB	108	57	38			
CMYK	19	79	84	61		

Notes   In current color palette.

Proximity	Related Colors		Page
6.44	Earth Orange		36
10.09	Medium Brown		32
11.42	Brown		34
12.77	Rust		28
18.29	Brick Red		31
21.07	Dark Brown		27

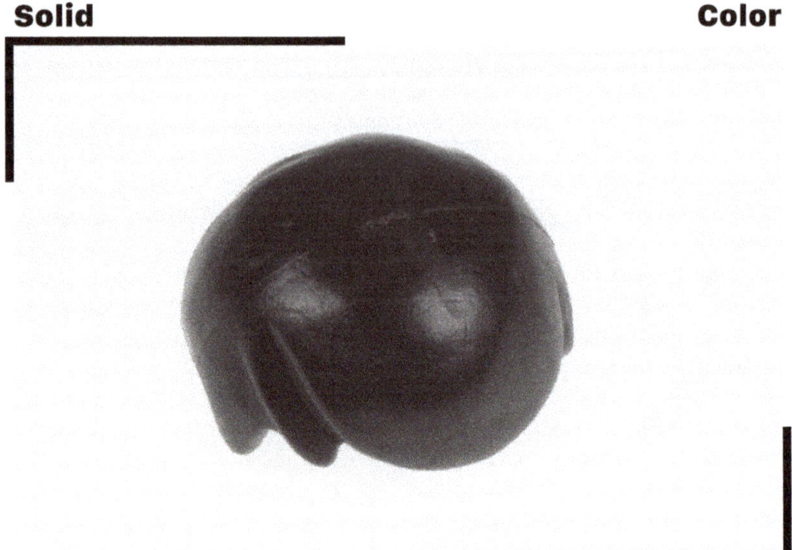

Homemaker Brown   14

Lego					
Bricklink					
UUID	94A7852B-EC7A-492B-AF51-8790F666D37C				
Year	1974	**to**	1980	**Availability**	Rare

LAB	21	7	97	**Pantone**	7533 C
sRGB	71	55	49		
CMYK	56	64	69	55	

Notes   Only in homemaker sets.

Proximity	Related Colors		Page
50.92	Curry		52
54.60	Dark Orange		40
58.96	Flame Yellowish Orange		50
59.57	Bright Yellowish Orange		46
60.51	Light Orange Brown		41
61.48	Bright Yellow		53

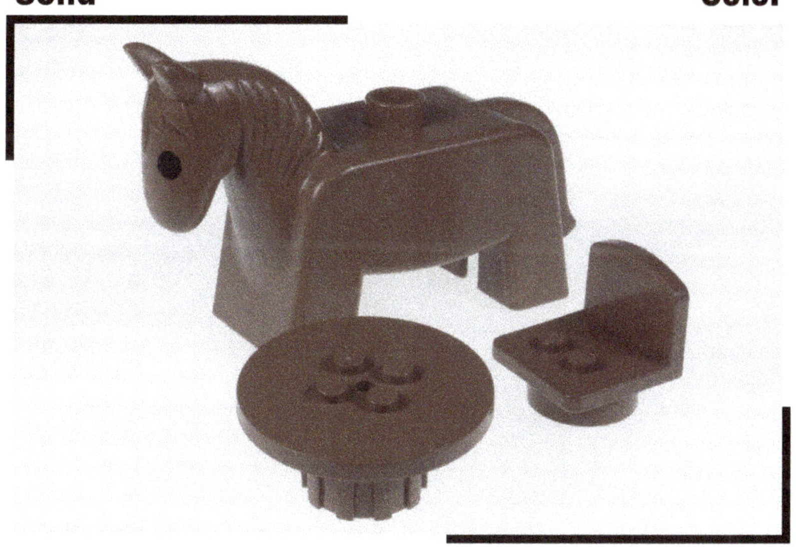

Brick Red   15

Lego	Brick Red					4
Bricklink	Fabuland Brown					106
UUID	EF84AA28-0E49-473E-AF56-AEA156DFCFEA					
Year	1979	**to**	1989	**Availability**		Few

				Pantone	7525 C
LAB	49	26	29		
sRGB	159	95	68		
CMYK	13	56	61	32	

Notes   Only used in Fabuland.

Proximity	Related Colors		Page
4.03	Dark Nougat		33
6.87	Rust		28
10.92	Medium Nougat		39
14.16	Light Brown		42
15.47	Brown		34
17.26	Light Yellowish Orange		44

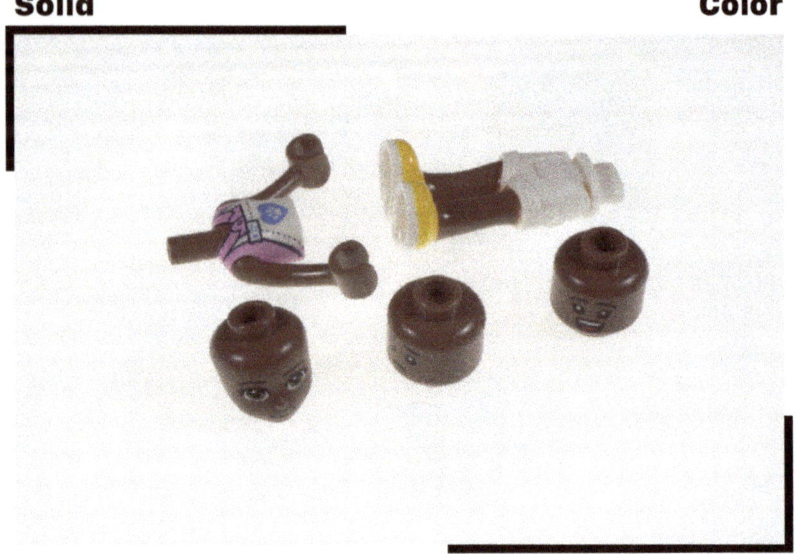

Medium Brown   16

Lego	Medium Brown			370
Bricklink	Medium Brown			240
UUID	8B4C66C0-B526-4E9B-B9B2-356CDB456CB3			
Year	2022 **to** current	**Availability**		Few

LAB	34	15	18	**Pantone**	148 1 5 C
sRGB	106	71	54		
CMYK	43	65	74	39	

Notes   Introduced in 2022 as a skin color.

Proximity	Related Colors		Page
6.84	Brown		34
10.09	Reddish Brown		29
12.00	Earth Orange		36
16.24	Dark Brown		27
16.57	Rust		28
19.67	Dark Grey		118

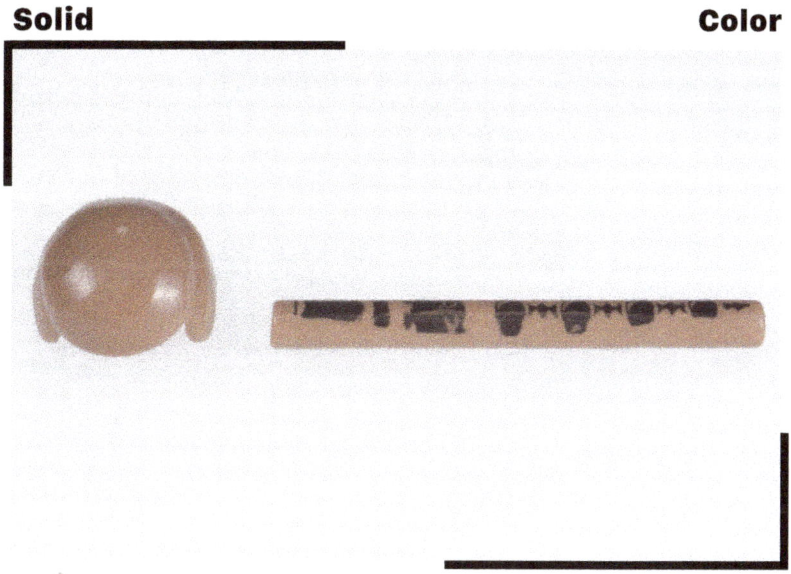

Dark Nougat   17

Lego	Dark Nougat	128
Bricklink	Dark Nougat	225
UUID	19E9982E-3714-48F8-AD88-CD089A33A7A0	

Year	2001	to	2002	Availability	Few

					Pantone	7525 C
LAB	52	26	31			
sRGB	169	104	72			
CMYK	13	56	61	32		

Notes	Know as "Vernon Dursley's hair".

Proximity	Related Colors		Page
4.03	Brick Red		31
8.00	Medium Nougat		39
10.86	Rust		28
11.98	Light Brown		42
14.81	Light Yellowish Orange		44
16.36	Nougat		35

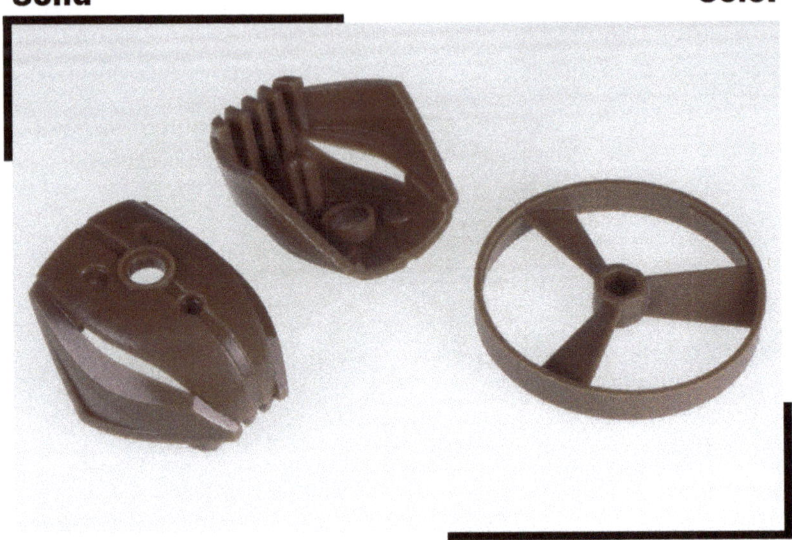

Brown   18

Lego	Brown	217
Bricklink	Dark Flesh	91

UUID   1DD7E3D0-70BD-45B5-942C-F6C7EC7531D0

Year	2004	to	2006	Availability	Some

				Pantone	4705 C
LAB	40	15	22		
sRGB	123	83	60		
CMYK	24	70	71	58	

Notes   Mainly Bionicle color.

Proximity	Related Colors		Page
6.84	Medium Brown		32
11.42	Reddish Brown		29
12.66	Rust		28
13.60	Earth Orange		36
15.47	Brick Red		31
17.51	Sand Red		24

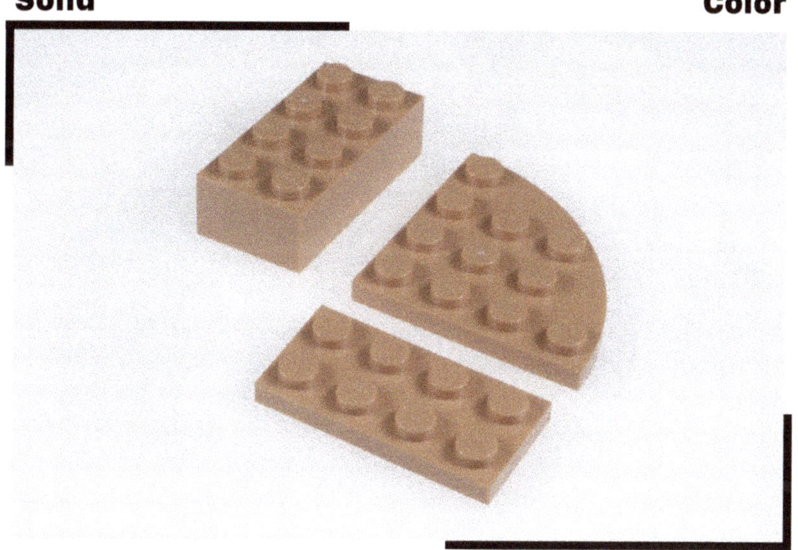

Nougat   19

Lego	Nougat	18
Bricklink	Flesh	28

UUID   3B553772-4A71-43E7-BB5A-7CE9981AEB3F

Year	1979	**to**	current	**Availability**	Several

LAB	65	30	39	**Pantone**	472 C
sRGB	214	135	88		
CMYK	1	46	63	1	

Notes   In current color palette.

Proximity	Related Colors		Page
14.76	Medium Nougat		39
16.36	Dark Nougat		33
16.36	Light Brown		42
16.99	Light Orange Brown		41
18.39	Light Yellowish Orange		44
18.98	Medium Red		21

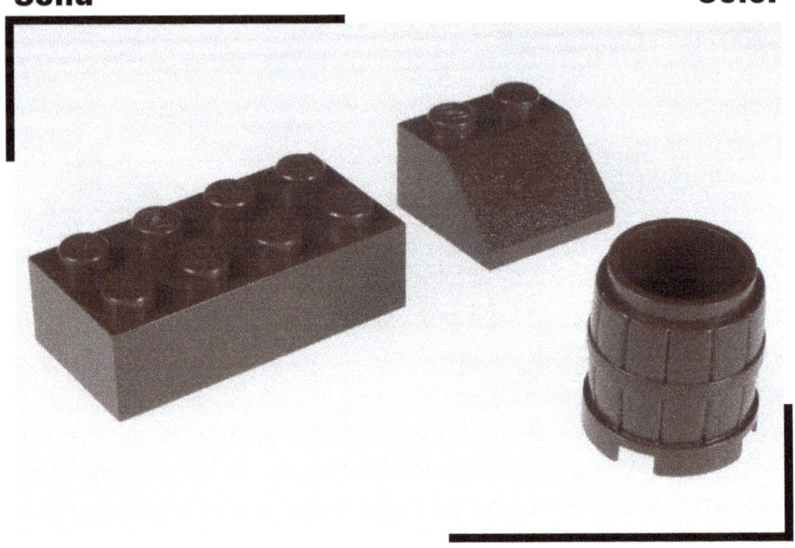

Earth Orange   20

Lego	Earth Orange				25
Bricklink	Brown				8
UUID	A4B78A0C-4ED6-4124-9C8A-8AB13AB6157F				
Year	1978	to	2006	Availability	Several

				Pantone	732 C
LAB	28	18	27		
sRGB	96	52	25		
CMYK	16	69	100	71	

Notes   Replaced by 192 Reddish Brown starting in 2003.

Proximity	Related Colors		Page
6.44	Reddish Brown		29
12.00	Medium Brown		32
13.60	Brown		34
17.78	Rust		28
20.50	Dark Brown		27
22.01	Brick Red		31

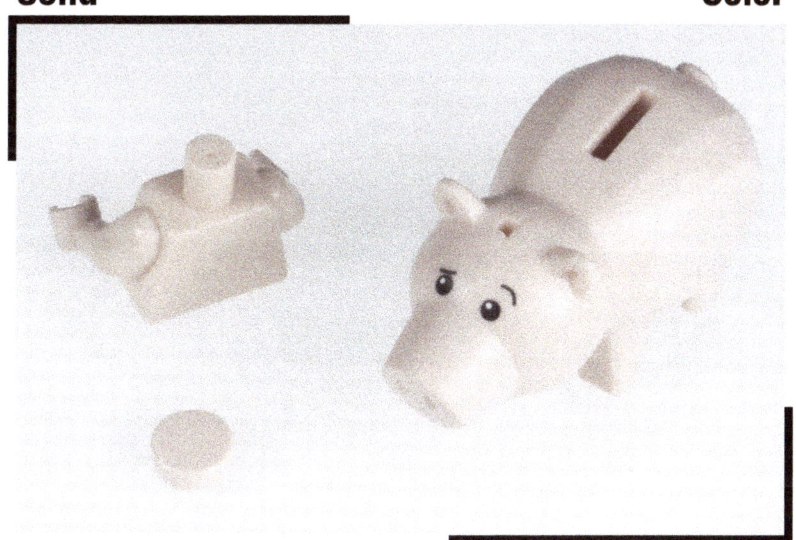

Light Nougat   21

Lego	Light Nougat				283
Bricklink	Light Flesh				90
UUID	AB293CBD-AE54-4CB2-B30B-0B2978B3F5C0				
Year	2003	**to**	current	**Availability**	Many

				Pantone	473 C
LAB	80	13	23		
sRGB	232	187	157		
CMYK	0	32	42	0	

Notes   In current color palette.

Proximity	Related Colors		Page
9.94	Light Brick Yellow		48
11.13	Brick Yellow		49
12.88	Light Red		20
18.12	Rose		115
24.67	Light Yellow		51
25.73	Sand Yellow		47

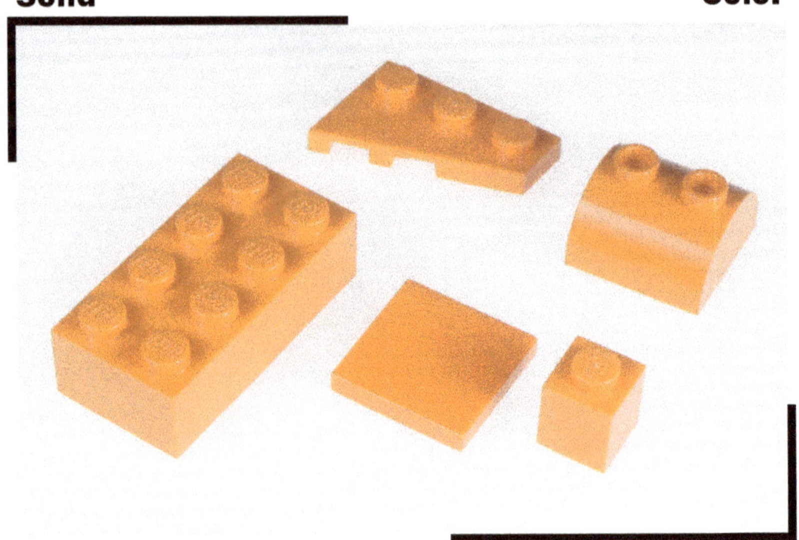

Bright Orange   22

Lego	Bright Orange				106
Bricklink	Orange				4
UUID	C8FB7639-E34B-45E7-A678-73C81DA6FBA1				
Year	1998	**to**	current	**Availability**	Many

LAB	65	50	79	**Pantone**	151 C
sRGB	245	107	0		
CMYK	0	60	100	0	

Notes   In current color palette.

Proximity	Related Colors		Page
17.22	Bright Yellowish Orange		46
25.80	Bright Reddish Orange		26
30.79	Flame Yellowish Orange		50
31.86	Medium Yellowish Orange		43
32.39	Light Orange Brown		41
34.65	Curry		52

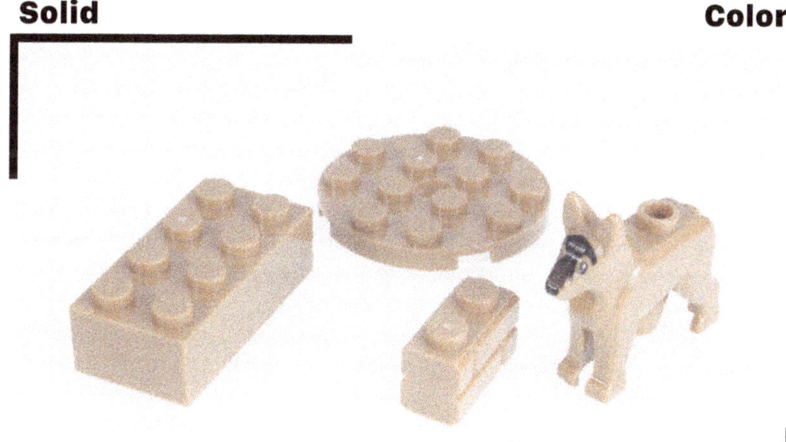

Medium Nougat   23

Lego	Medium Nougat				312
Bricklink	Medium Dark Flesh				150
UUID	EB7956DC-A43E-4BF7-99C6-E19A35FC594C				
Year	2010	**to**	current	**Availability**	Several

LAB	54	21	37	**Pantone**	730 C
sRGB	171	112	66		
CMYK	10	55	83	35	

Notes   In current color palette.

Proximity	Related Colors		Page
6.48	Light Brown		42
7.30	Light Yellowish Orange		44
8.00	Dark Nougat		33
10.92	Brick Red		31
14.76	Nougat		35
17.39	Rust		28

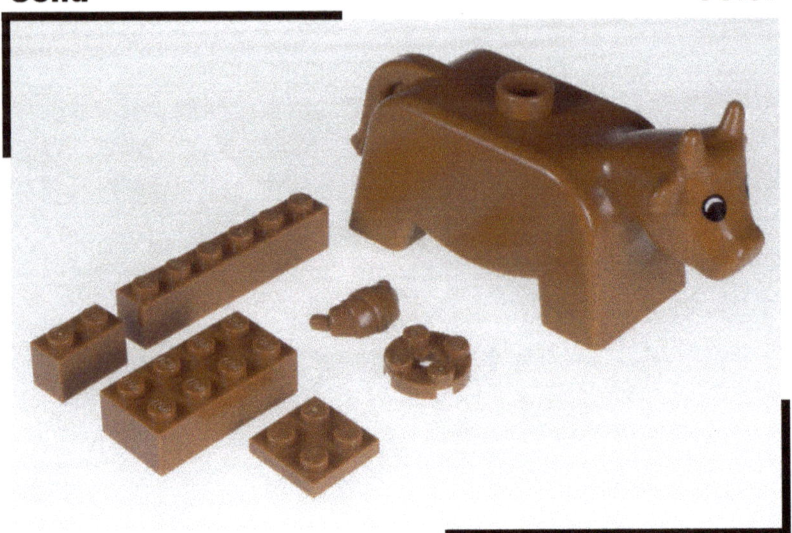

Dark Orange   24

Lego	Dark Orange	38
Bricklink	Dark Orange	68
UUID	77CCE53B-ED39-44DA-8F75-8A2D8C9F869F	
Year	1994 **to** current **Availability** Several	

LAB	44	35	56	**Pantone**	724 C
sRGB	160	72	0		
CMYK	7	70	100	42	

Notes   In current color palette.

Proximity	Related Colors		Page
16.85	Light Orange Brown		41
18.84	Red Orange		25
20.06	Light Brown		42
24.01	Rust		22
25.81	Bright Reddish Orange		26
26.02	Medium Nougat		39

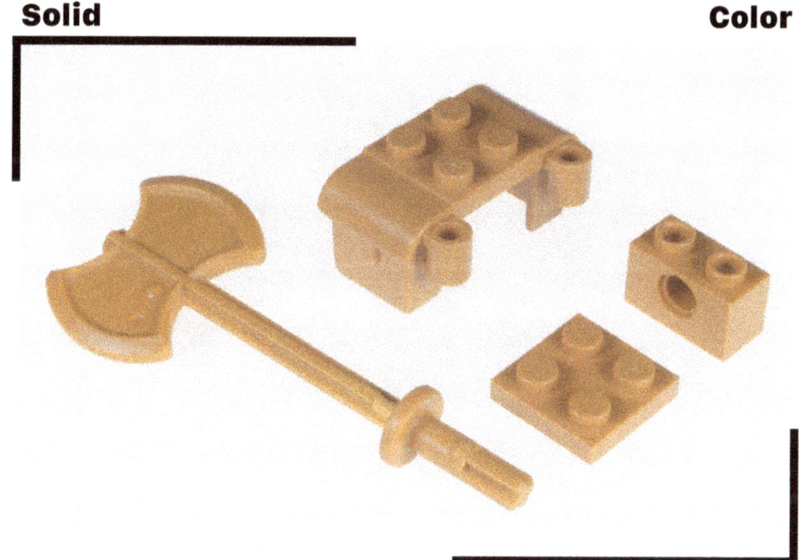

Light Orange Brown   25

Lego	Light Orange Brown	12
Bricklink	Earth Orange	29
UUID	CE04D921-8BDE-4D7B-8E9A-159E0D6995E0	

Year	1979	to	2008	Availability	Some

LAB	59	29	55	Pantone	7412 C
sRGB	200	115	44		
CMYK	2	58	96	10	

Notes   No 2x4 brick available.

Proximity	Related Colors		Page
16.63	Light Brown		42
16.85	Dark Orange		40
16.99	Nougat		35
20.69	Medium Yellowish Orange		43
20.91	Medium Nougat		39
22.38	Light Yellowish Orange		44

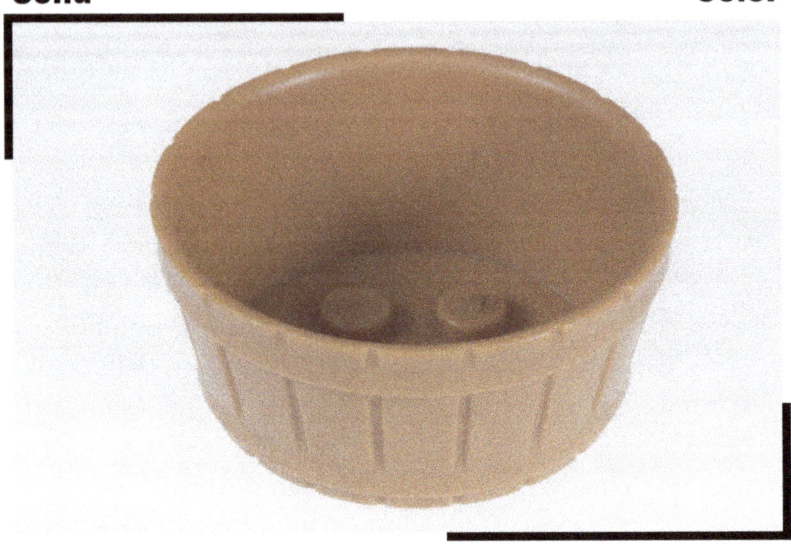

Light Brown   26

Lego	Light Brown	19
Bricklink	Fabuland Orange	160
UUID	9719931A-450F-4257-9065-39B3C822030D	

Year	1987	**to**	1987	**Availability**	Few

					Pantone	730 C
LAB	51	22	42			
sRGB	166	103	48			
CMYK	10	55	83	35		

Notes   Appeared only in a few Fabuland parts.

Proximity	Related Colors		Page
6.48	Medium Nougat		39
10.09	Light Yellowish Orange		44
11.98	Dark Nougat		33
14.16	Brick Red		31
16.36	Nougat		35
16.63	Light Orange Brown		41

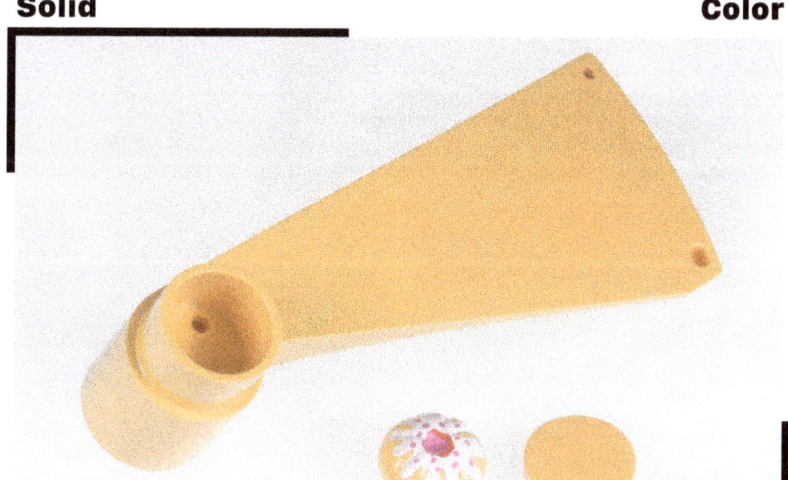

Medium Yellowish Orange   27

Lego	Medium Yellowish Orange	121
Bricklink	Light Orange	32

UUID	CD4877B5-E1BD-4C15-B20B-48856E4C04B6				
Year	1998	**to**	2004	**Availability**	Some

				Pantone	150 C
LAB	78	26	62		
sRGB	255	165	78		
CMYK	0	41	78	0	

Notes	Mainly a Scala and DUPLO color.

Proximity	Related Colors		Page
17.21	Warm Yellowish Orange		45
20.69	Light Orange Brown		41
23.27	Curry		52
23.62	Bright Yellowish Orange		46
26.71	Nougat		35
29.45	Flame Yellowish Orange		50

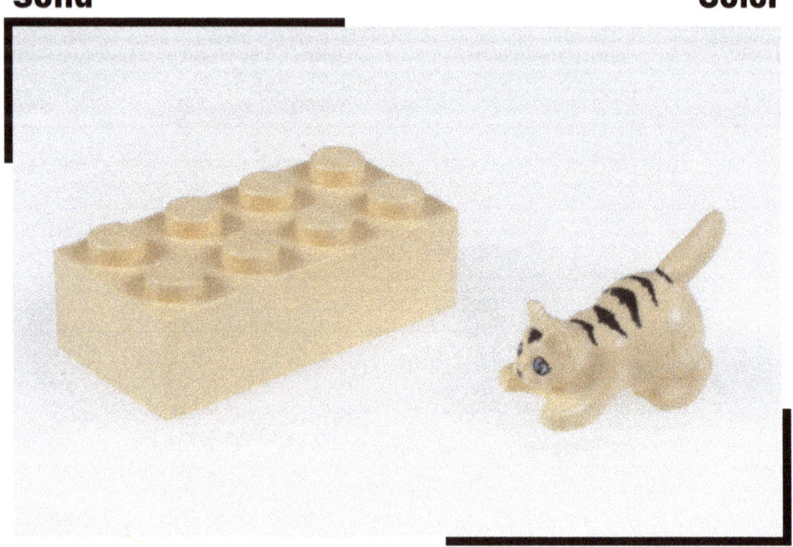

Light Yellowish Orange   28

Lego	Light Yellowish Orange			36
Bricklink	Very Light Orange			96
UUID	1B65C85B-C593-4F93-99CC-20FAE16B4EB1			
Year	1999	**to**	2001	**Availability** Few

LAB	56	14	39	**Pantone**	148 C
sRGB	255	199	143		
CMYK	0	17	43	0	

Notes   Rare color, such as the striped cat. Also available from LEGOLANDs.

Proximity	Related Colors		Page
7.30	Medium Nougat		39
10.09	Light Brown		42
14.81	Dark Nougat		33
17.26	Brick Red		31
18.39	Nougat		35
19.87	Sand Yellow		47

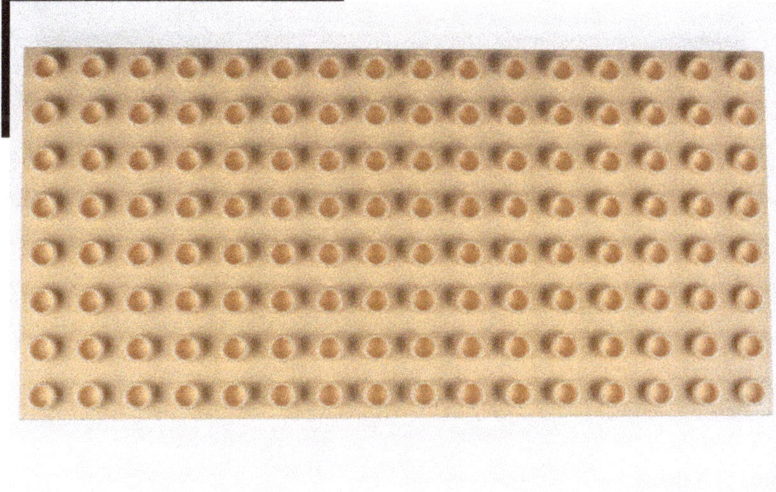

Warm Yellowish Orange   29

Lego	Warm Yellowish Orange				225
Bricklink					
UUID	8A06D3C2-FBA2-4212-89CA-5C7FA728A31C				
Year	2004	**to**	2004	**Availability**	Rare

LAB	84	19	48	**Pantone**	149 C
sRGB	255	189	121		
CMYK	0	24	51	0	

Notes   Only safe match is the DUPLO 8x16 plate from 4689.

Proximity	Related Colors		Page
15.82	Light Yellow		51
17.21	Medium Yellowish Orange		43
22.83	Cool Yellow		54
23.02	Nougat		35
23.15	Light Brick Yellow		48
25.59	Brick Yellow		49

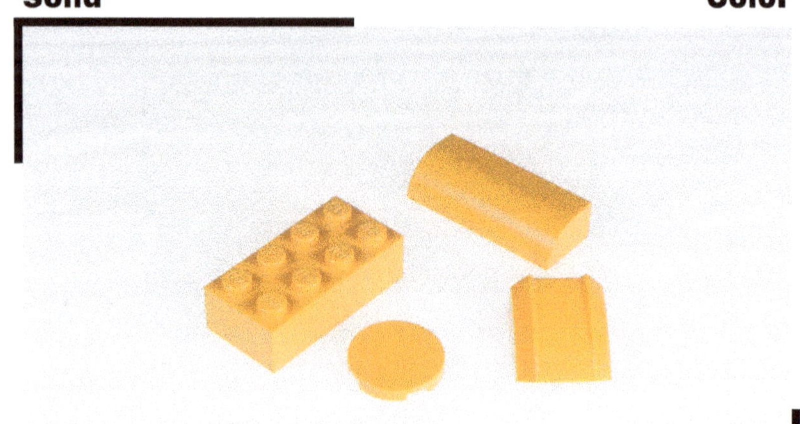

Bright Yellowish Orange   30

Lego	Bright Yellowish Orange				105
Bricklink	Medium Orange				31
UUID	D1EEA688-A181-4E25-BF9F-117A7801B6D5				
Year	1997	**to**	2008	**Availability**	Several

LAB	72	35	83	**Pantone**	137 C
sRGB	251	141	0		
CMYK	0	41	100	0	

Notes   Replaced by 191 Flame Yellowish Orange starting in 2004.

Proximity	Related Colors		Page
14.09	Flame Yellowish Orange		50
17.22	Bright Orange		38
19.88	Curry		52
23.62	Medium Yellowish Orange		43
29.93	Bright Yellow		53
31.73	Light Orange Brown		41

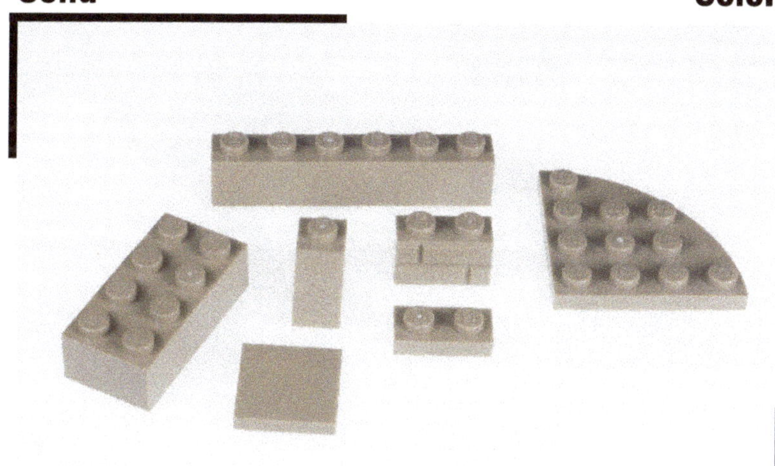

Sand Yellow   31

Lego	Sand Yellow			138
Bricklink	Dark Tan			69
UUID	2375F388-A717-4AC1-B51D-F176499AE585			
Year	2000 **to** current	**Availability**		Several

LAB	56	5	21	**Pantone**	7504 C
sRGB	152	128	97		
CMYK	17	36	52	38	

Notes   In current color palette.

Proximity	Related Colors		Page
11.78	Olive Green		55
12.76	Dark Army Green		57
16.42	Sand Red		24
18.37	Brown		34
19.87	Light Yellowish Orange		44
21.29	Dark Grey		118

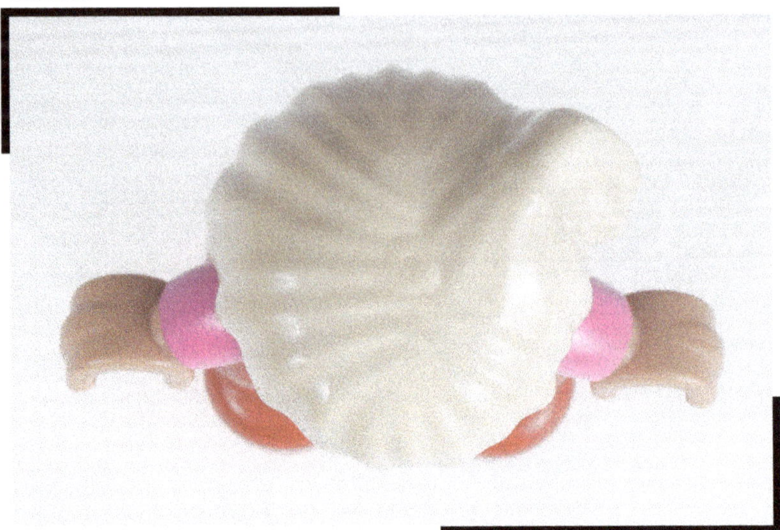

Light Brick Yellow   32

Lego	Light Brick Yellow			224
Bricklink				
UUID	C720268E-AB4B-4D2A-BECB-D0B8446DF36E			
Year	2004	**to**	2006	**Availability** Rare

LAB	81	6	29	**Pantone**	7508 C
sRGB	228	193	147		
CMYK	2	19	46	4	

Notes   Hair of one DUPLO figure.

Proximity	Related Colors		Page
3.91	Brick Yellow		49
9.94	Light Nougat		37
16.90	Light Yellow		51
19.04	Light Yellowish Green		61
22.76	Light Red		20
23.15	Warm Yellowish Orange		45

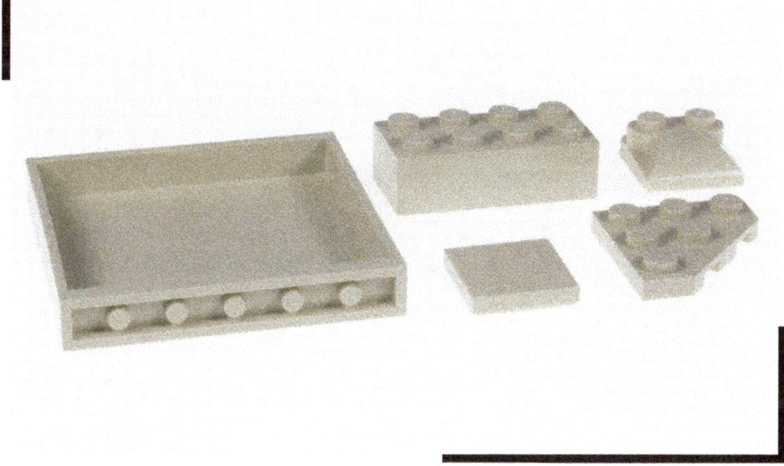

Brick Yellow 33

Lego	Brick Yellow					5
Bricklink	Tan					2
UUID	EF4B3B0A-6A03-440B-AC99-A7AA500145F5					
Year	1981	**to**	current	**Availability**		Many

LAB	78	4	28	**Pantone**	467 C
sRGB	215	186	140		
CMYK	6	15	41	10	

Notes In current color palette.

Proximity	Related Colors		Page
3.91	Light Brick Yellow		48
11.13	Light Nougat		37
18.85	Light Yellowish Green		61
19.35	Light Yellow		51
23.58	Sand Yellow		47
23.75	Light Red		20

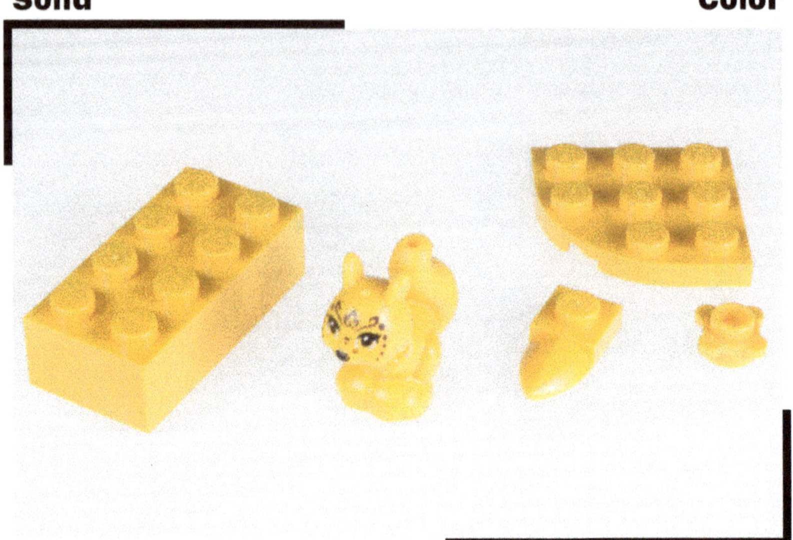

Flame Yellowish Orange   34

Lego	Flame Yellowish Orange				191
Bricklink	Bright Light Orange				110
UUID	39215277-E73C-4B27-8C16-9A9C7DD4C389				
Year	2004	**to**	current	**Availability**	Several

LAB	77	25	92	**Pantone**	130 C
sRGB	255	162	0		
CMYK	0	32	100	0	

Notes   In current color palette.

Proximity	Related Colors		Page
14.09	Bright Yellowish Orange		46
16.79	Curry		52
17.69	Bright Yellow		53
29.45	Medium Yellowish Orange		43
30.79	Bright Orange		38
41.05	Light Orange Brown		41

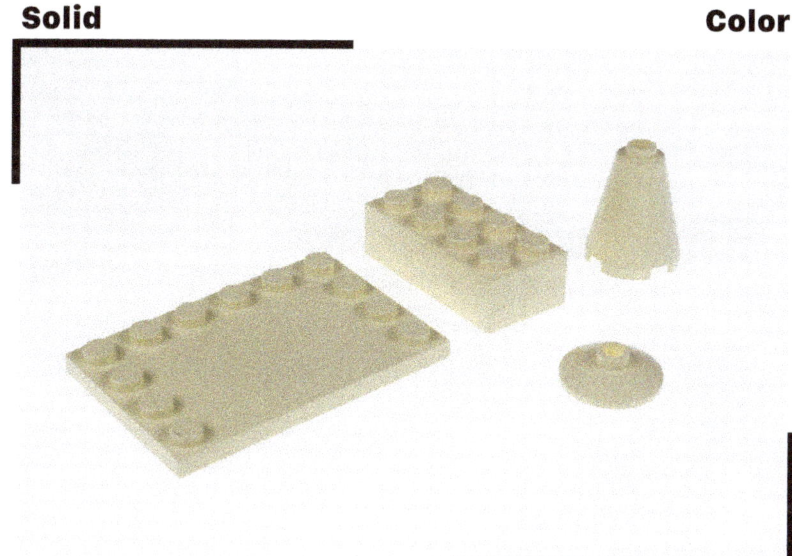

Light Yellow   35

Lego	Light Yellow		3
Bricklink	Light Yellow		33
UUID	CB1E2D97-A8E8-4CAD-94A0-B12CB1F9D9ED		
Year	1994 **to** 2011	**Availability**	Some

LAB	89	5	44	**Pantone**	1215 C
sRGB	255	213	139		
CMYK	0	6	53	0	

Notes   Phased out in 2003 and replaced by 226 Cool Yellow around 2004.

Proximity	Related Colors		Page
12.82	Cool Yellow		54
15.82	Warm Yellowish Orange		45
16.90	Light Brick Yellow		48
19.35	Brick Yellow		49
20.58	Light Yellowish Green		61
22.45	Lemon		56

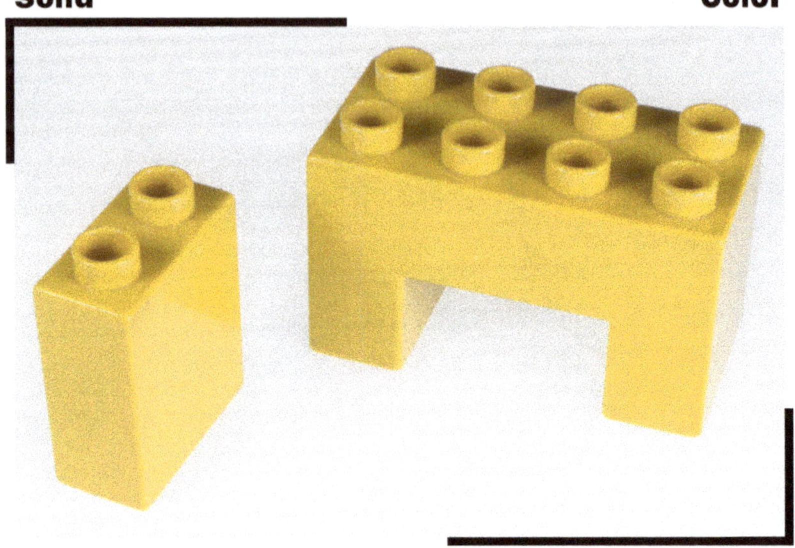

Curry   36

Lego	Curry	180
Bricklink	Dark Yellow	161
UUID	FFA7D259-4254-4527-8CA9-EFE5028B4052	

Year	2004	**to**	2005	**Availability**	Few

LAB	69	16	81	**Pantone**	117 C
sRGB	218	146	0		
CMYK	6	27	100	12	

Notes	Only used in for a few DUPLO parts.

Proximity	**Related Colors**		**Page**
16.79	Flame Yellowish Orange		50
18.86	Bright Yellow		53
19.88	Bright Yellowish Orange		46
23.27	Medium Yellowish Orange		43
28.34	Lemon		56
30.29	Light Orange Brown		41

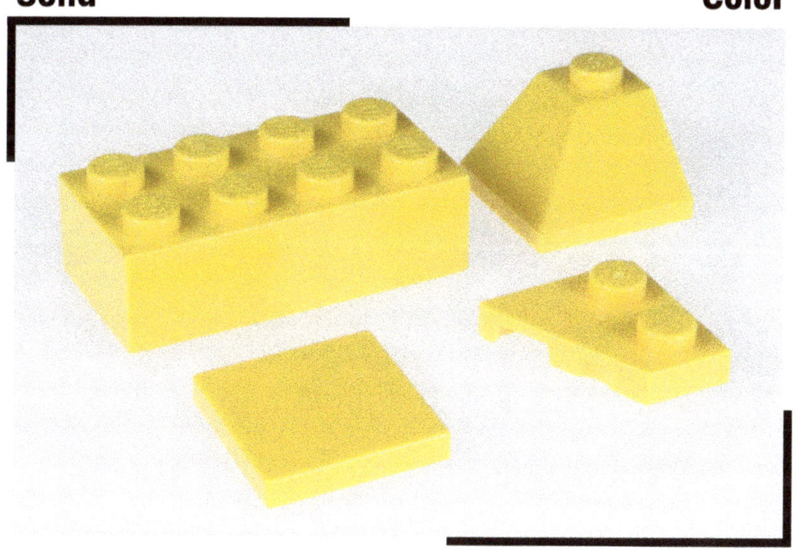

Bright Yellow   37

Lego	Bright Yellow	24
Bricklink	Yellow	3

UUID   9D2BC82E-50EA-49B1-A8B6-F1596FA3E357

Year	1950	**to**	current	**Availability**	Many

LAB	82	8	91	**Pantone**	116 C
sRGB	250	189	0		
CMYK	0	14	100	0	

Notes   In current color palette.

Proximity	Related Colors		Page
17.69	Flame Yellowish Orange		50
18.86	Curry		52
25.37	Vibrant Yellow		58
29.67	Medium Yellowish Green		59
29.93	Bright Yellowish Orange		46
31.50	Lemon		56

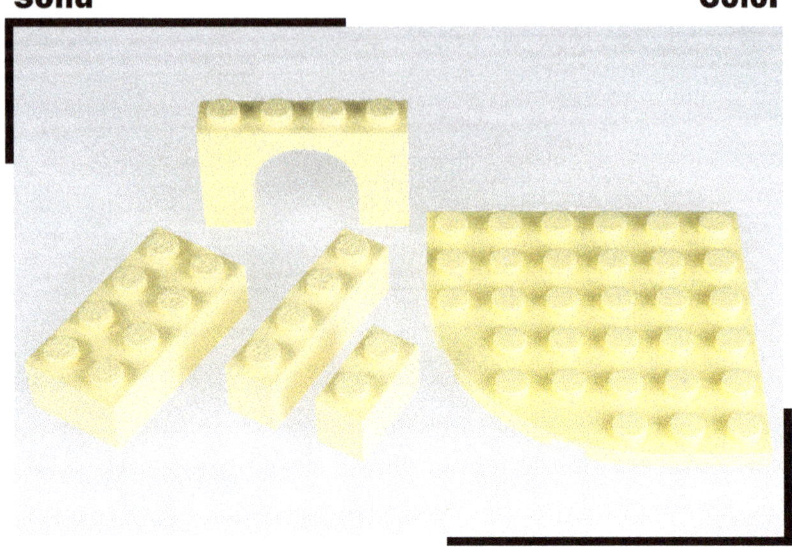

Cool Yellow   38

Lego	Cool Yellow	226
Bricklink	Bright Light Yellow	103
UUID	2DF1256B-1041-48AD-BFF6-18E063FA8365	

Year	2004	**to**	current	**Availability**	Several

				Pantone	120 C
LAB	92	-1	55		
sRGB	255	225	121		
CMYK	0	5	64	0	

Notes   In current color palette.

Proximity	Related Colors		Page
12.82	Light Yellow		51
15.81	Lemon		56
22.83	Warm Yellowish Orange		45
23.96	Spring Yellowish Green		63
26.24	Light Yellowish Green		61
29.13	Light Brick Yellow		48

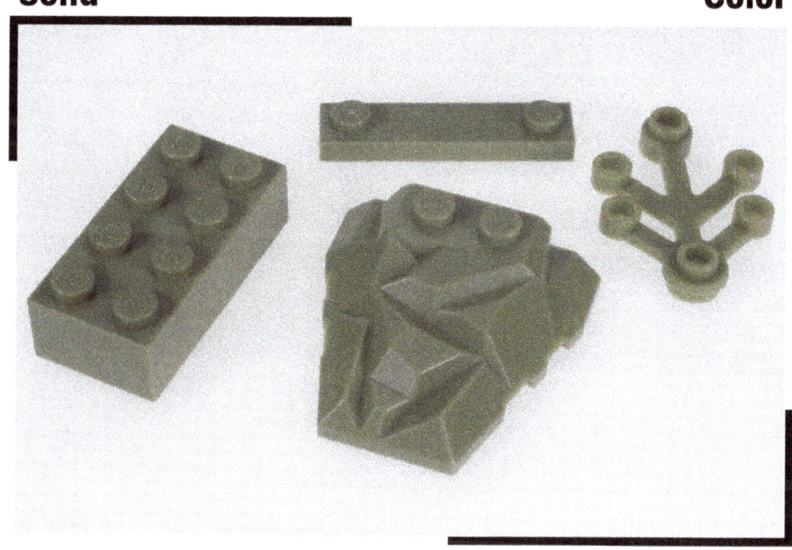

Olive Green   39

Lego	Olive Green	330
Bricklink	Olive Green	155

UUID   580741E5-2748-47AA-AD68-8121CE5E3E51

Year	2012	**to**	current	**Availability**	Several

LAB	54	-4	28	**Pantone**	5825 C
sRGB	138	127	79		
CMYK	22	15	86	47	

Notes   In current color palette.

Proximity	Related Colors		Page
11.78	Sand Yellow		47
12.12	Dark Army Green		57
20.95	Light Yellowish Orange		44
22.68	Sand Green		68
24.16	Brown		34
25.13	Dark Grey		118

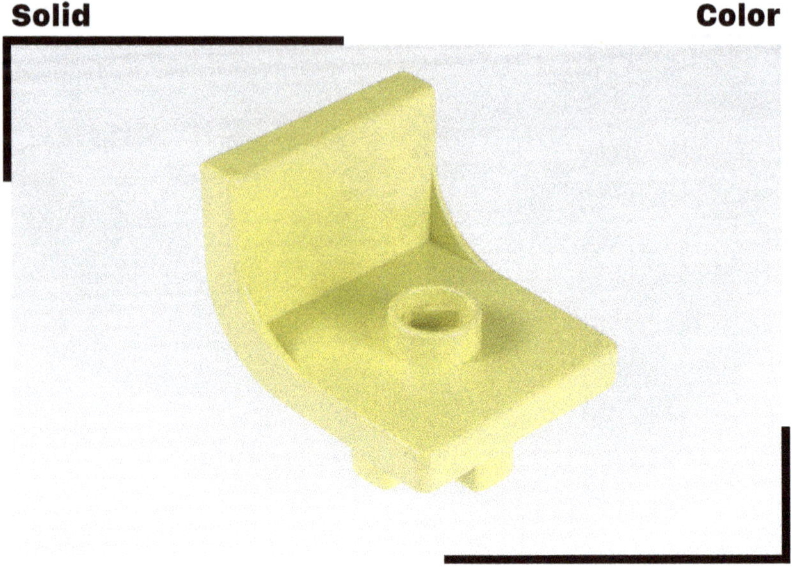

Lemon   40

Lego	Lemon					15
Bricklink						
UUID	3DA1C2BC-B534-4D77-AB29-994AAAD8E5B4					
Year	1992	**to**	1992	**Availability**		Rare

LAB	78	-4	62	**Pantone**	611 C
sRGB	216	188	65		
CMYK	7	1	89	10	

Notes   Used in only a few DUPLO parts.

Proximity	Related Colors		Page
15.81	Cool Yellow		54
22.33	Medium Yellowish Green		59
22.45	Light Yellow		51
23.10	Bright Yellowish Green		60
27.50	Warm Yellowish Orange		45
28.34	Curry		52

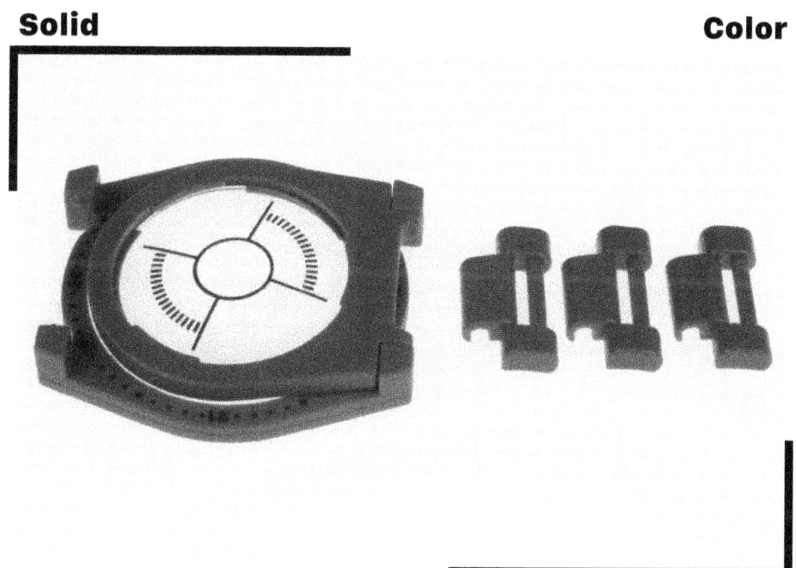

Dark Army Green   41

Lego	Dark Army Green				144
Bricklink					
UUID	3FDF06B6-F073-43AA-9E8B-1322191FFD1E				
Year	2000	**to**	2000	**Availability**	Rare

				Pantone	7497 C
LAB	47	-4	18		
sRGB	117	111	82		
CMYK	49	45	67	18	

Notes Only used for X-Tracker watch.

Proximity	Related Colors		Page
12.12	Olive Green		55
12.76	Sand Yellow		47
13.18	Dark Grey		118
18.05	Sand Green		68
19.86	Dark Stone Grey		121
20.25	Brown		34

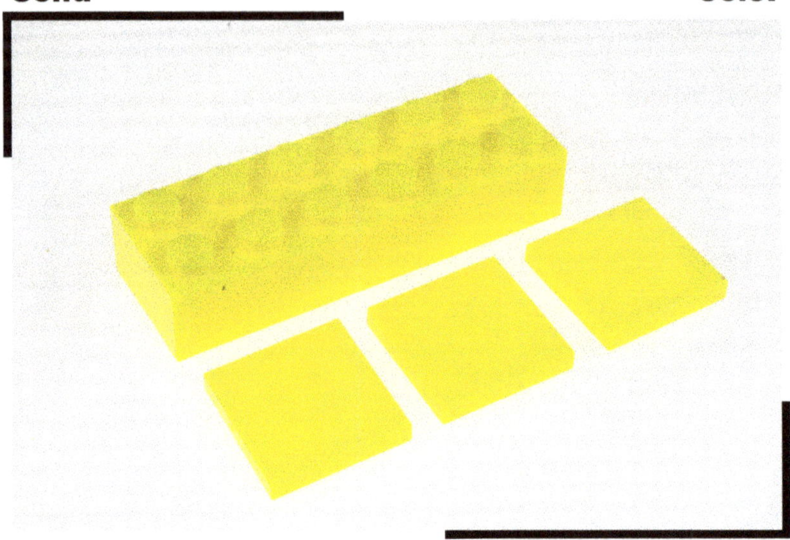

Vibrant Yellow   42

Lego	Vibrant Yellow	368
Bricklink	Neon Yellow	236
UUID	09DE35F7-53E0-4B22-BDAF-339EF971FE2A	

Year	2022	**to**	current	**Availability**	Some

				Pantone	115 C
LAB	89	-16	98		
sRGB	238	220	0		
CMYK	2	10	85	0	

Notes

Proximity	**Related Colors**		**Page**
21.37	Medium Yellowish Green		59
25.37	Bright Yellow		53
32.90	Bright Yellowish Green		60
38.86	Lemon		56
40.86	Curry		52
42.62	Flame Yellowish Orange		50

Medium Yellowish Green   43

Lego	Medium Yellowish Green	115
Bricklink	Medium Lime	76
UUID	3A31BB17-00A5-4934-A0E1-D2F934934AC7	

Year	1998	**to**	2005	**Availability**	Some

				Pantone	382 C
LAB	80	-19	79		
sRGB	202	198	0		
CMYK	28	0	100	0	

Notes   Mainly Scale and DUPLO color.

Proximity	Related Colors		Page
12.56	Bright Yellowish Green		60
21.37	Vibrant Yellow		58
22.33	Lemon		56
29.67	Bright Yellow		53
30.76	Neon Green		64
31.98	Cool Yellow		54

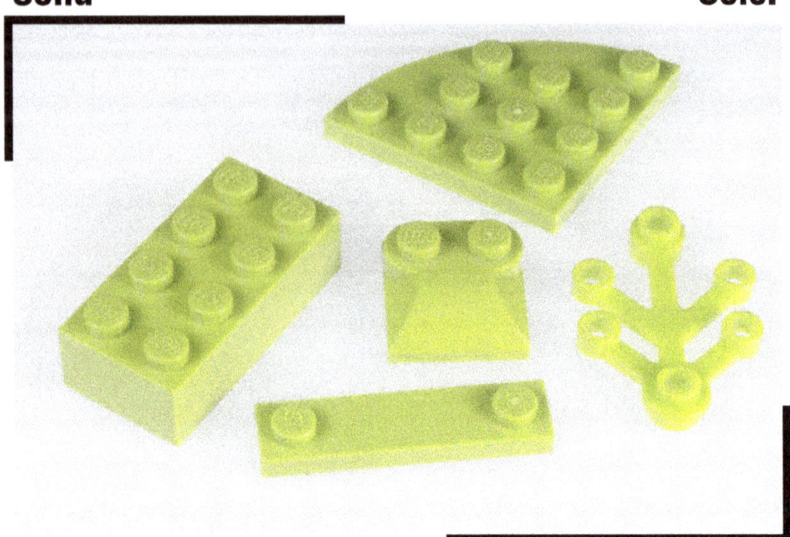

Bright Yellowish Green   44

Lego	Bright Yellowish Green				119
Bricklink	Lime				34
UUID	F81B7FCF-427C-4EB7-80CA-3D6E76817087				
Year	2000	**to**	current	**Availability**	Many

LAB	70	-23	72	**Pantone**	583 C
sRGB	169	174	0		
CMYK	26	1	100	10	

Notes   In current color palette.

Proximity	Related Colors		Page
12.56	Medium Yellowish Green		59
23.10	Lemon		56
25.33	Neon Green		64
29.07	Pastel Green		62
32.90	Vibrant Yellow		58
35.39	Cool Yellow		54

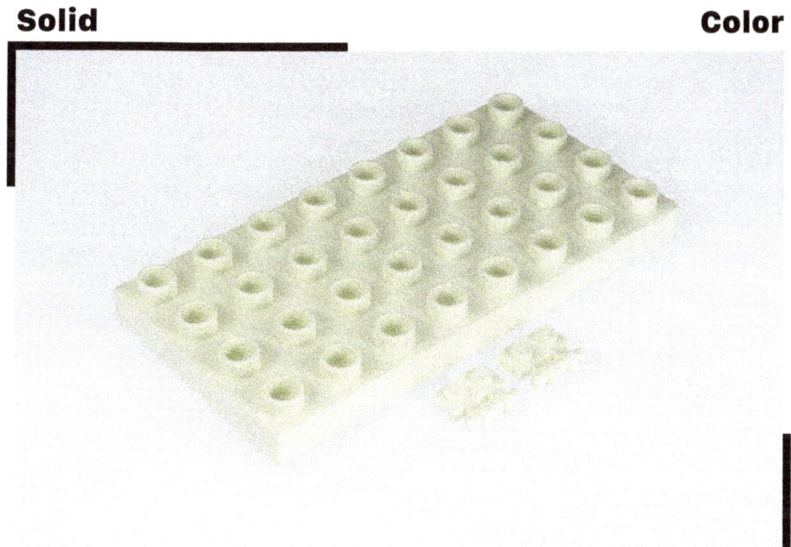

Light Yellowish Green   45

Lego	Light Yellowish Green				120
Bricklink	Light Lime				35
UUID	14FE6153-9489-4303-A7A0-F4618765F998				
Year	1998	**to**	2007	**Availability**	Some

LAB	87	-12	32	**Pantone**	372 C
sRGB	217	222	152		
CMYK	16	0	41	0	

Notes   Mainly a Scala and DUPLO color.

Proximity	Related Colors		Page
13.41	Spring Yellowish Green		63
18.85	Brick Yellow		49
18.92	Light Green		66
19.04	Light Brick Yellow		48
19.66	Light Faded Green		65
20.58	Light Yellow		51

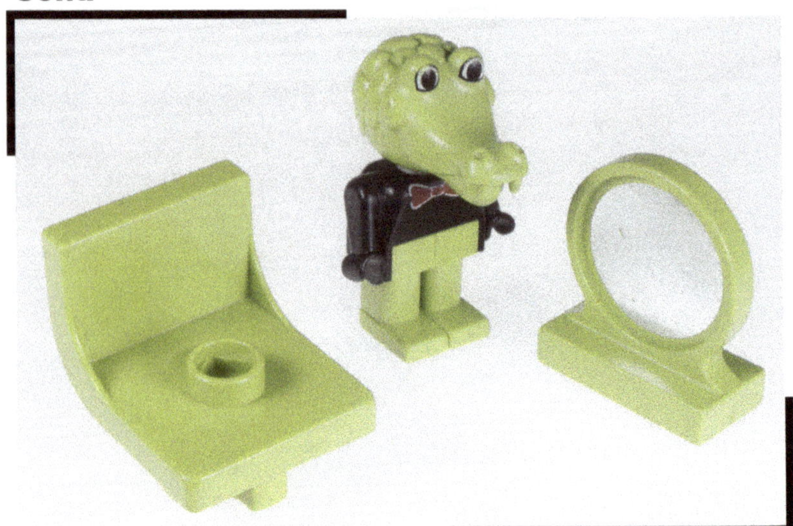

Pastel Green   **46**

Lego	Pastel Green					14
Bricklink						
UUID	5DDACC83-C6E8-4D69-8506-54FFD49912EA					
Year	1982	**to**	1989	**Availability**		Rare

LAB	63	-22	44	**Pantone**	7495 C
sRGB	142	156	67		
CMYK	42	5	98	29	

Notes   Not listed on Bricklink.

Proximity	Related Colors		Page
17.21	Light Faded Green		65
25.56	Olive Green		55
27.87	Spring Yellowish Green		63
28.47	Medium Green		67
28.58	Faded Green		69
28.91	Light Yellowish Green		61

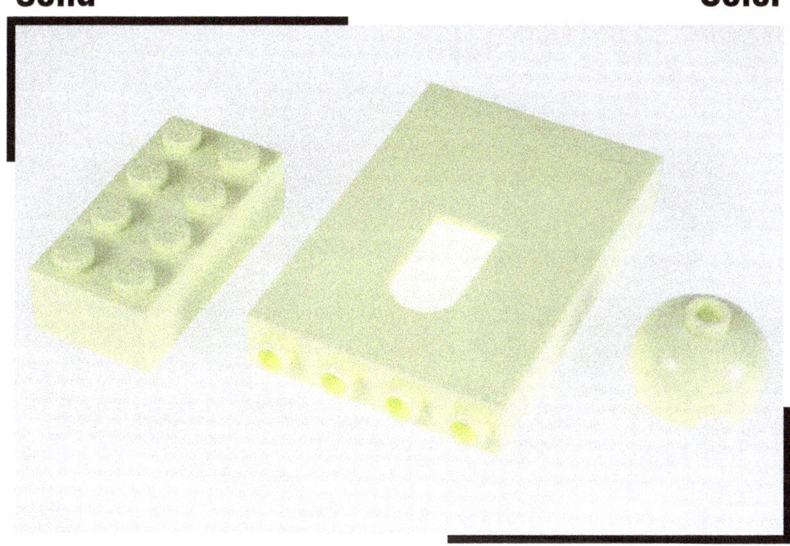

Spring Yellowish Green   47

Lego	Spring Yellowish Green	326
Bricklink	Yellowish Green	158
UUID	FFA4A187-7BB7-45D2-8FB1-7CE2141417C6	

Year	2012	**to**	current	**Availability**	Several

				Pantone	373 C
LAB	90	-21	42		
sRGB	216	235	139		
CMYK	21	0	48	0	

Notes   In current color palette.

Proximity	Related Colors		Page
13.41	Light Yellowish Green		61
22.68	Light Faded Green		65
23.96	Cool Yellow		54
24.58	Light Green		66
25.32	Light Yellow		51
27.87	Pastel Green		62

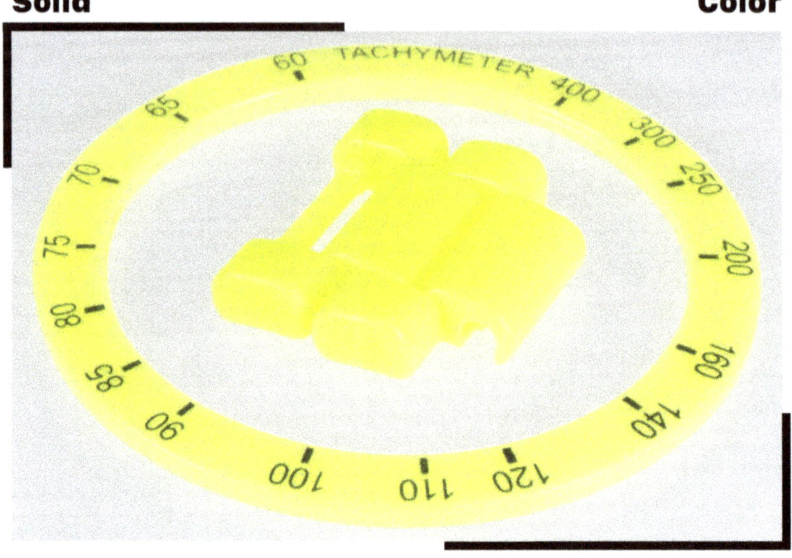

Neon Green   48

Lego	Neon Green				134
Bricklink	Neon Green				166
UUID	B2D53C27-4A77-47E1-8FA7-071049A0131A				
Year	1997	**to**	2001	**Availability**	Rare

LAB	81	-42	58	**Pantone**	367 C
sRGB	152	219	57		
CMYK	41	0	68	0	

Notes   Only used in UFO Cyclone Master Watch.

Proximity	Related Colors		Page
25.33	Bright Yellowish Green		60
28.16	Spring Yellowish Green		63
29.90	Medium Green		67
30.34	Pastel Green		62
30.76	Medium Yellowish Green		59
34.79	Light Faded Green		65

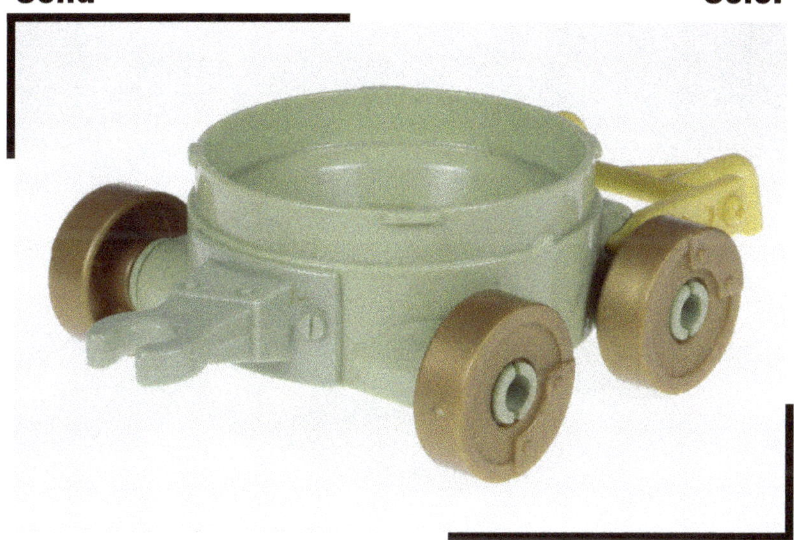

Light Faded Green   49

Lego	Light Faded Green				233
Bricklink					
UUID	AF130B7A-3B20-4208-B8DD-08F27D7B30E7				
Year	2004	**to**	2004	**Availability**	Rare

				Pantone	577 C
LAB	72	-24	29		
sRGB	155	186	118		
CMYK	35	2	58	0	

Notes   Not listed on Bricklink and used for only one part.

Proximity	Related Colors		Page
16.49	Light Green		66
17.21	Pastel Green		62
19.66	Light Yellowish Green		61
19.70	Medium Green		67
21.70	Faded Green		69
22.68	Spring Yellowish Green		63

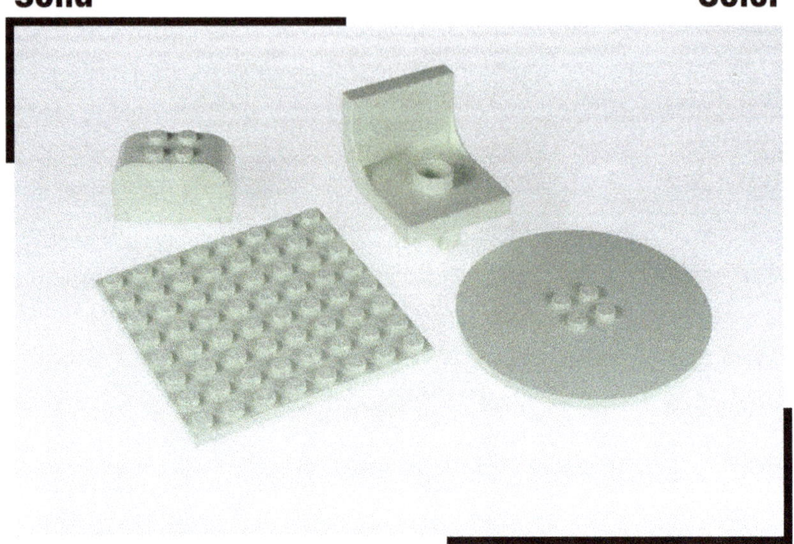

Light Green   50

Lego	Light Green	6
Bricklink	Light Green	38

| UUID | 87D6CC2D-A71C-4961-BBC2-DD62BE4B5771 |

Year	1992	to	2007	Availability	Some

				Pantone	351 C
LAB	85	-25	19		
sRGB	181	223	172		
CMYK	27	0	23	0	

Notes   Mainly a Scala, DUPLO and Clikits color.

Proximity	Related Colors		Page
16.49	Light Faded Green		65
18.92	Light Yellowish Green		61
21.88	Aqua		73
23.96	Medium Green		67
24.58	Spring Yellowish Green		63
25.20	Light Grey		117

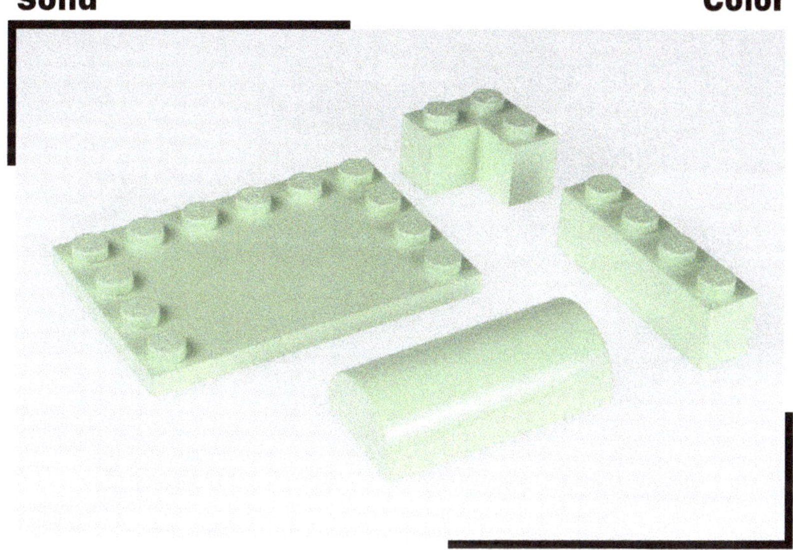

Medium Green   51

Lego	Medium Green	29
Bricklink	Medium Green	37

UUID	11008E1F-E8D5-47CF-8D08-0A5C6CBC8ADD				
Year	1994	to	2004	Availability	Several

				Pantone	7479 C
LAB	74	-44	29		
sRGB	118	202	120		
CMYK	56	0	58	0	

Notes   No 2x4 brick available.

Proximity	Related Colors		Page
19.70	Light Faded Green		65
23.96	Light Green		66
23.98	Bright Green		70
24.63	Faded Green		69
28.47	Pastel Green		62
29.90	Neon Green		64

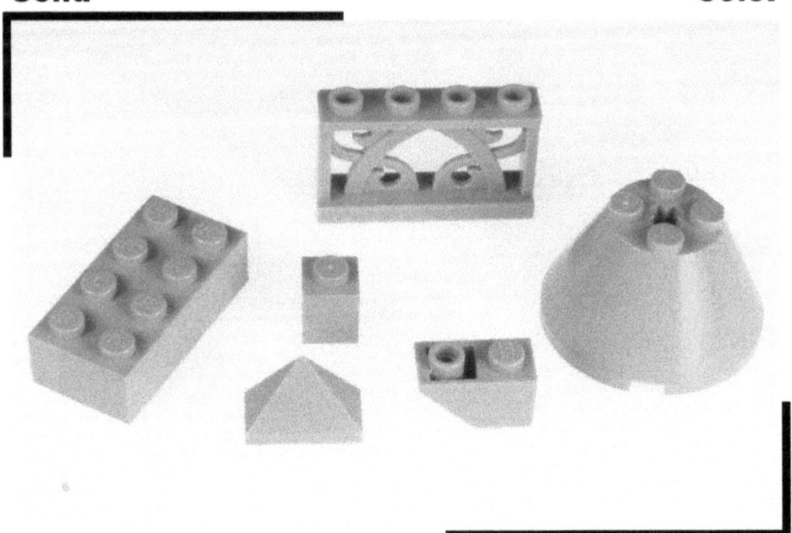

Sand Green   52

Lego	Sand Green	151
Bricklink	Sand Green	48

UUID   A665DC5E-05FC-4A3B-8637-2E8E256CA190

Year	2000	**to**	current	**Availability**	Several

				Pantone	5555 C
LAB	56	-17	9		
sRGB	114	142	115		
CMYK	51	12	39	37	

Notes   In current color palette.

Proximity	Related Colors		Page
17.32	Faded Green		69
18.05	Dark Army Green		57
18.09	Grey		119
21.03	Light Grey		117
22.02	Medium Stone Grey		122
22.68	Olive Green		55

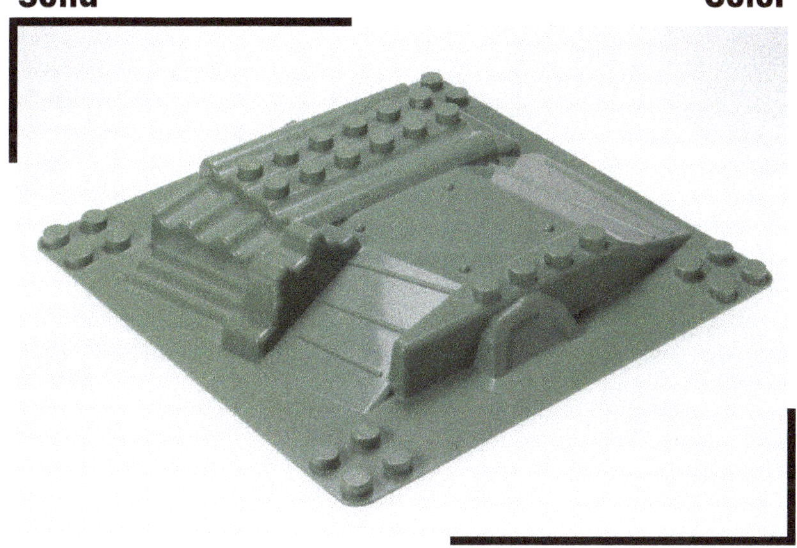

Faded Green   53

Lego	Faded Green					210

Bricklink

UUID   A1689EAE-D390-443C-A844-4533F7F02024

Year	2003	to	2003	Availability	Rare

					Pantone	362 C
LAB	56	-32	18			
sRGB	92	146	98			
CMYK	78	0	100	2		

Notes   Not listed on Bricklink and used for only one part.

Proximity	Related Colors		Page
17.32	Sand Green		68
21.70	Light Faded Green		65
24.63	Medium Green		67
28.58	Pastel Green		62
29.81	Dark Army Green		57
29.99	Light Green		66

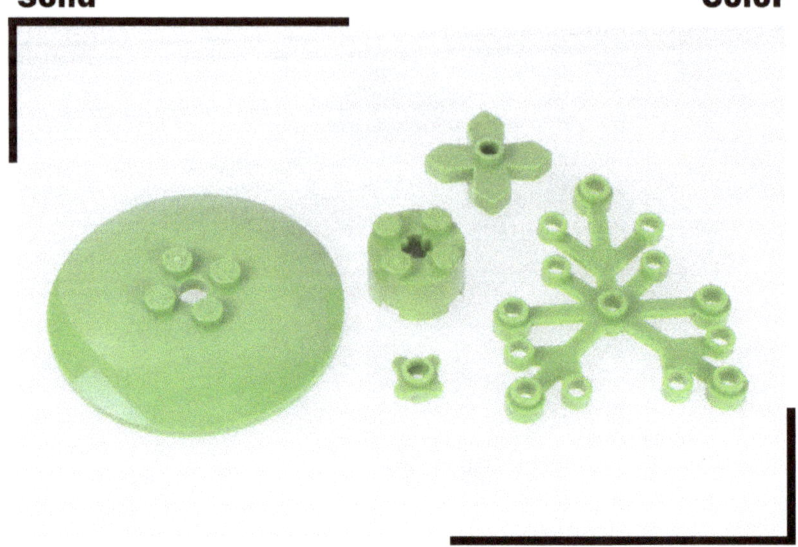

Bright Green   54

Lego	Bright Green	37
Bricklink	Bright Green	36

UUID	6916626B-3D0F-4234-8FBF-201545B7A922

Year	1995	**to**	current	**Availability**	Several

				Pantone	354 C
LAB	58	-60	36		
sRGB	21	162	59		
CMYK	81	0	92	0	

Notes   In current color palette.

Proximity	Related Colors		Page
19.38	Dark Green		71
23.98	Medium Green		67
33.59	Faded Green		69
36.39	Neon Green		64
38.83	Pastel Green		62
39.13	Light Faded Green		65

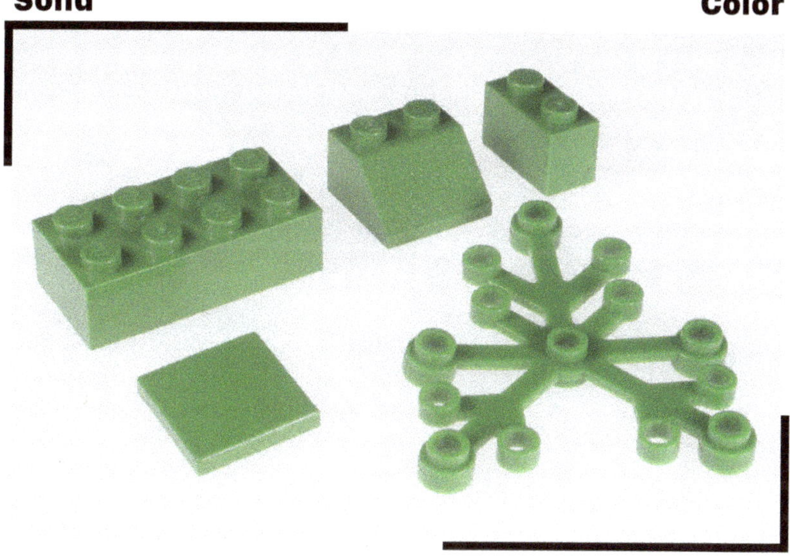

Dark Green   55

Lego	Dark Green	28
Bricklink	Green	6
UUID	EA4D04EE-7E40-4CDC-997A-E906D4A8CCE6	

Year	1950	**to**	current	**Availability**	Many

LAB	43	-68	28	**Pantone**	348 C
sRGB	0	125	40		
CMYK	96	2	100	12	

Notes　　In current color palette.

Proximity	**Related Colors**		**Page**
19.38	Bright Green		70
39.20	Faded Green		69
39.61	Medium Green		67
44.63	Bright Bluish Green		75
48.94	Medium Bluish Green		76
52.44	Pastel Green		62

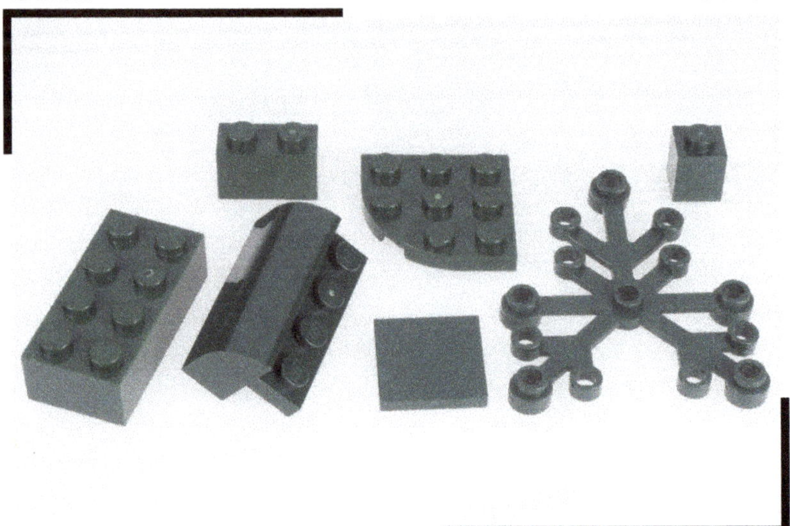

Earth Green   56

Lego	Earth Green			141
Bricklink	Dark Green			80
UUID	18B69A8B-AB78-4A01-B587-EAA52B0D3F41			
Year	2002	**to** current	**Availability**	Several

LAB	22	-21	5		**Pantone**	3435 C
sRGB	16	61	42			
CMYK	93	24	85	68		

Notes   In current color palette.

Proximity	Related Colors		Page
28.42	Dark Grey		118
28.61	Black		123
29.50	Dark Stone Grey		121
30.92	Ultra-Dark Blue		97
30.92	Reddish Lilac		103
30.92	Light Pink		106

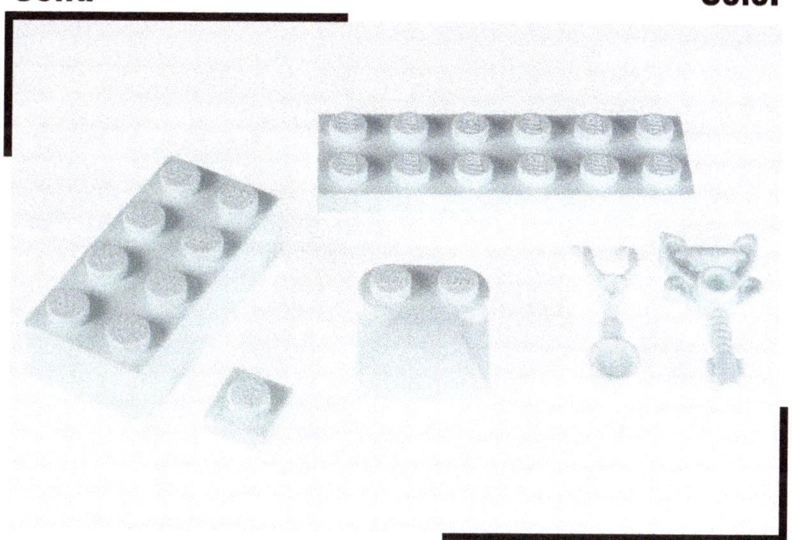

Aqua   57

Lego	Aqua	323
Bricklink	Light Aqua	152

UUID	C835FCFB-236B-417C-BE2E-FD997B0F33B3		
Year	2011 **to** current	**Availability**	Several

LAB	91	-14	1	**Pantone**	573 C
sRGB	204	237	225		
CMYK	20	0	14	0	

Notes	In current color palette.

Proximity	Related Colors		Page
13.73	Light Bluish Green		74
15.89	White		116
17.29	Light Stone Grey		120
18.49	Light Grey		117
19.08	Light Blue		83
21.41	Light Bluish Violet		93

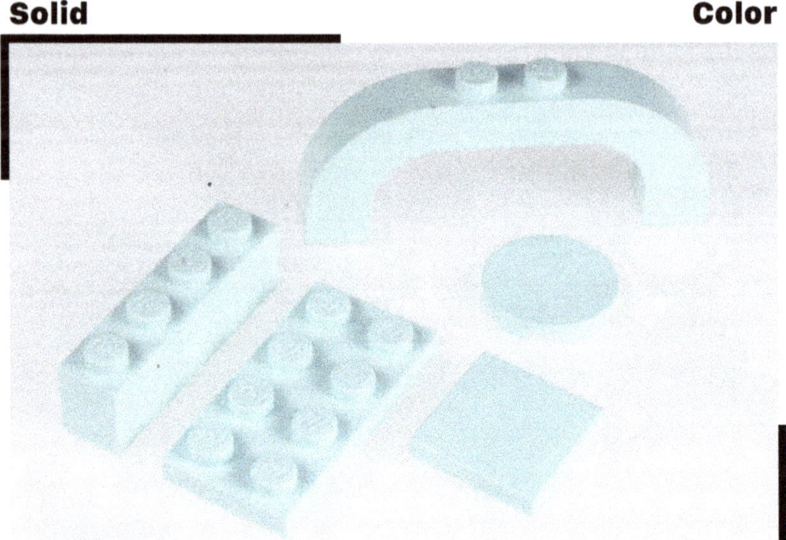

Light Bluish Green   58

Lego	Light Bluish Green				118
Bricklink	Aqua				41

UUID   FB5F0671-474E-4AFF-A431-F9A6A5684063

Year	1998	**to**	2006	**Availability**	Some

LAB	83	-23	-6	**Pantone**	324 C
sRGB	157	221	215		
CMYK	35	0	14	0	

Notes   Mainly Clikits and Scala color.

Proximity	Related Colors		Page
13.73	Aqua		73
15.53	Light Blue		83
21.18	Light Grey		117
22.10	Pastel Blue		79
22.52	Light Stone Grey		120
23.40	Light Bluish Violet		93

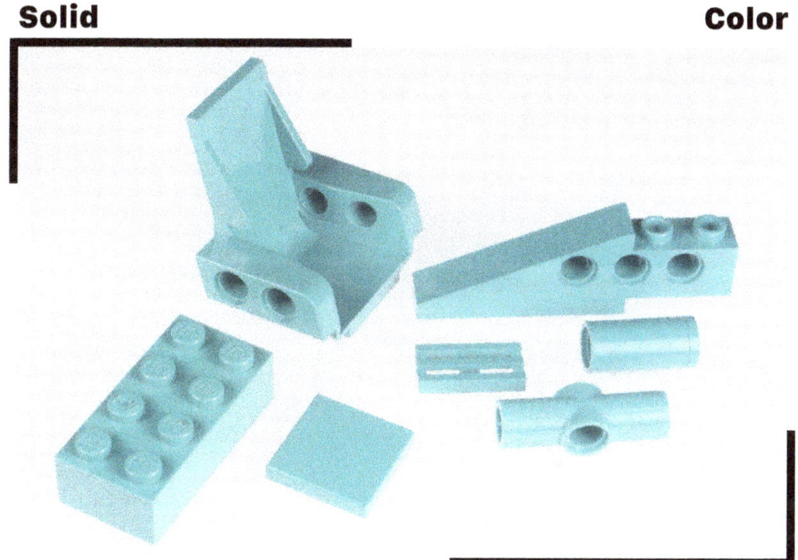

Bright Bluish Green   59

Lego	Bright Bluish Green				107
Bricklink	Dark Turquoise				39
UUID	D0F38567-B649-44E0-B881-1F94FFAEAFFF				
Year	1998	**to**	2005	**Availability**	Several

LAB	49	-52	-14	**Pantone**	3282 C
sRGB	0	146	134		
CMYK	100	4	56	8	

Notes   Popular in Technic.

Proximity	Related Colors		Page
12.55	Medium Bluish Green		76
27.14	Dove Blue		77
27.34	Medium Azure		78
30.50	Tiny Blue		80
33.64	Pastel Blue		79
37.69	Faded Green		69

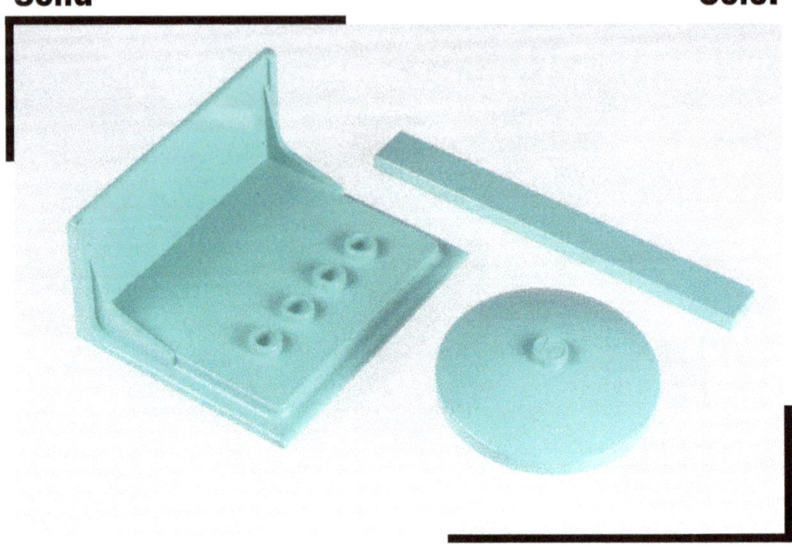

Medium Bluish Green   60

Lego	Medium Bluish Green				116
Bricklink	Light Turquoise				40
UUID	29604DD9-3AAC-4D03-B9E0-D11CE2E7FCCF				
Year	1998	**to**	2003	**Availability**	Some

LAB	62	-51	-14	**Pantone**	326 C
sRGB	0	180	167		
CMYK	80	0	36	0	

Notes   Mainly Scala, Belville and DUPLO parts.

Proximity	Related Colors		Page
12.55	Bright Bluish Green		75
21.04	Medium Azure		78
22.76	Dove Blue		77
29.04	Tiny Blue		80
29.49	Pastel Blue		79
36.10	Light Bluish Green		74

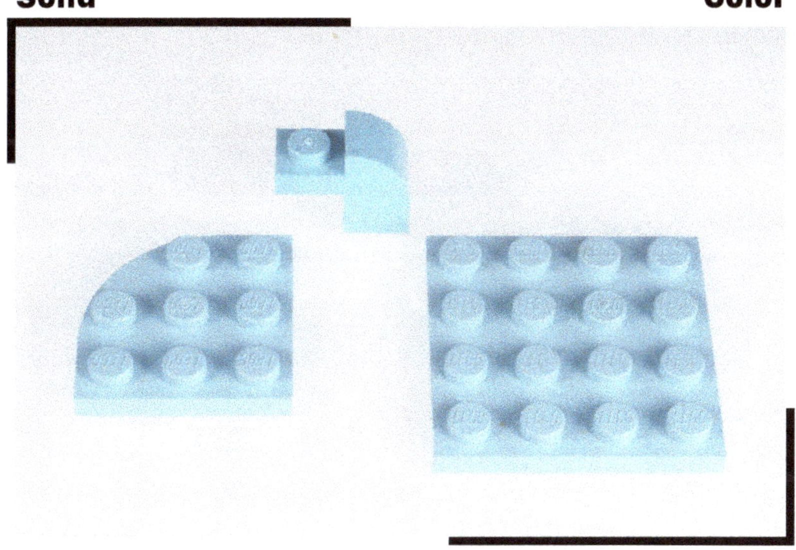

Dove Blue   61

Lego	Dove Blue	232
Bricklink	Sky Blue	87

UUID	87C1EA3A-24DC-405D-9D2B-84983A684EF5				
Year	2004	to	2007	Availability	Some

				Pantone	631 C
LAB	62	-30	-23		
sRGB	22	174	189		
CMYK	74	0	13	0	

Notes   No 2x4 brick available.

Proximity	Related Colors		Page
6.62	Medium Azure		78
9.01	Tiny Blue		80
9.95	Pastel Blue		79
16.61	Tiny-Medium Blue		82
20.65	Medium Blue		85
22.76	Medium Bluish Green		76

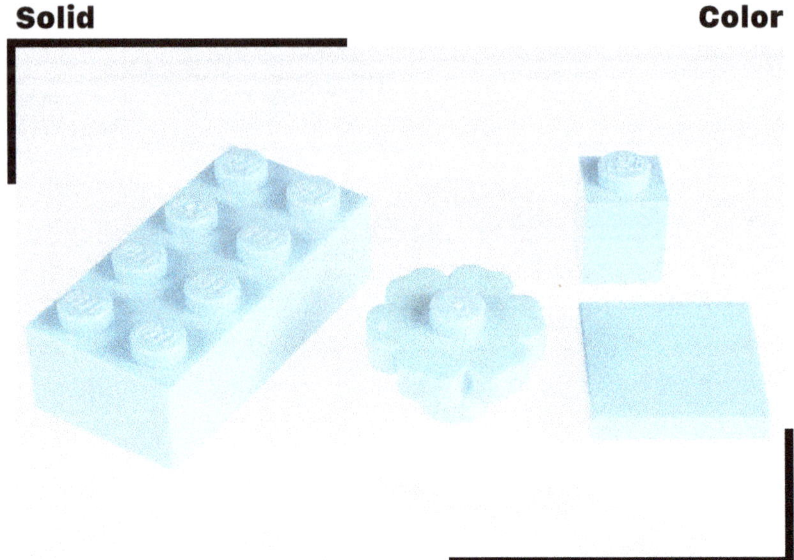

Medium Azure   62

Lego	Medium Azure			322
Bricklink	Medium Azure			156
UUID	BB91F0ED-51AB-47D4-A7A7-C35AEAD73331			
Year	2012	**to**	current	**Availability** Several

LAB	66	-35	-27	**Pantone**	631 C
sRGB	0	186	205		
CMYK	74	0	13	0	

Notes   In current color palette.

Proximity	Related Colors		Page
6.62	Dove Blue		77
12.49	Tiny Blue		80
15.55	Pastel Blue		79
21.04	Medium Bluish Green		76
22.32	Tiny-Medium Blue		82
24.52	Medium Blue		85

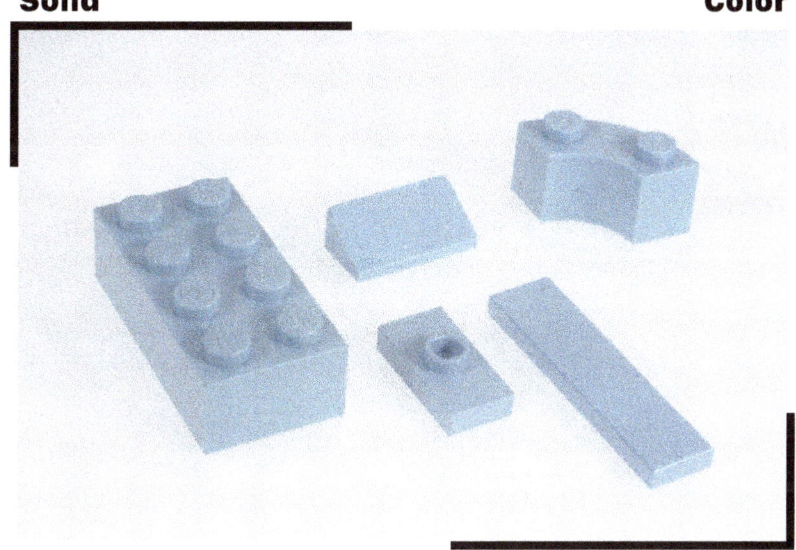

Pastel Blue   63

Lego	Pastel Blue	11
Bricklink	Maersk Blue	72
UUID	B2793479-6556-4476-88ED-57E6BF203994	

Year	1974	to	2011	Availability	Some

				Pantone	
LAB	64	-22	-18		631 C
sRGB	88	172	184		
CMYK	74	0	13	0	

Notes   Used mainly for Maersk branded sets.

Proximity	Related Colors		Page
8.46	Tiny-Medium Blue		82
9.95	Dove Blue		77
14.27	Tiny Blue		80
15.55	Medium Azure		78
16.16	Light Lilac		87
17.16	Medium Blue		85

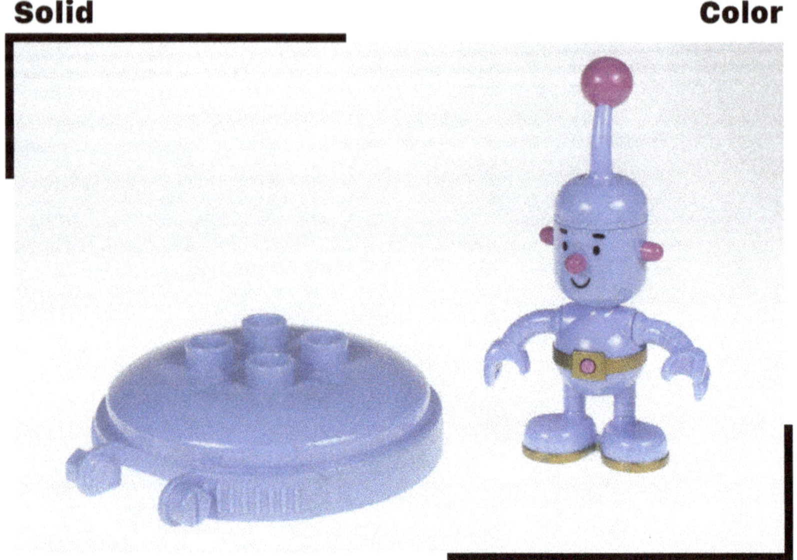

Tiny Blue   64

Lego	Tiny Blue				188
Bricklink					
UUID	99505CED-9FE6-42E1-B6CA-7E0622C0ED5A				
Year	2003	**to**	2004	**Availability**	Rare

LAB	57	-27	-29	**Pantone**	7459 C
sRGB	0	158	184		
CMYK	72	9	9	13	

Notes   Only used in one set. Not listed on Bricklink.

Proximity	Related Colors		Page
9.01	Dove Blue		77
12.49	Medium Azure		78
14.27	Pastel Blue		79
16.23	Medium Blue		85
16.44	Dark Azure		81
16.61	Tiny-Medium Blue		82

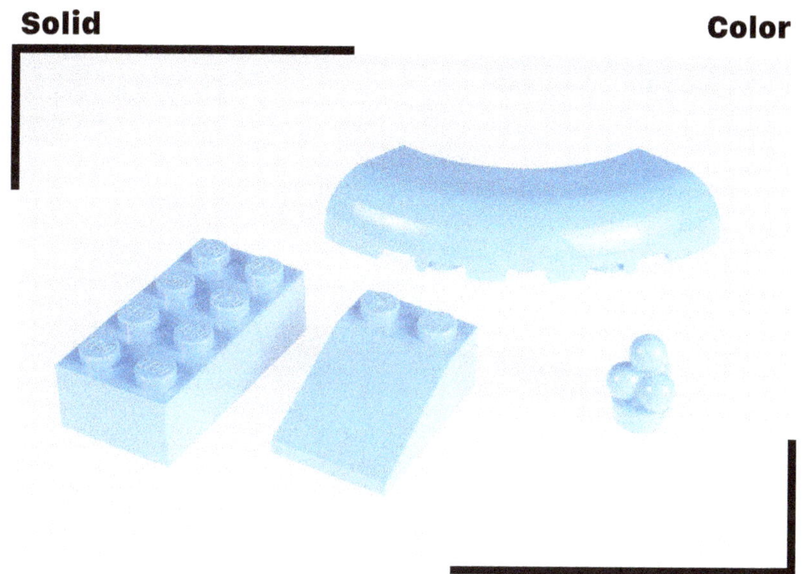

Dark Azure   65

Lego	Dark Azure					321
Bricklink	Dark Azure					153

UUID 261FAAD1-D07C-4268-A18E-A4131785A9D1

Year	2011	**to**	current	**Availability**	Several

LAB	52	-24	-45		**Pantone**	7461 C
sRGB	0	150	200			
CMYK	98	24	1	3		

Notes In current color palette.

Proximity	Related Colors		Page
16.44	Tiny Blue		80
20.91	Medium Blue		85
24.61	Dove Blue		77
24.92	Medium Royal Blue		91
25.02	Medium Azure		78
28.75	Tiny-Medium Blue		82

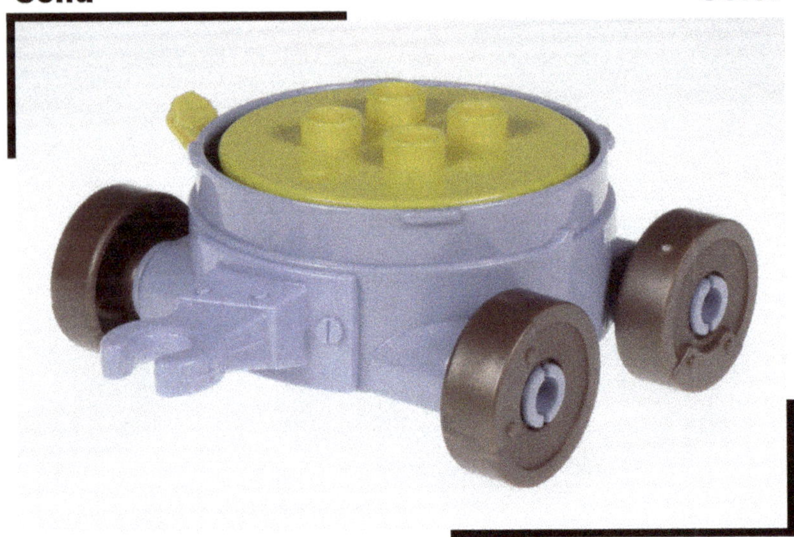

Tiny-Medium Blue   66

Lego	Tiny-Medium Blue				269
Bricklink					
UUID	F720B58D-7795-4522-8489-862520A6D896				
Year	2004	**to**	2004	**Availability**	Rare

LAB	61	-14	-20	**Pantone**	549 C
sRGB	100	160	180		
CMYK	56	8	9	21	

Notes   Used in only one set. Not listed on Bricklink.

Proximity	Related Colors		Page
8.46	Pastel Blue		79
11.53	Light Lilac		87
11.80	Medium Blue		85
13.68	Sand Blue		88
15.87	Light Royal Blue		86
16.61	Tiny Blue		80

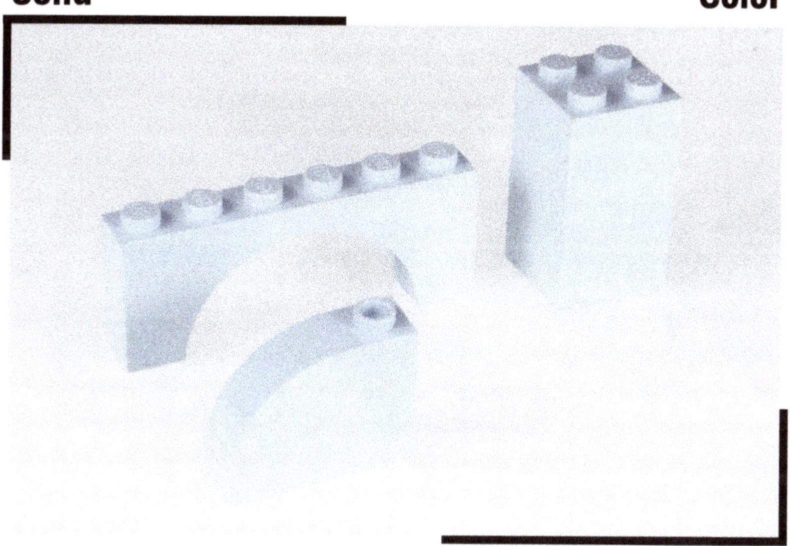

Light Blue   67

Lego	Light Blue				45
Bricklink	Light Blue				62
UUID	9A42358D-25BA-44C0-9E38-0A494FE0680F				
Year	1995	**to**	2002	**Availability**	Some

LAB	79	-10	-14	**Pantone**	551 C
sRGB	163	205	219		
CMYK	35	3	8	7	

Notes This color was replaced by 212 Light Royal Blue in 2004.

Proximity	Related Colors		Page
9.87	Light Bluish Violet		93
13.85	Light Royal Blue		86
14.52	Light Lilac		87
15.53	Light Bluish Green		74
15.66	Light Stone Grey		120
19.08	Aqua		73

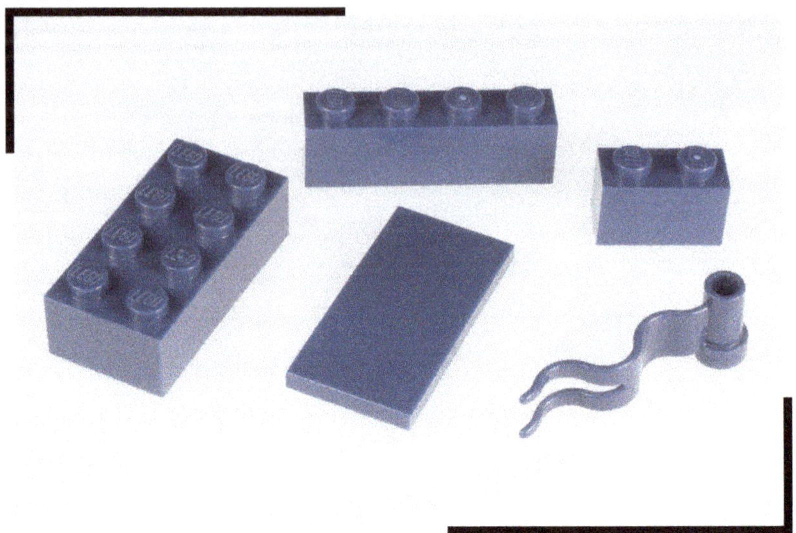

Earth Blue   68

Lego	Earth Blue	140
Bricklink	Dark Blue	63

UUID   CB2D76E1-3806-4758-A2F6-4A0A682A7EEC

Year	2001	**to**	current	**Availability**	Many

				Pantone	7463 C
LAB	18	-8	-27		
sRGB	0	56	82		
CMYK	100	63	12	67	

Notes   In current color palette.

Proximity	Related Colors		Page
22.73	Bright Bluish Violet		96
26.28	Dark Royal Blue		92
29.39	Black		123
31.76	Bright Lilac		98
33.28	Ultra-Dark Blue		97
33.28	Reddish Lilac		103

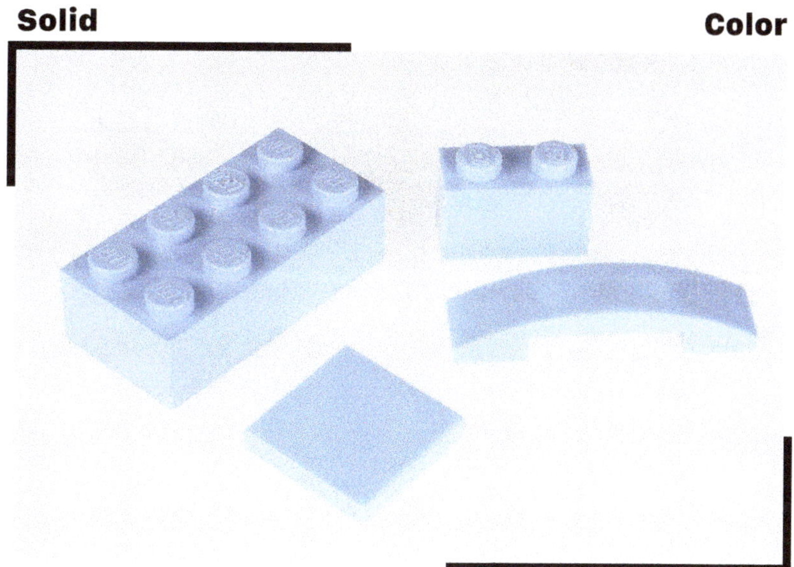

Medium Blue 69

Lego	Medium Blue	102
Bricklink	Medium Blue	42

UUID	FAD9FB60-C7B2-435C-8508-FEBAB37CB679

Year	1997	**to**	current	**Availability**	Several

					Pantone	542 C
LAB	60	-11	-31		**Pantone**	542 C
sRGB	83	161	199			
CMYK	60	19	1	4		

Notes In current color palette.

Proximity	Related Colors		Page
11.28	Light Lilac		87
11.80	Tiny-Medium Blue		82
14.54	Light Royal Blue		86
16.23	Tiny Blue		80
17.16	Pastel Blue		79
18.95	Medium Royal Blue		91

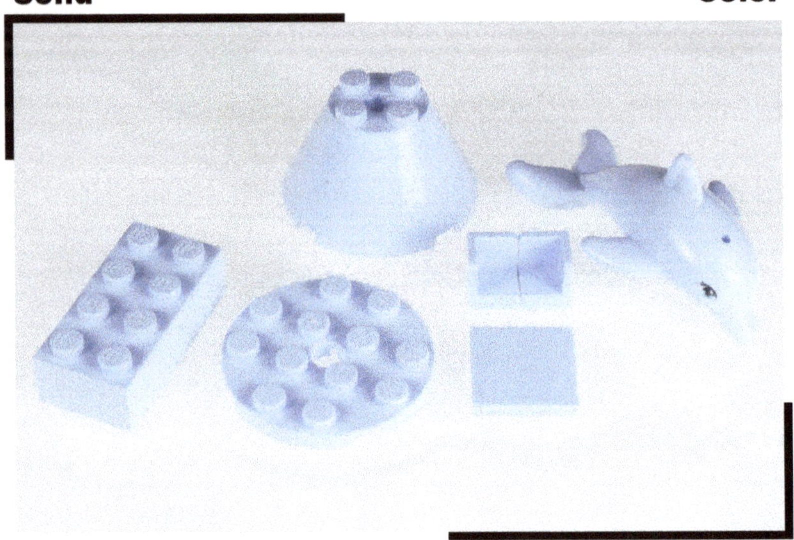

Light Royal Blue   70

Lego	Light Royal Blue	212
Bricklink	Bright Light Blue	105
UUID	08E897E0-4FE4-49A0-A82D-28E0A518BBAC	

Year	2004	**to**	current	**Availability**	Several

				Pantone	278 C
LAB	74	-9	-27		
sRGB	137	195	231		
CMYK	45	14	0	0	

Notes	In current color palette.

Proximity	Related Colors		Page
5.30	Light Lilac		87
13.85	Light Blue		83
14.54	Medium Blue		85
15.87	Tiny-Medium Blue		82
18.51	Pastel Blue		79
19.00	Light Bluish Violet		93

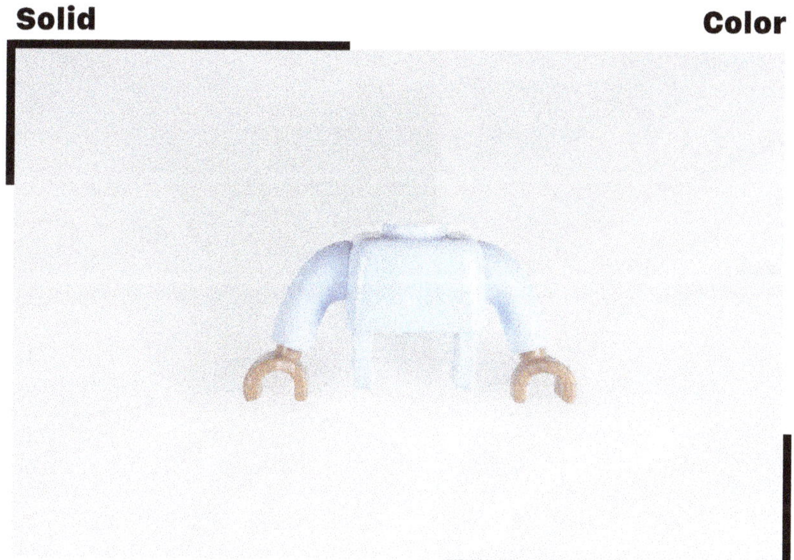

Light Lilac   71

Lego	Light Lilac				220
Bricklink					
UUID	E0570ED0-495B-4EBC-8CDD-429CFF22EC9E				
Year	2004	**to**	2006	**Availability**	Rare

				Pantone	278 C
LAB	69	-8	-25		
sRGB	129	181	214		
CMYK	45	14	0	0	

Notes   On the torso of one DUPLO figure. Not listed on Bricklink.

Proximity	Related Colors		Page
5.30	Light Royal Blue		86
11.28	Medium Blue		85
11.53	Tiny-Medium Blue		82
14.52	Light Blue		83
16.16	Pastel Blue		79
18.87	Light Bluish Violet		93

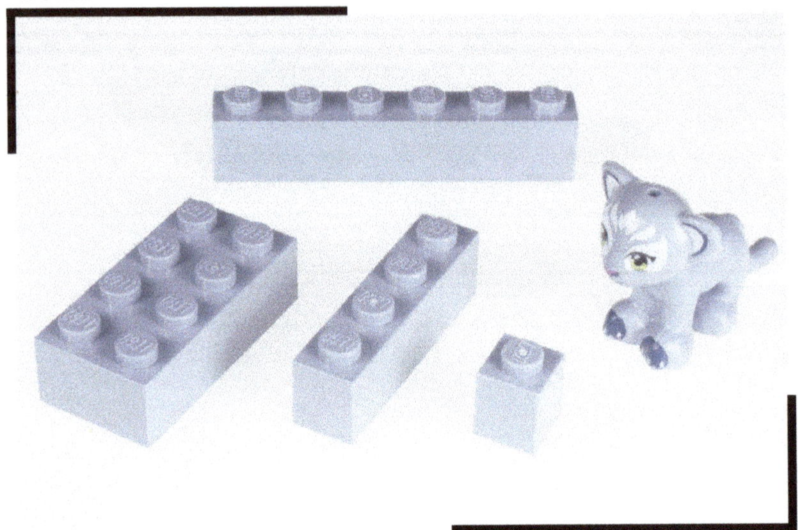

Sand Blue   72

Lego	Sand Blue	135
Bricklink	Sand Blue	55

UUID   A0B9C685-9949-4A43-A89C-369725951D4A

Year	2001	**to**	current	**Availability**	Several

				Pantone	8201 C
LAB	53	-4	-15		
sRGB	106	133	151		
CMYK	56	24	11	34	

Notes   In current color palette. There is no Pantone CP match for 8201C.

Proximity	Related Colors		Page
13.68	Tiny-Medium Blue		82
17.35	Sand Violet		104
17.39	Dark Stone Grey		121
19.31	Medium Blue		85
19.48	Medium Stone Grey		122
19.83	Light Lilac		87

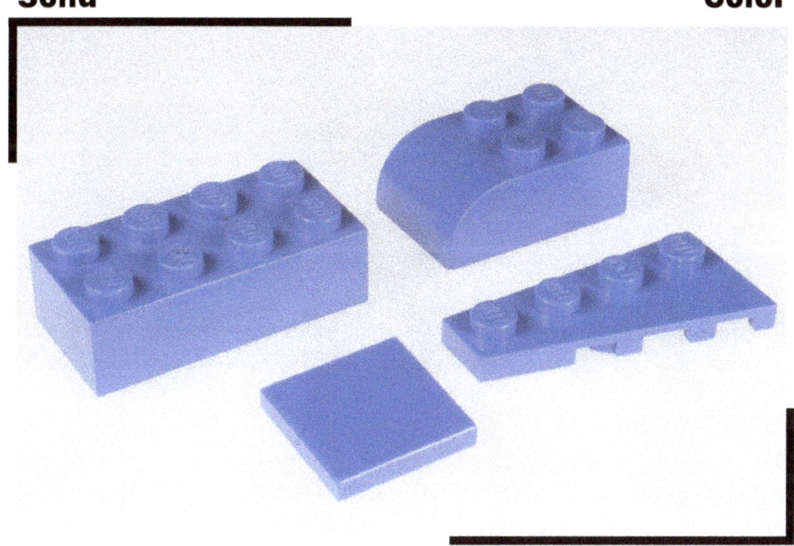

Bright Blue　　　　　　　　　　　　　　　　　73

Lego	Bright Blue	23
Bricklink	Blue	7

UUID　　4C8BB399-8D2E-4094-9EED-182C26B35710

Year	1950	**to**	current	**Availability**	Many

LAB	35	-4	-57	**Pantone**	2945 C
sRGB	0	103	173		
CMYK	100	53	2	16	

Notes　　In current color palette.

Proximity	Related Colors		Page
13.77	Royal Blue		90
22.12	Dark Royal Blue		92
23.33	Medium Royal Blue		91
24.68	Lilac		94
28.78	Dark Azure		81
28.91	Medium Bluish Violet		95

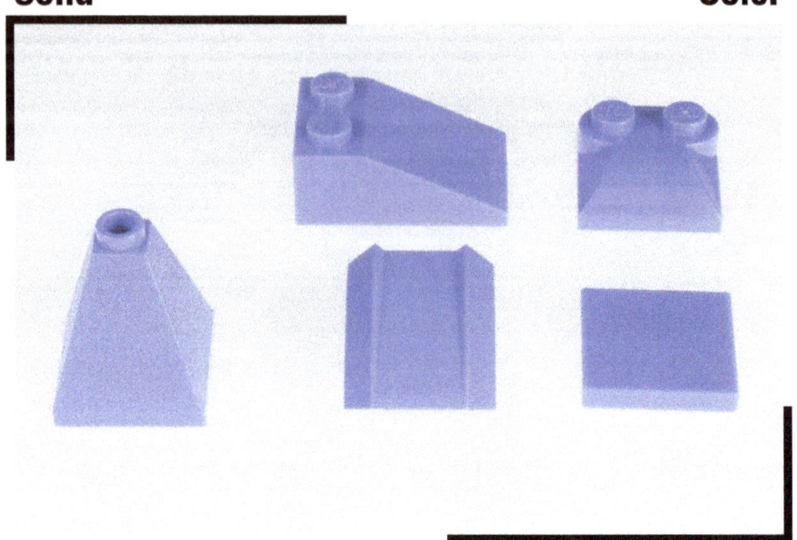

Royal Blue   74

Lego	Royal Blue	195
Bricklink	Blue-Violet	97
UUID	743C84FA-B789-40C7-A257-55A9EE2A8B40	

Year	2004	to	2005	Availability	Some

				Pantone	7455 C
LAB	41	8	-54		
sRGB	15	108	188		
CMYK	90	66	0	0	

Notes   Available only during two years.

Proximity	Related Colors		Page
13.77	Bright Blue		89
14.39	Lilac		94
15.76	Medium Bluish Violet		95
18.33	Medium Royal Blue		91
19.65	Dark Royal Blue		92
25.80	Bright Lilac		98

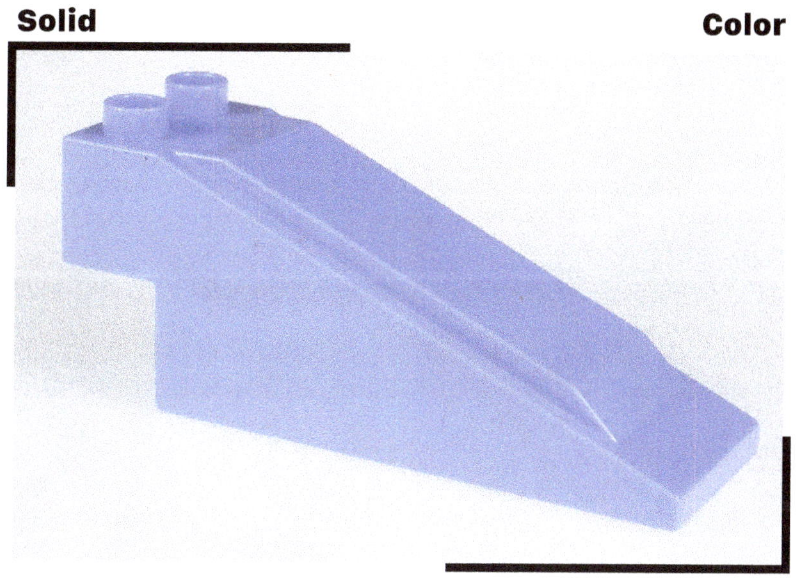

Medium Royal Blue 75

Lego	Medium Royal Blue	213
Bricklink		
UUID	0B8EFCA1-C5F0-47B3-AD7E-E3B529C8D75A	

Year	2004	**to**	2004	**Availability**	Rare

LAB	55	0	-45	**Pantone**	2718 C
sRGB	71	144	209		
CMYK	65	45	0	0	

Notes   Only used for one part. Not listed on Bricklink.

Proximity	Related Colors		Page
14.35	Lilac		94
18.33	Royal Blue		90
18.95	Medium Blue		85
22.87	Medium Bluish Violet		95
23.33	Bright Blue		89
24.92	Dark Azure		81

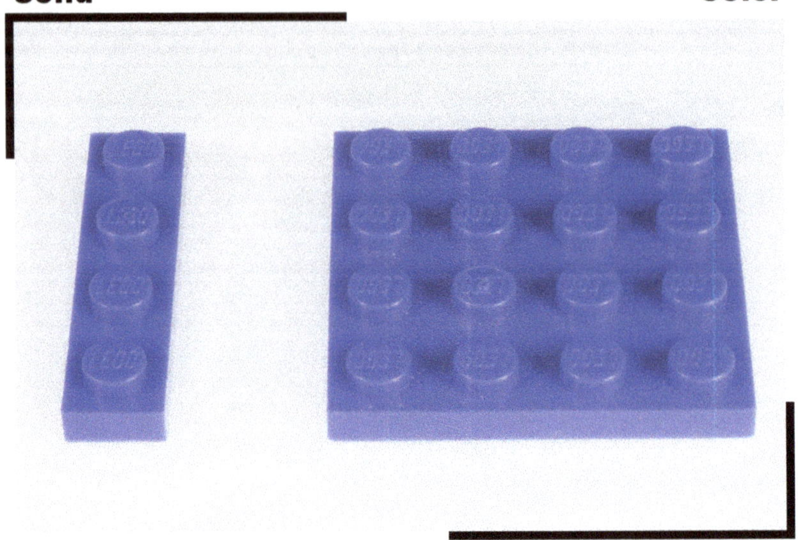

Dark Royal Blue   76

Lego	Dark Royal Blue				196
Bricklink	Dark Blue-Violet				109
UUID	6CEADE99-199D-4F7A-9F31-0BF388DD7A1A				
Year	2004	**to**	2006	**Availability**	Few

LAB	24	11	-45	**Pantone**	534 C
sRGB	0	63	126		
CMYK	95	74	7	44	

Notes   No 2x4 brick available.

Proximity	Related Colors		Page
14.83	Bright Lilac		98
19.13	Medium Lilac		99
19.65	Royal Blue		90
22.12	Bright Blue		89
23.02	Lilac		94
23.18	Medium Bluish Violet		95

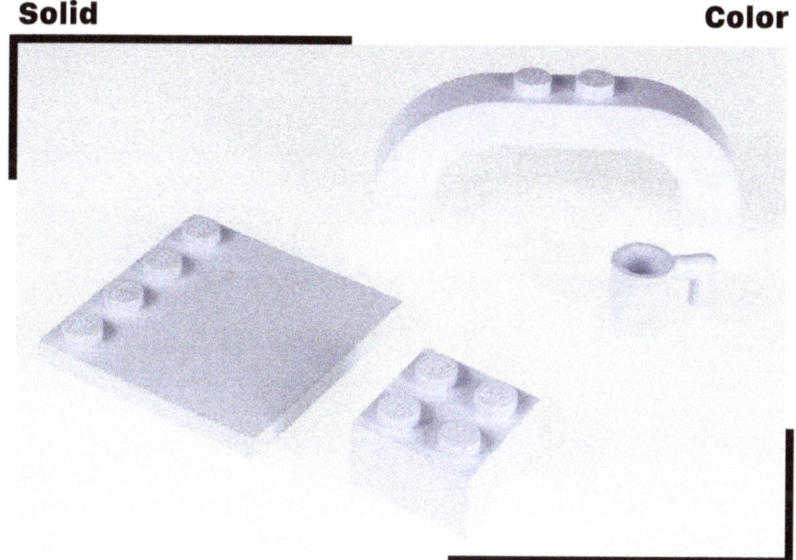

Light Bluish Violet   77

Lego	Light Bluish Violet	39
Bricklink	Light Violet	44
UUID	8C2E39DD-D92E-4FB4-9B95-BE6B64208AB7	

Year	1994	**to**	2004	**Availability**	Some

LAB	79	0	-11	**Pantone**	537 C
sRGB	187	200	217		
CMYK	21	7	2	3	

Notes   Mainly Belville and Scala parts.

Proximity	Related Colors		Page
9.87	Light Blue		83
10.91	Light Stone Grey		120
16.12	Medium Stone Grey		122
18.09	Light Grey		117
18.87	Light Lilac		87
19.00	Light Royal Blue		86

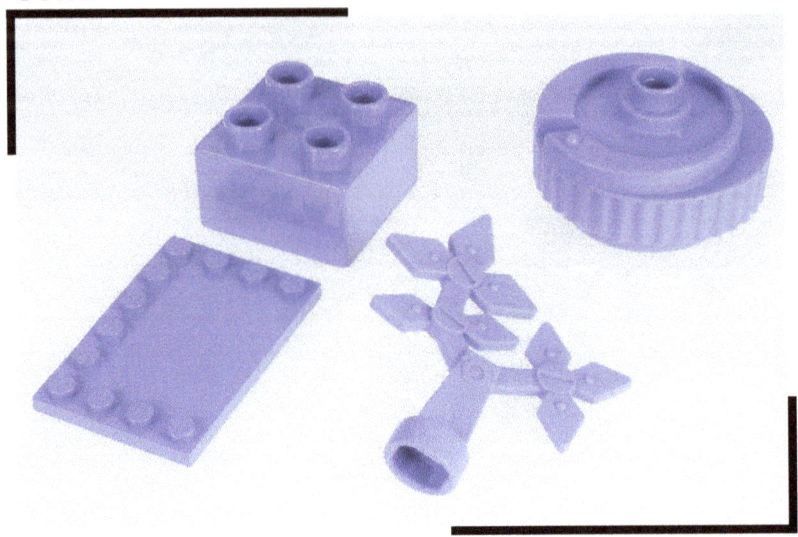

Lilac   78

Lego	Lilac				219
Bricklink	Medium Violet				73
UUID	E628FA3A-E3CB-4585-B0DE-68E909F9580B				
Year	2003	**to**	2005	**Availability**	Some

LAB	46	12	-41	**Pantone**	7456 C
sRGB	87	114	182		
CMYK	72	55	0	0	

Notes   Replaced 112 Medium Bluish Violet around 2003. Both listed as Medium Violet 73 on Bricklink.

Proximity	Related Colors		Page
10.50	Medium Bluish Violet		95
14.35	Medium Royal Blue		91
14.39	Royal Blue		90
21.09	Bright Lilac		98
22.52	Medium Lilac		99
23.02	Dark Royal Blue		92

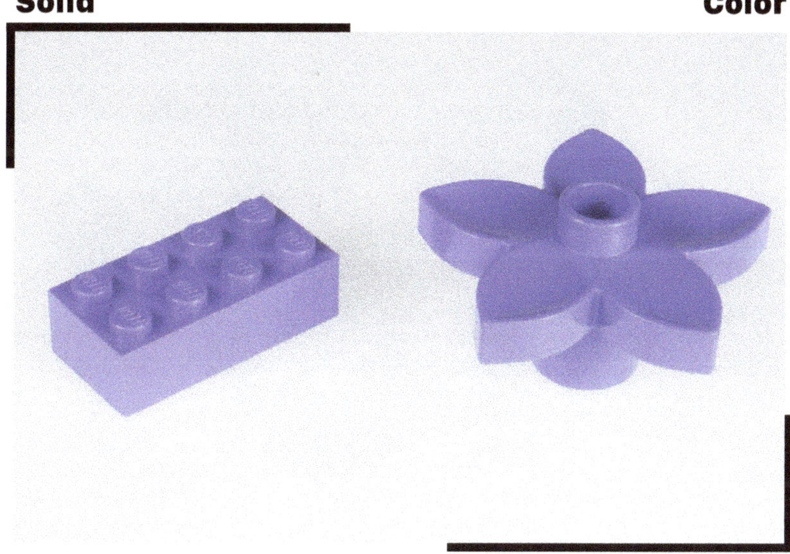

Medium Bluish Violet   79

Lego	Medium Bluish Violet	112
Bricklink	Medium Violet	73
UUID	3D09A049-0738-4635-8AF3-C61E3A081F4A	

Year	1999	to	2005	Availability	Some

LAB	45	21	-46	Pantone	2725 C
sRGB	95	105	186		
CMYK	76	76	0	0	

Notes Replaced by 219 Lilac around 2003. Both listed as Medium Violet 73 on Bricklink.

Proximity	Related Colors		Page
10.50	Lilac		94
15.76	Royal Blue		90
16.33	Medium Lilac		99
18.87	Bright Lilac		98
20.87	Medium Lavender		101
22.87	Medium Royal Blue		91

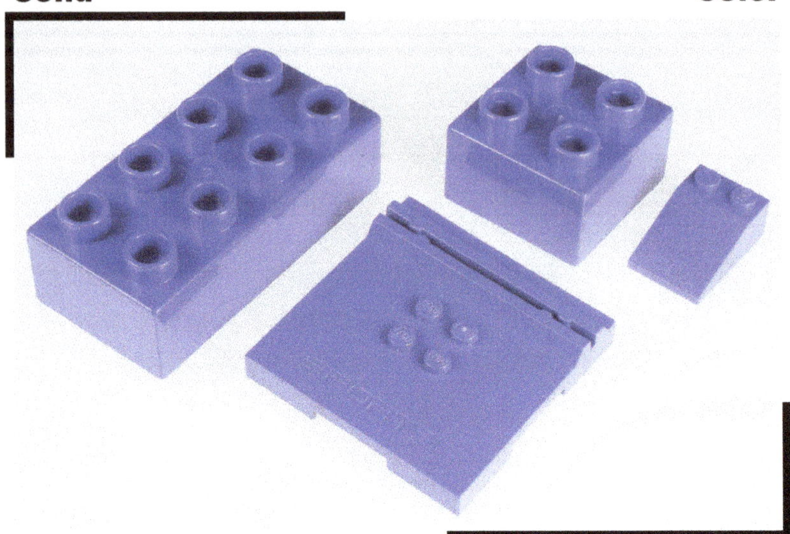

Bright Bluish Violet   80

Lego	Bright Bluish Violet				110
Bricklink	Violet				43
UUID	33CCC401-F044-4B7E-ACCD-8D1C6425414C				
Year	1999	**to**	2004	**Availability**	Some

LAB	30	11	-22	**Pantone**	5265 C
sRGB	69	71	106		
CMYK	86	83	9	45	

Notes   No 2x4 brick available.

Proximity	Related Colors		Page
17.23	Bright Lilac		98
22.73	Earth Blue		84
24.10	Dark Royal Blue		92
24.66	Medium Lilac		99
25.25	Sand Violet		104
25.35	Lilac		94

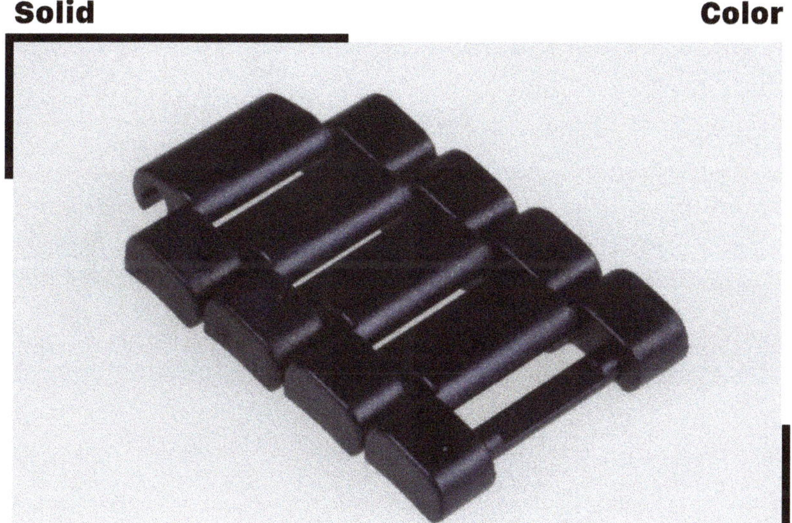

Ultra-Dark Blue   81

Lego

Bricklink

UUID   54FFE1B2-8257-4000-815C-282C01A735BD

Year	2000	**to**	2000	**Availability**	Rare

				Pantone	Black 6 C
LAB					
sRGB	0	0	10		
CMYK	82	71	59	75	

Notes   Only used in the X-Tracker watch.

Proximity	**Related Colors**		**Page**
	Neon Orange		17
	New Dark Red		18
	Fabuland Red		19
	Light Red		20
	Medium Red		21
	Rust		22

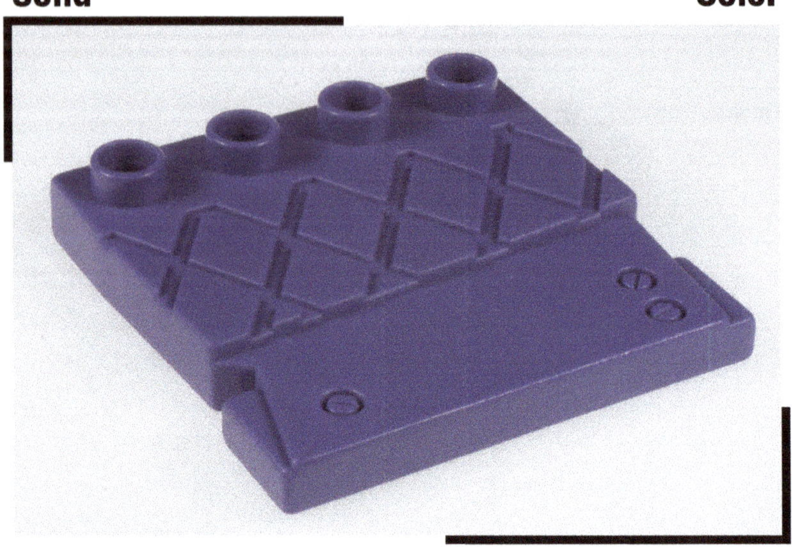

Bright Lilac   82

Lego	Bright Lilac					197

Bricklink

UUID   46644F70-FDD6-45B9-A163-38A9B1573BB0

Year	2003	to	2003	Availability		Rare

LAB	29	21	-36	**Pantone**		269 C
sRGB	68	64	126			
CMYK	80	98	5	27		

Notes   Used for only one part.

Proximity	Related Colors		Page
8.18	Medium Lilac		99
14.83	Dark Royal Blue		92
17.23	Bright Bluish Violet		96
18.87	Medium Bluish Violet		95
21.09	Lilac		94
25.80	Royal Blue		90

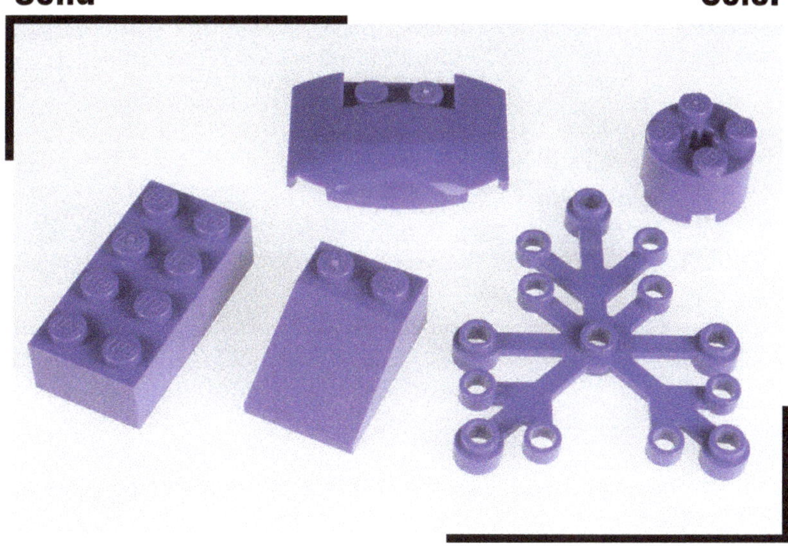

Medium Lilac   83

Lego	Medium Lilac				268
Bricklink	Dark Purple				89
UUID	8DFEF0EF-934C-48FA-878F-5CDF35361CB4				
Year	2004	**to**	current	**Availability**	Several

LAB	31	28	-40	**Pantone**	268 C
sRGB	79	66	140		
CMYK	82	98	0	12	

Notes   In current color palette.

Proximity	Related Colors		Page
8.18	Bright Lilac		98
16.33	Medium Bluish Violet		95
19.13	Dark Royal Blue		92
22.52	Lilac		94
24.66	Bright Bluish Violet		96
25.08	Bright Violet		102

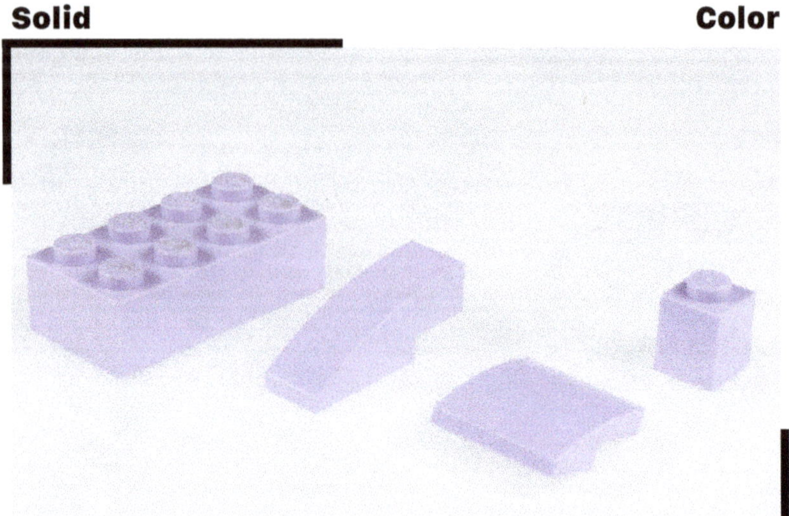

Lavender   84

Lego	Lavender	325
Bricklink	Lavender	154

UUID   78E5CC62-4911-4480-817D-5BECC991F6C2

Year	2011	**to**	current	**Availability**	Several

LAB	71	14	-20	**Pantone**	264 C
sRGB	179	171	212		
CMYK	26	37	0	0	

Notes   In current color palette.

Proximity	Related Colors		Page
19.18	Light Bluish Violet		93
21.61	Light Purple		107
22.13	Light Reddish Violet		112
23.24	Light Lilac		87
24.61	Medium Lavender		101
24.85	Light Royal Blue		86

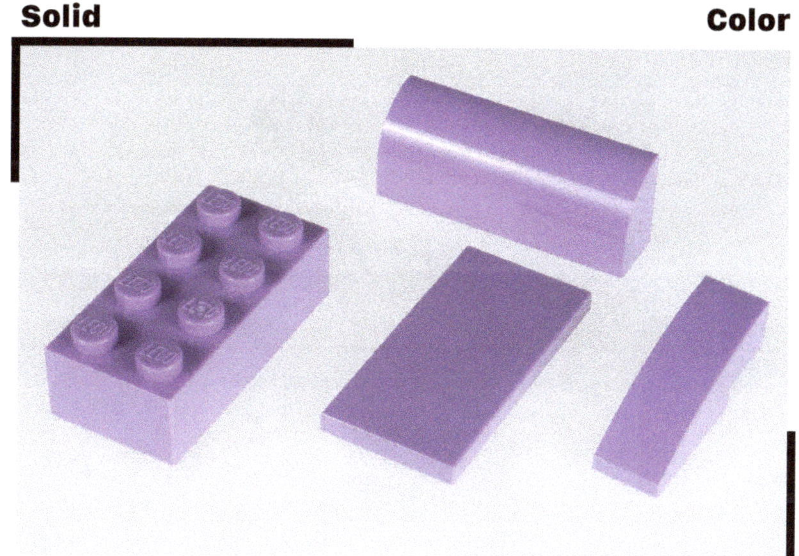

Medium Lavender   85

Lego	Medium Lavender	324
Bricklink	Medium Lavender	157

UUID	D4949AFE-5522-416A-B2E4-C5A23D8844E3

Year	2012	**to**	current	**Availability**	Several

				Pantone	2577 C
LAB	55	30	-30		
sRGB	153	121	188		
CMYK	40	54	0	0	

Notes   In current color palette.

Proximity	Related Colors		Page
20.87	Medium Bluish Violet		95
23.33	Lilac		94
24.61	Lavender		100
26.15	Medium Lilac		99
27.13	Bright Reddish Lilac		105
28.44	Bright Lilac		98

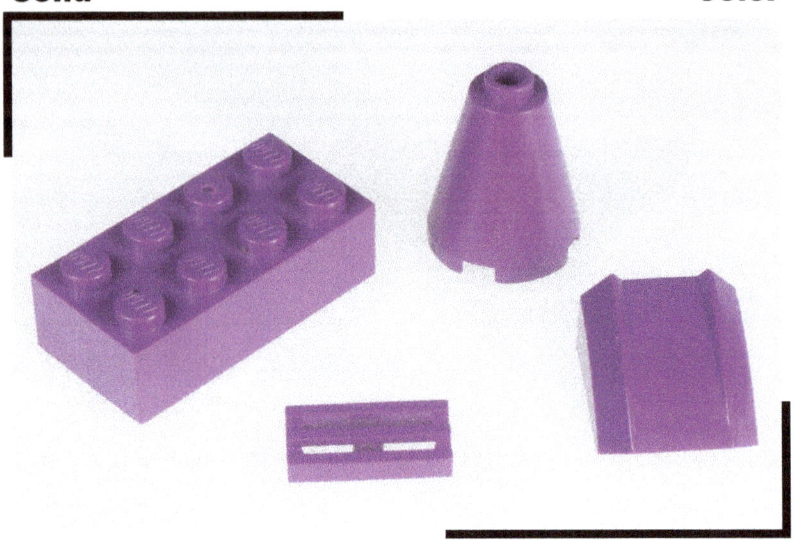

Bright Violet   86

Lego	Bright Violet				104
Bricklink	Purple				24
UUID	EFBDEE2A-0430-4037-9884-4B36355019D2				
Year	1997	to	2006	Availability	Several

				Pantone	2612 C
LAB	31	52	-33		
sRGB	115	39	129		
CMYK	67	100	0	5	

Notes	Used in many themes.

Proximity	Related Colors		Page
14.71	Bright Reddish Lilac		105
25.08	Medium Lilac		99
28.51	Bright Reddish Violet		108
30.64	Bright Lilac		98
32.39	Medium Lavender		101
33.24	Bright Purple		109

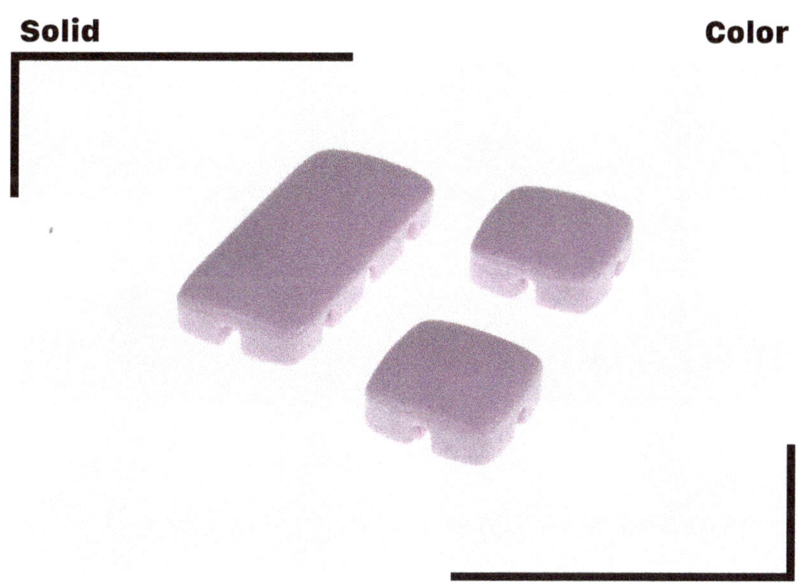

Reddish Lilac   87

Lego	Reddish Lilac			218
Bricklink	Clikits Lavender			227
UUID	C83CD563-2AE5-418B-AA3F-FA87B9AC8036			
Year	2005	**to**	2005	**Availability** Few

LAB				**Pantone**	2573 C
sRGB	142	85	151		
CMYK	40	66	4	0	

Notes   Only in Clikits.

Proximity	Related Colors		Page
	Neon Orange		17
	New Dark Red		18
	Fabuland Red		19
	Light Red		20
	Medium Red		21
	Rust		22

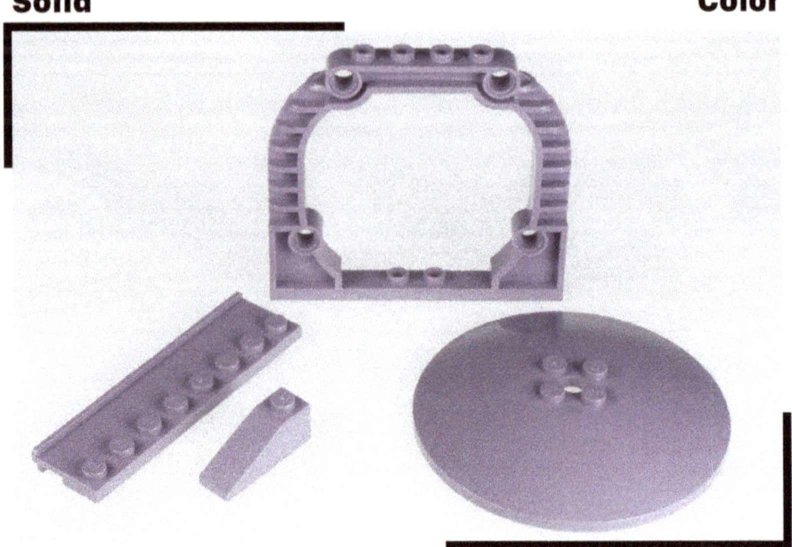

Sand Violet   88

Lego	Sand Violet	136
Bricklink	Sand Purple	54
UUID	E379738A-0FE5-4FA4-ABAF-AB26919274D6	

Year	2001	to	2002	Availability	Some

					Pantone	8100 C
LAB	50	11	-6			
sRGB	131	115	132			
CMYK	36	29	2	5		

Notes   No matching Pantone CP available. CMYK value from 666C used.

Proximity	Related Colors		Page
15.12	Dark Stone Grey		121
17.35	Sand Blue		88
18.98	Sand Red		24
19.46	Dark Grey		118
20.52	Pink		113
20.78	Medium Stone Grey		122

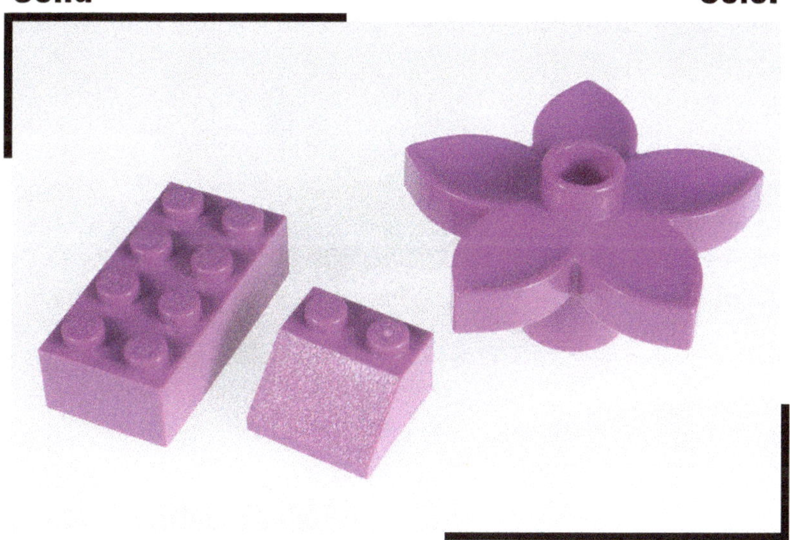

Bright Reddish Lilac 89

Lego	Bright Reddish Lilac		198
Bricklink	Light Purple		93
UUID	A2388759-B090-4DC9-911F-07C9F3F17E64		

Year	2004	to	2007	Availability	Some

				Pantone	248 C
LAB	41	52	-22		
sRGB	148	63	137		
CMYK	42	100	0	0	

Notes Only used for a few parts across several themes.

Proximity	Related Colors		Page
14.71	Bright Violet		102
18.62	Bright Purple		109
18.62	Medium Reddish Violet		110
18.64	Bright Reddish Violet		108
27.13	Medium Lavender		101
31.89	Medium Lilac		99

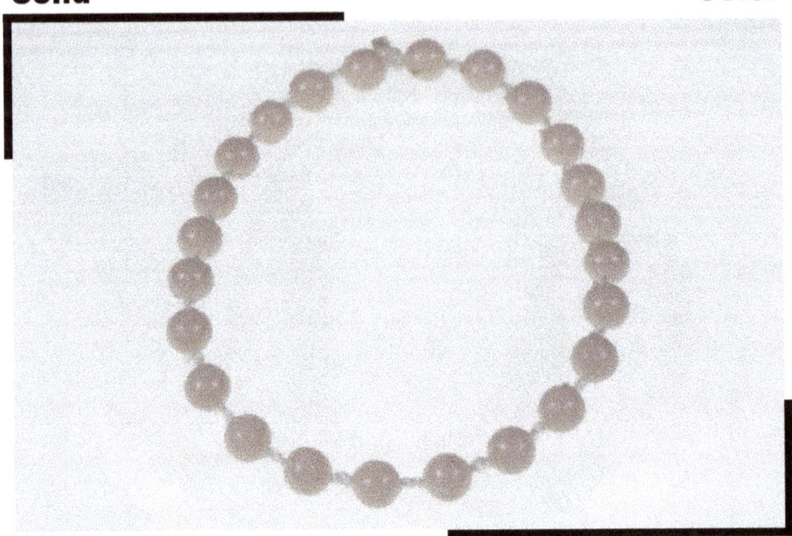

Light Pink   90

Lego

Bricklink Light Pink   56

UUID   3B155AEA-F345-425E-95B5-6C80424285DB

| **Year** | 1994 | **to** | 2007 | **Availability** | Few |

LAB				**Pantone**	183 C
sRGB	238	218	234		
CMYK					

Notes   Bricklink only lists two plastic parts of this color.

Proximity	**Related Colors**		**Page**
	Neon Orange		17
	New Dark Red		18
	Fabuland Red		19
	Light Red		20
	Medium Red		21
	Rust		22

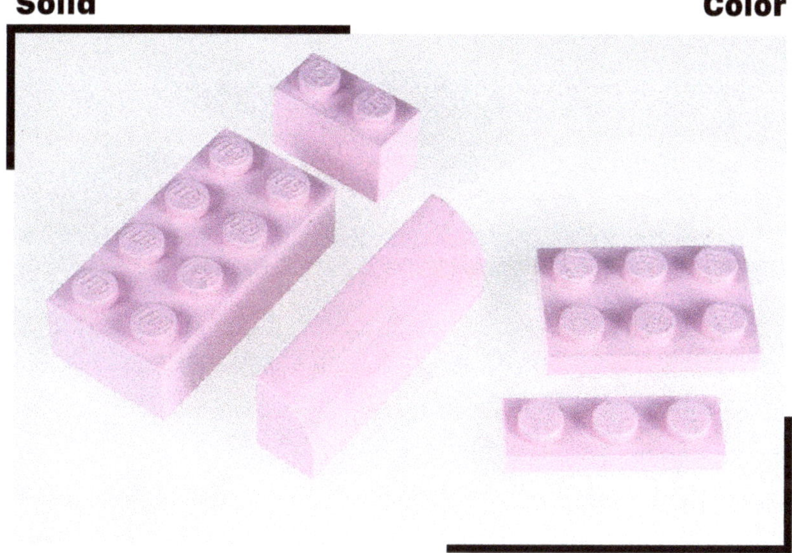

Light Purple   91

Lego	Light Purple	222
Bricklink	Bright Pink	104
UUID	CCB53C8C-A979-4CCA-B6B6-87435C4CBF75	

Year	2004	**to**	current	**Availability**	Several

LAB	75	33	-10	**Pantone**	672 C
sRGB	228	167	209		
CMYK	6	46	0	0	

Notes   Replaced 9 Light Reddish Violet around 2004.

Proximity	Related Colors		Page
13.62	Light Reddish Violet		112
21.43	Rose		115
21.61	Lavender		100
22.59	Flamingo Pink		111
27.02	Light Red		20
27.25	Pink		113

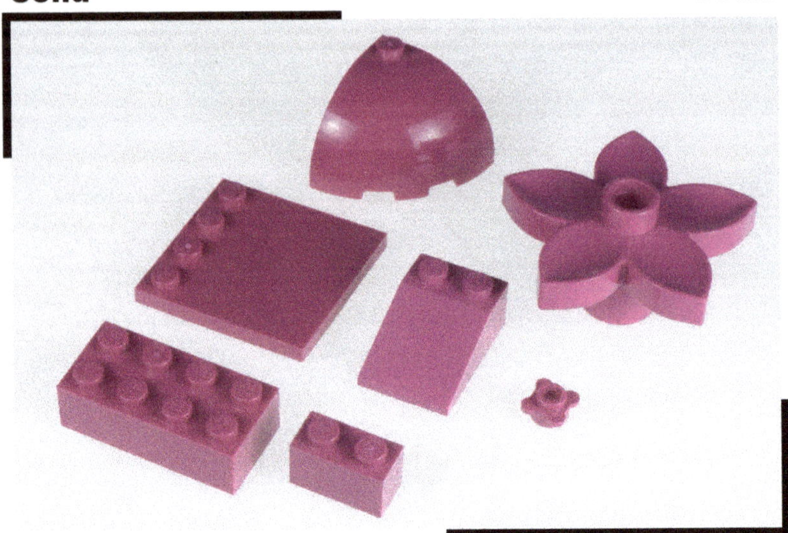

Bright Reddish Violet   92

Lego	Bright Reddish Violet			124
Bricklink	Magenta			71
UUID	8B1D370A-61BE-460C-9CEE-6DE0B9750273			
Year	2000	**to** current	**Availability**	Several

				Pantone	234 C
LAB	37	63	-7		
sRGB	155	31	105		
CMYK	18	100	6	18	

Notes   In current color palette.

Proximity	Related Colors		Page
18.64	Bright Reddish Lilac		105
21.44	Bright Purple		109
21.44	Medium Reddish Violet		110
28.51	Bright Violet		102
33.93	Flamingo Pink		111
36.47	Pink		113

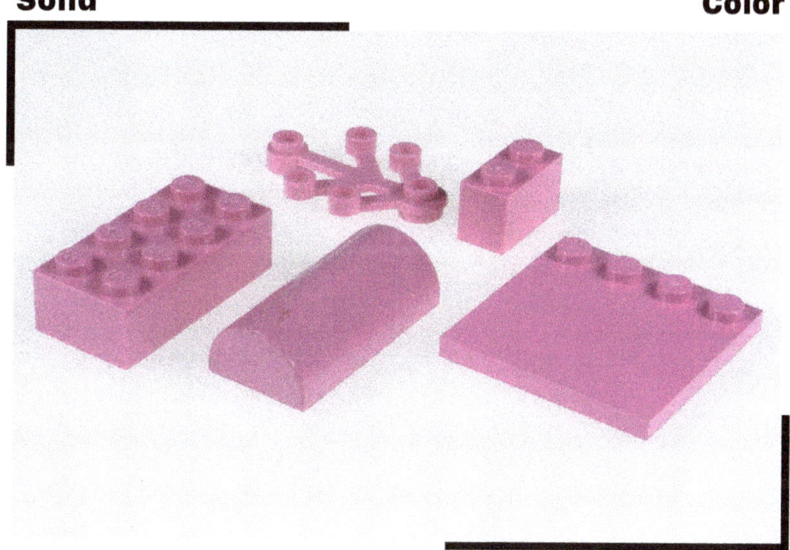

Bright Purple   93

Lego	Bright Purple	221
Bricklink	Dark Pink	47
UUID	41950F51-B274-4A59-87C2-CB8BF7B284FB	

Year	?	**to**	current	**Availability**	Several

LAB	56	52	-11	**Pantone**	674 C
sRGB	194	100	156		
CMYK	16	83	0	0	

Notes Replaced the extremely similar Medium Reddish Violet 22 around 2004.

Proximity	Related Colors		Page
0.00	Medium Reddish Violet		110
16.09	Flamingo Pink		111
18.62	Bright Reddish Lilac		105
21.44	Bright Reddish Violet		108
25.74	Pink		113
27.51	Light Purple		107

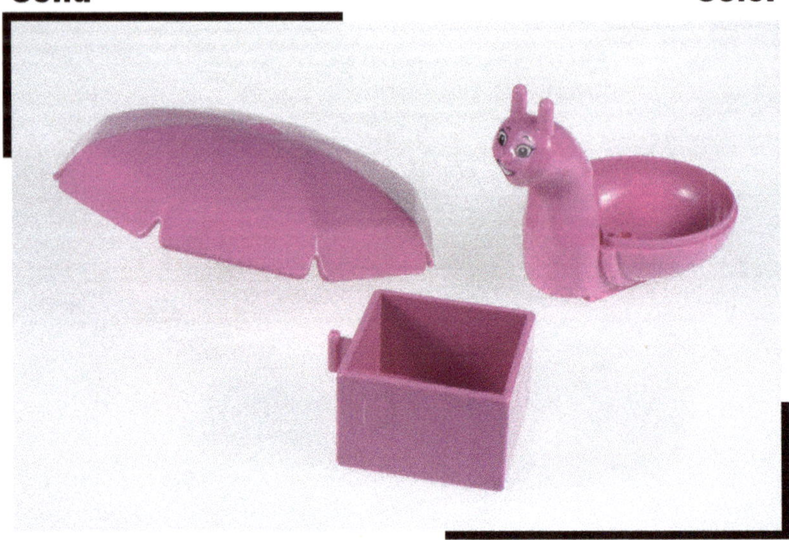

Medium Reddish Violet   94

Lego	Medium Reddish Violet				22
Bricklink	Dark Pink				47
UUID	D7D69DA8-38AB-4D33-96E8-F6E75B106FB5				
Year	1994	**to**	2004	**Availability**	Several

LAB	56	52	-11	**Pantone**	674 C
sRGB	194	100	156		
CMYK	16	83	0	0	

Notes   Replaced by the extremely similar Bright Purple
221 around 2004.

Proximity	Related Colors		Page
0.00	Bright Purple		109
16.09	Flamingo Pink		111
18.62	Bright Reddish Lilac		105
21.44	Bright Reddish Violet		108
25.74	Pink		113
27.51	Light Purple		107

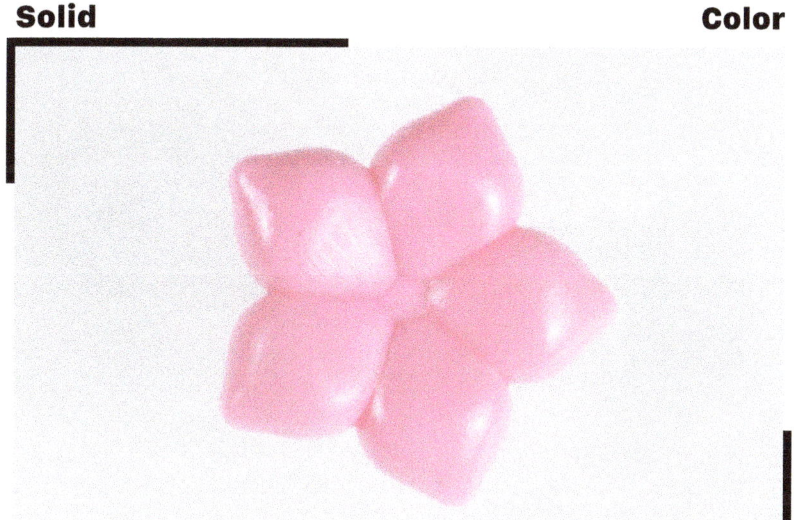

Flamingo Pink   95

Lego	Flamingo Pink				295
Bricklink					
UUID	F790690B-9D7F-457D-94A6-8B3288046A97				
Year	2006	**to**	2006	**Availability**	Rare

				Pantone	211 C
LAB	70	54	-3		
sRGB	245	129	183		
CMYK	0	61	6	0	

Notes   Clikits only color.

Proximity	Related Colors		Page
16.09	Bright Purple		109
16.09	Medium Reddish Violet		110
22.59	Light Purple		107
30.59	Pink		113
32.17	Light Reddish Violet		112
33.93	Bright Reddish Violet		108

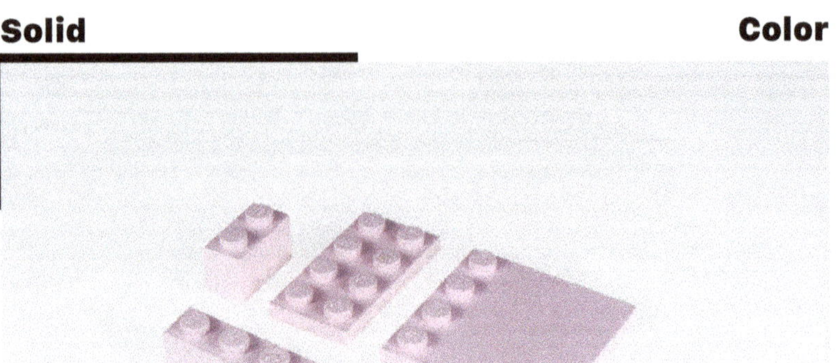

Light Reddish Violet   96

Lego	Light Reddish Violet				9
Bricklink	Pink				23
UUID	C6AB527E-9CD9-4959-84DC-1C5EC6A0EFE5				
Year	1994	to	2006	Availability	Several

				Pantone	1895 C
LAB	80	23	-2		
sRGB	231	185	205		
CMYK	0	30	2	0	

Notes   Replaced 17 Rose starting in 1994 and was replaced by Light Purple 222 around 2004.

Proximity	Related Colors		Page
8.85	Rose		115
13.62	Light Purple		107
16.31	Light Red		20
22.13	Lavender		100
24.61	Light Stone Grey		120
24.73	Light Bluish Violet		93

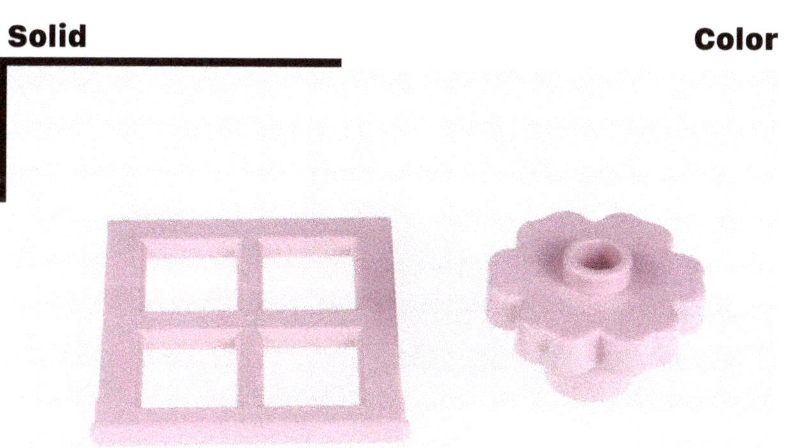

Pink   97

Lego	Pink				16
Bricklink	Medium Dark Pink				94
UUID	4BC5BB3F-63BC-4EAA-9854-EC57448C4BCD				
Year	1992	**to**	1996	**Availability**	Some

LAB	51	30	1	**Pantone**	4995 C
sRGB	160	105	121		
CMYK	15	62	30	38	

Notes   Mainly used in DUPLO parts.

Proximity	Related Colors		Page
15.17	Sand Red		24
20.52	Sand Violet		104
24.88	Rust		28
25.74	Bright Purple		109
25.74	Medium Reddish Violet		110
27.25	Light Purple		107

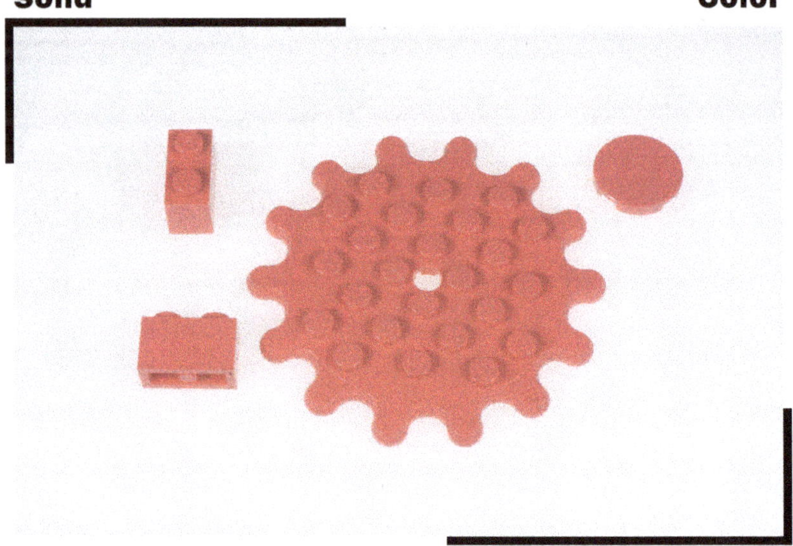

Vibrant Coral   98

Lego	Vibrant Coral		353
Bricklink	Coral		220
UUID	8491FA6E-C1FE-4857-80A4-93142378703E		
Year	2019	**to** current	**Availability** Several

				Pantone	177C
LAB	71	70	28		
sRGB	255	107	135		
CMYK	0	54	38	0	

Notes   In current color palette.

Proximity	Related Colors		Page
14.18	Neon Orange		17
23.58	Medium Red		21
32.03	Bright Reddish Orange		26
34.94	Red Orange		25
35.42	Flamingo Pink		111
36.82	Fabuland Red		19

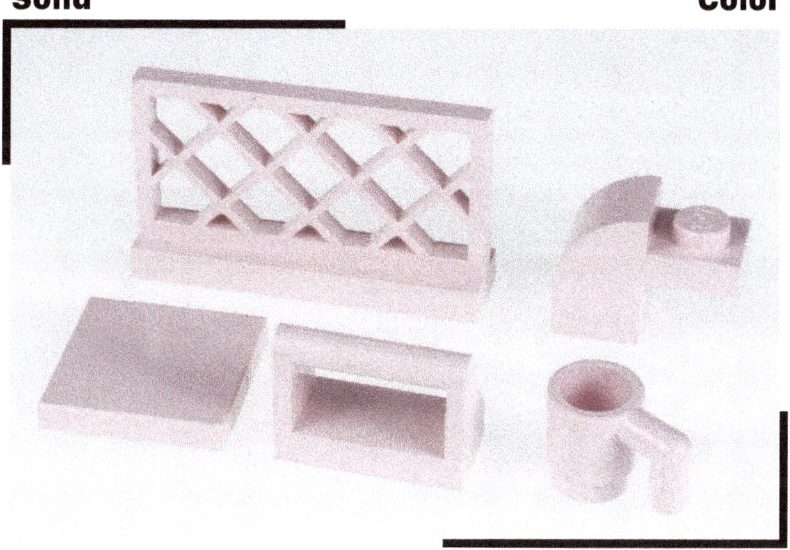

Rose   99

Lego	Rose				17
Bricklink					
UUID	F1332F3A-62EB-46B7-B087-E8EBF1DAB2A0				
Year	1991	**to**	1995	**Availability**	Rare

LAB	79	20	6	**Pantone**	495 C
sRGB	229	184	187		
CMYK	0	32	6	0	

Notes This color often is listed on Bricklink as Light Pink. It was replaced by Light Reddish Violet 9 starting in 1994.

Proximity	Related Colors		Page
8.65	Light Red		20
8.85	Light Reddish Violet		112
18.12	Light Nougat		37
21.43	Light Purple		107
22.10	Light Stone Grey		120
24.37	White		116

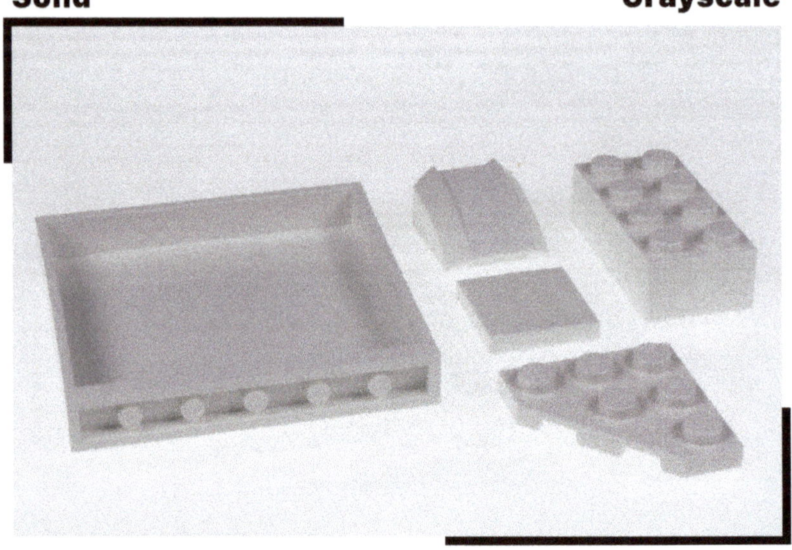

White   100

Lego	White	1
Bricklink	White	1

UUID   64E736F8-8B81-4882-955A-6943383C4D83

Year	1950	**to**	current	**Availability**	Many

LAB	94	1	6	**Pantone**	Warm
sRGB	244	238	228		
CMYK	3	3	6	7	

Notes   In current color palette.

Proximity	Related Colors		Page
15.89	Aqua		73
16.86	Light Stone Grey		120
21.87	Light Grey		117
22.45	Light Bluish Violet		93
24.37	Rose		115
25.79	Light Nougat		37

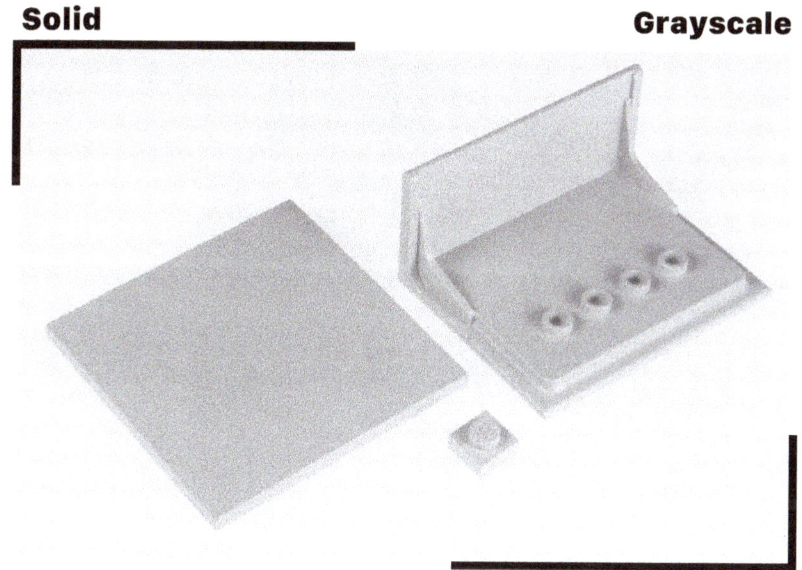

Light Grey   101

Lego	Light Grey				103
Bricklink	Very Light Gray				49
UUID	48273B34-12E9-4807-83FB-2BBBB018459B				
Year	1997	**to**	2004	**Availability**	Some

LAB	74	-7	5	**Pantone**	414 C
sRGB	185	181	173		
CMYK	13	8	17	26	

Notes   Replaced by 208 Light Stone Grey in 2004.

Proximity	Related Colors		Page
8.89	Light Stone Grey		120
10.62	Grey		119
11.23	Medium Stone Grey		122
18.09	Light Bluish Violet		93
18.49	Aqua		73
19.18	Light Blue		83

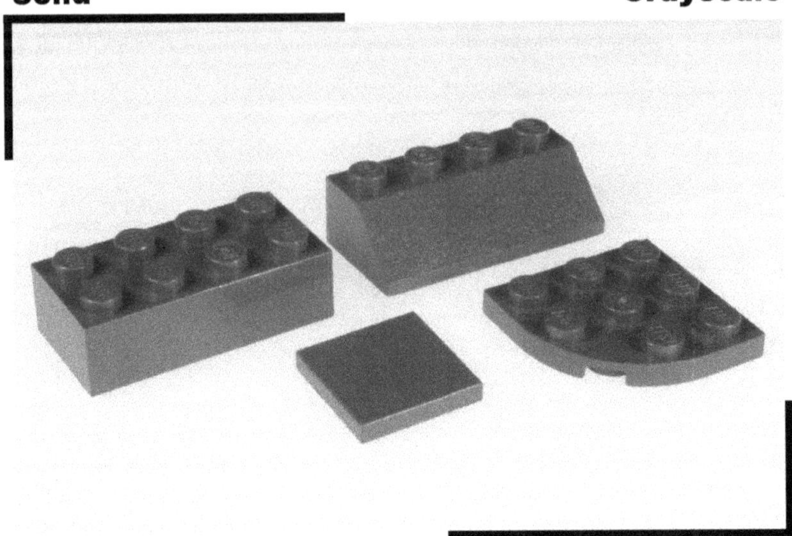

Dark Grey   102

Lego	Dark Grey	27
Bricklink	Dark Gray	10
UUID	FCFE18B7-5159-4C14-B387-D9283B59AA19	

Year	1978	**to**	2006	**Availability**	Many

				Pantone	418 C
LAB	41	-0	7		
sRGB	100	96	86		
CMYK	38	26	40	72	

Notes   Replaced by Dark Stone Grey 199 starting in 2003.

Proximity	Related Colors		Page
8.01	Dark Stone Grey		121
13.18	Dark Army Green		57
19.46	Sand Violet		104
19.67	Medium Brown		32
21.29	Sand Yellow		47
21.44	Brown		34

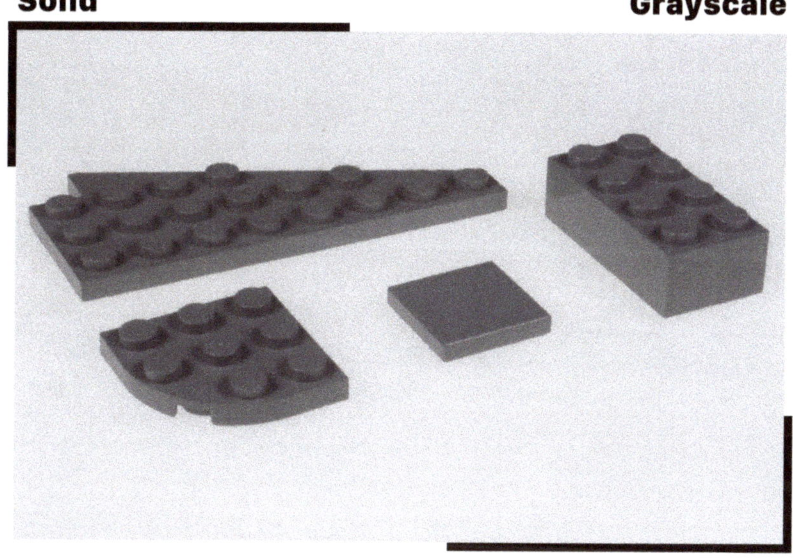

Grey   103

Lego	Grey	2
Bricklink	Light Gray	9

UUID	63743670-ED0A-47C2-B26B-4037B7E44E50

Year	1954	**to**	2004	**Availability**	Many

LAB	65	-3	3	**Pantone**	7538 C
sRGB	154	158	151		
CMYK	24	11	24	33	

Notes	Replaced by Medium Stone Grey 194 starting in 2003.

Proximity	Related Colors		Page
4.66	Medium Stone Grey		122
10.62	Light Grey		117
14.53	Light Stone Grey		120
18.09	Sand Green		68
20.32	Light Bluish Violet		93
20.82	Sand Blue		88

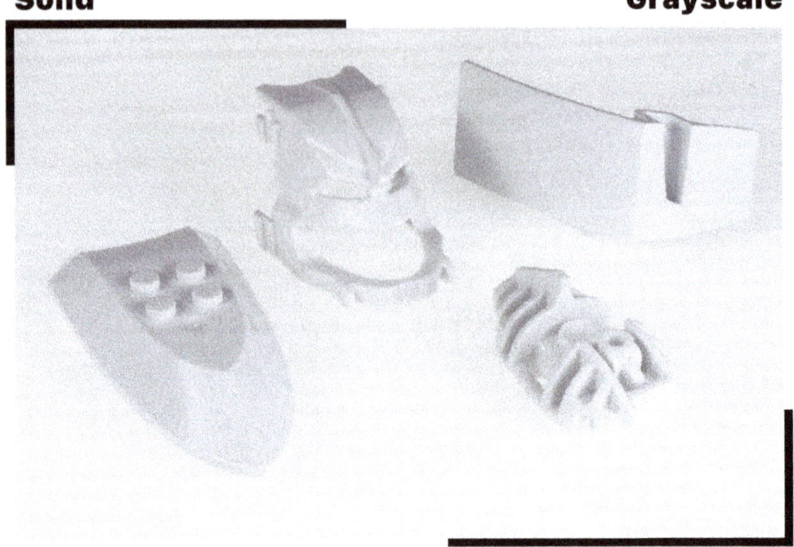

Light Stone Grey   104

Lego	Light Stone Grey				208
Bricklink	Very Light Bluish Gray				99
UUID	692AAC14-785D-485D-88BB-73A353F2E268				
Year	2004	**to**	2010	**Availability**	Some

LAB	79	-1	-0	**Pantone**	428 C
sRGB	193	196	196		
CMYK	10	4	4	14	

Notes   Replaced Light Grey 103 in 2004.

Proximity	Related Colors		Page
8.89	Light Grey		117
10.91	Light Bluish Violet		93
12.15	Medium Stone Grey		122
14.53	Grey		119
15.66	Light Blue		83
16.86	White		116

Dark Stone Grey   105

Lego	Dark Stone Grey	199
Bricklink	Dark Bluish Gray	85

UUID AD1FFC80-364D-4980-9384-594D21EC51E3

Year	2003	**to**	current	**Availability**	Many

				Pantone	Cool Gray
LAB	42	-1	-1		
sRGB	98	101	102		
CMYK	40	30	20	66	

Notes Replaced Dark Grey 27 starting in 2003.

Proximity	Related Colors		Page
8.01	Dark Grey		118
15.12	Sand Violet		104
17.39	Sand Blue		88
19.86	Dark Army Green		57
22.81	Grey		119
23.81	Sand Green		68

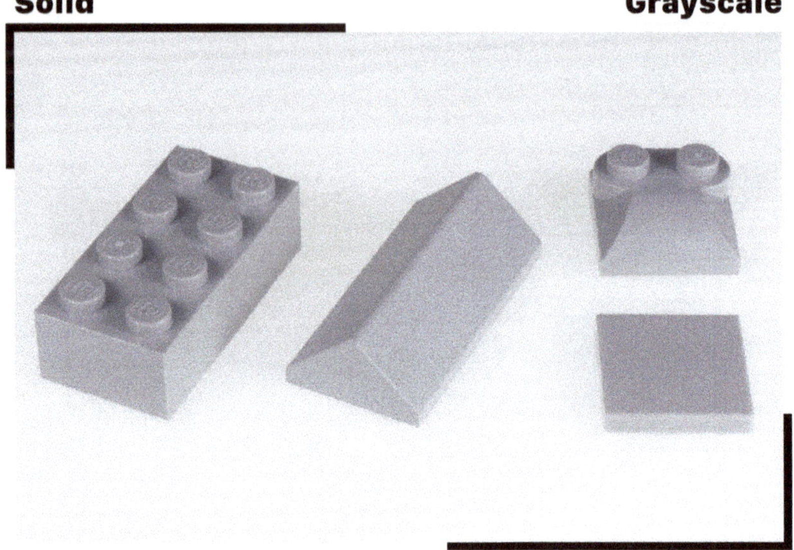

Medium Stone Grey   106

Lego	Medium Stone Grey	194
Bricklink	Light Bluish Gray	86
UUID	3917C8B8-6357-4570-9799-D13E4DAA8F23	
Year	2003 **to** current **Availability**	Many

LAB	67	-1	-1	**Pantone**	422 C
sRGB	160	163	164		
CMYK	19	12	13	34	

Notes   Replaced Grey 2 starting in 2003.

Proximity	Related Colors		Page
4.66	Grey		119
11.23	Light Grey		117
12.15	Light Stone Grey		120
16.12	Light Bluish Violet		93
19.45	Light Blue		83
19.48	Sand Blue		88

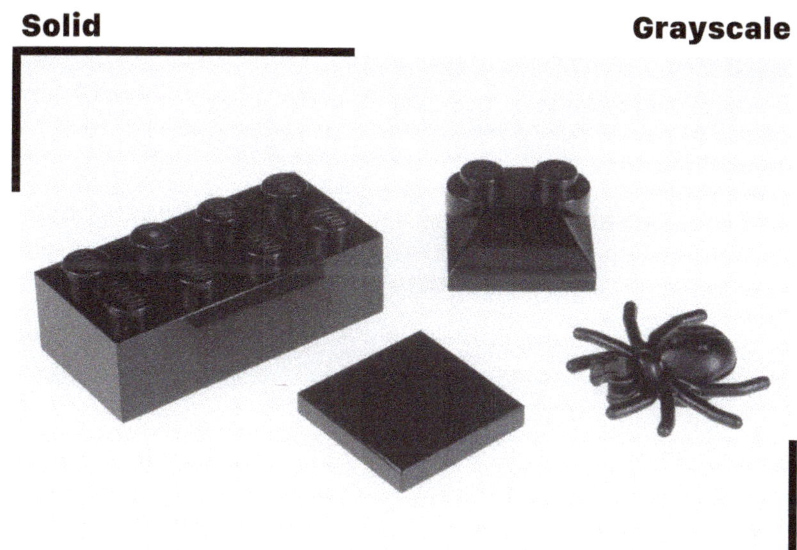

Black   107

Lego	Black	26
Bricklink	Black	11

UUID	9C63A043-4A5E-44E6-8CFD-C29E4035862E

Year	1958	**to**	current	**Availability**	Many

				Pantone	Process
LAB	5	1	-2		
sRGB	18	18	21		
CMYK	63	62	59	94	

Notes   In current color palette.

Proximity	Related Colors		Page
5.69	Ultra-Dark Blue		97
5.69	Reddish Lilac		103
5.69	Light Pink		106
21.53	Dark Brown		27
28.61	Earth Green		72
29.39	Earth Blue		84

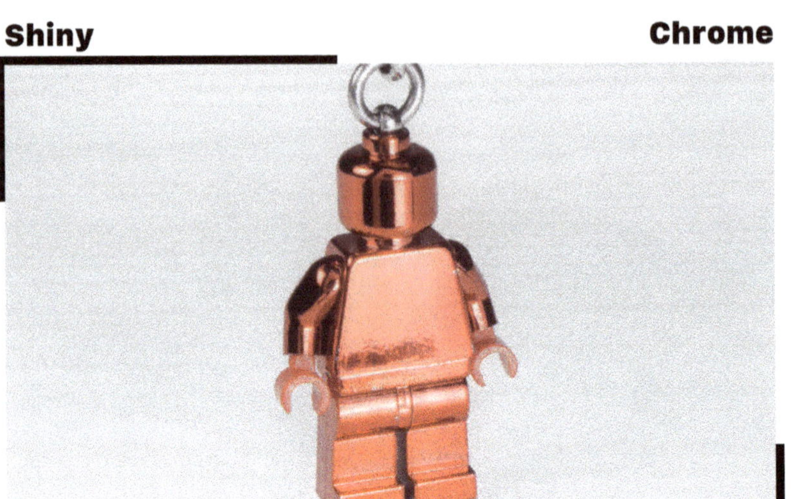

Chrome Red   108

Lego					
Bricklink					
UUID	CF46064A-B3C9-4702-89BC-03B6D2FAF330				
Year	2011	**to**	2011	**Availability**	Rare

LAB	17	11	5	**Pantone**
sRGB	55	35	35	
CMYK				

Notes   Only used for one keychain Minifigure.

Proximity	Related Colors		Page
6.68	Dark Brown		27
16.28	Black		123
20.30	Ultra-Dark Blue		97
20.30	Reddish Lilac		103
20.30	Light Pink		106
22.43	Medium Brown		32

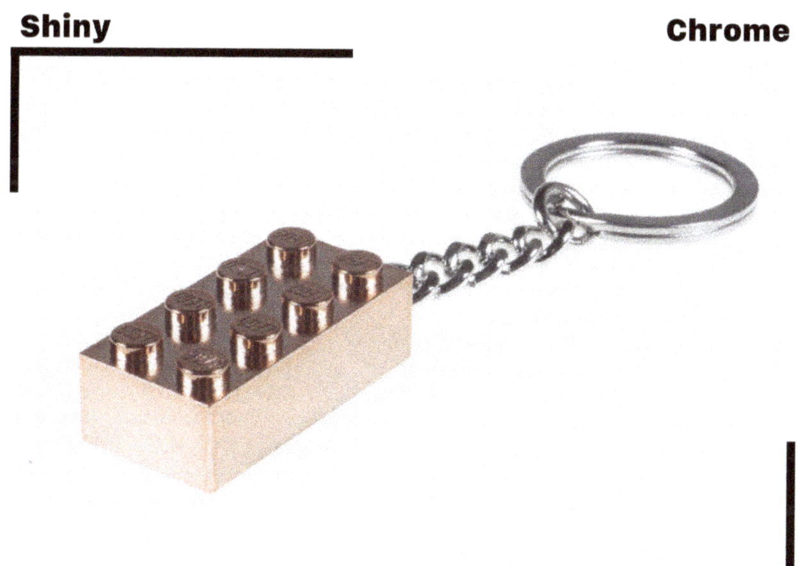

Rose Gold 109

Lego	Rose Gold
Bricklink	
UUID	A70990A4-4828-4743-AF22-680E8943FC6F

Year	2018	**to**	current	**Availability**	Rare

				Pantone	
LAB	19	6	8		
sRGB	58	43	36		
CMYK					

Notes Only used for one keychain.

Proximity	Related Colors		Page
5.25	Dark Brown		27
17.73	Black		123
20.08	Medium Brown		32
21.64	Ultra-Dark Blue		97
21.64	Reddish Lilac		103
21.64	Light Pink		106

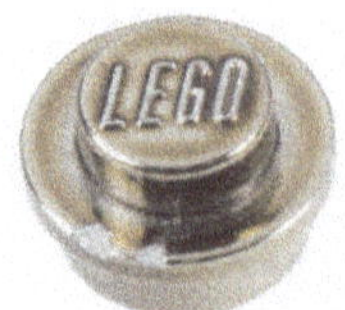

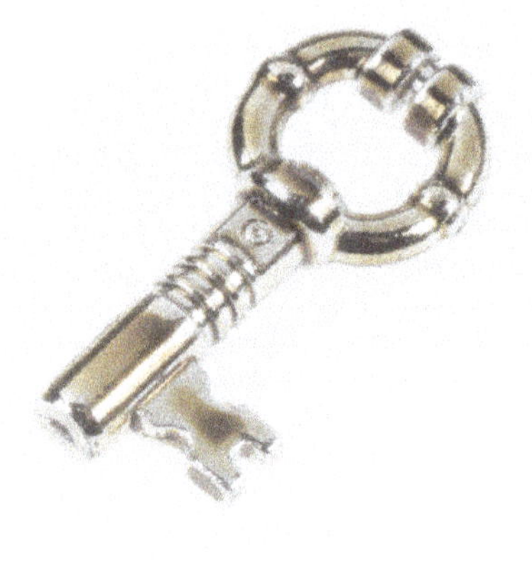

Antique Gold   110

Lego	Antique Gold				
Bricklink	Chrome Antique Brass				57
UUID	9987FD09-3C2B-4CA0-A72A-7B56B68F1DD4				
Year	2001	**to**	2005	**Availability**	Few

LAB	66	3	16	**Pantone**	7536 C
sRGB	174	157	131		
CMYK	11	13	30	32	

Notes   Only used for very few parts.

Proximity	Related Colors		Page
11.72	Sand Yellow		47
14.69	Grey		119
16.86	Brick Yellow		49
16.94	Light Grey		117
17.77	Medium Stone Grey		122
18.12	Olive Green		55

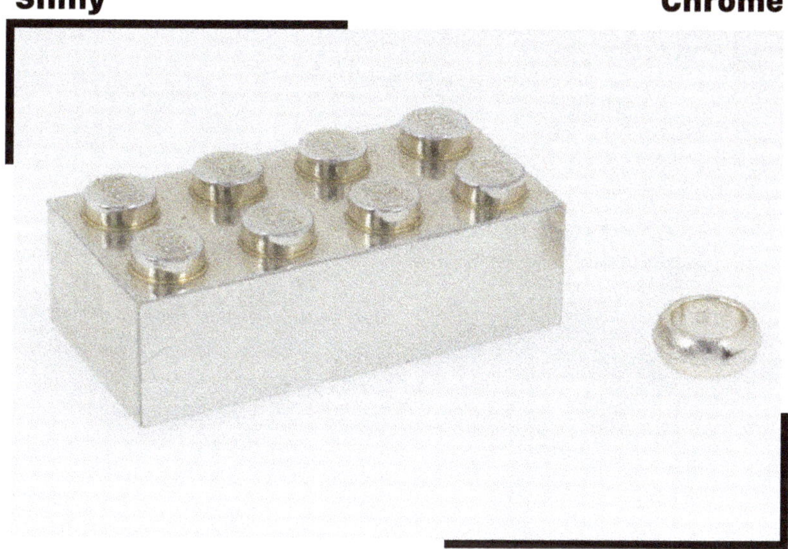

Metalized Gold   111

Lego	Metalized Gold				310
Bricklink	Chrome Gold				21
UUID	C006B643-10D6-4169-BA40-126BF4FE3FBC				
Year	1989	**to**	2021	**Availability**	Some

LAB	14	-1	3	**Pantone**	
sRGB	36	35	31		
CMYK					

Notes   Popular for jewellery.

Proximity	Related Colors		Page
9.49	Black		123
13.78	Ultra-Dark Blue		97
13.78	Reddish Lilac		103
13.78	Light Pink		106
14.90	Dark Brown		27
22.44	Earth Green		72

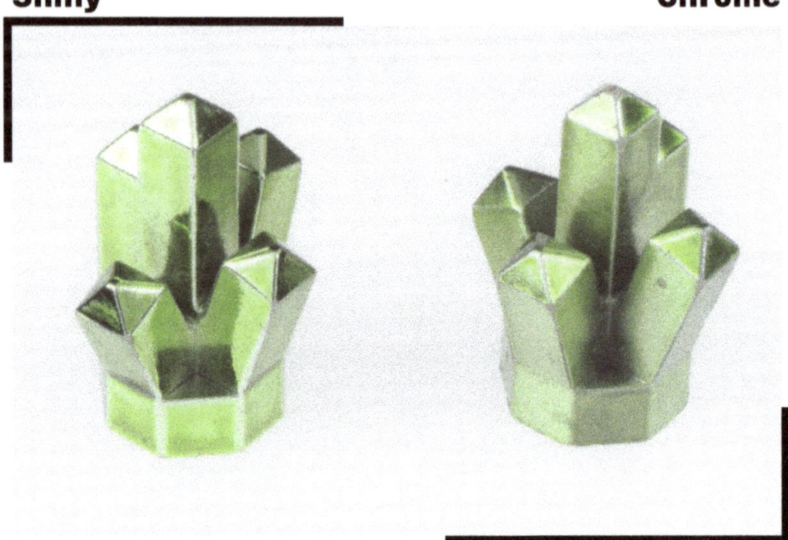

Chrome Green   112

Lego				
Bricklink	Chrome Green			64
UUID	FAEBE3EE-9A84-4938-856D-FABB6DE4D59E			
Year	1999	**to**	1999	**Availability** Few

LAB	25	-20	15	**Pantone**
sRGB	41	68	36	
CMYK				

Notes   Only used for crystal part.

Proximity	Related Colors		Page
10.35	Earth Green		72
26.81	Dark Grey		118
27.87	Dark Army Green		57
30.50	Dark Stone Grey		121
31.01	Dark Brown		27
31.75	Sand Green		68

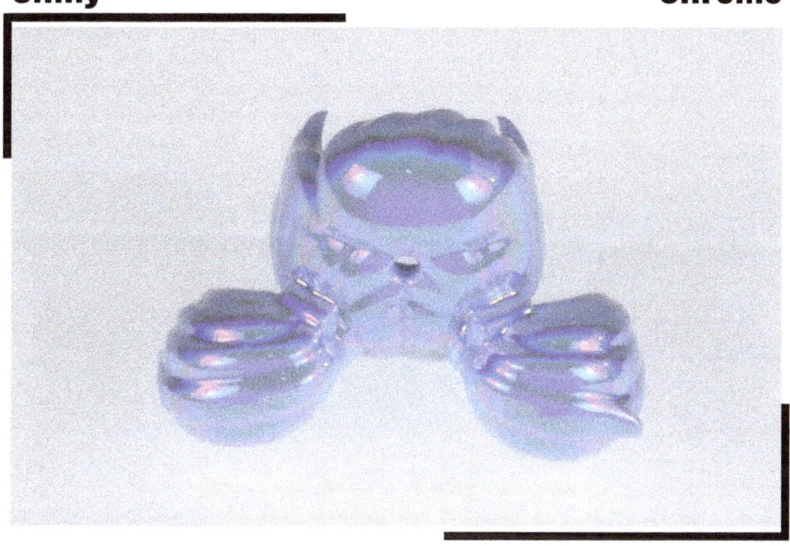

Rainbow Shimmer Ink   113

Lego	
Bricklink	
UUID	9A46CD48-92AE-47C6-AF72-8C3AA56BEF48

Year	2020	**to** present	**Availability**	Rare

				Pantone	278 C
LAB	74	0	-27		
sRGB	137	195	231		
CMYK	45	14	0	0	

Notes   The plastic itself is Light Royal Blue and only the outside has an iridescent effect.

Proximity	Related Colors		Page
9.41	Light Royal Blue		86
9.85	Light Lilac		87
16.16	Lavender		100
16.85	Light Bluish Violet		93
17.09	Light Blue		83
18.04	Medium Blue		85

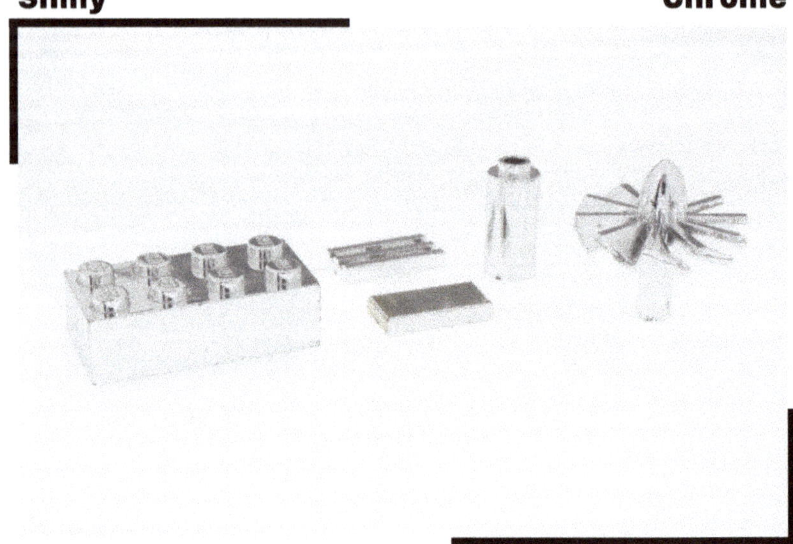

Metalized Silver   114

Lego	Metalized Silver		309
Bricklink	Chrome Silver		22
UUID	90E77EEF-6954-4999-8ABB-F7868EAC122B		
Year	1971 **to** current	**Availability**	Several

LAB	17	-0	-0	**Pantone**	
sRGB	41	44	47		
CMYK					

Notes   In current color palette.

Proximity	Related Colors		Page
12.26	Black		123
14.94	Dark Brown		27
17.41	Ultra-Dark Blue		97
17.41	Reddish Lilac		103
17.41	Light Pink		106
22.15	Earth Green		72

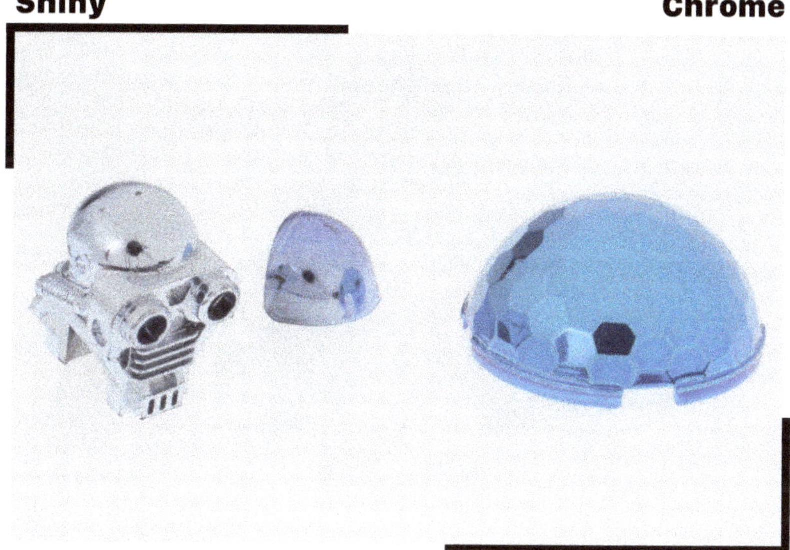

Bluemetal 115

Lego	Bluemetal	
Bricklink	Chrome Blue	52
UUID	BA6A6333-9A84-4DE2-856C-6E8B471FA15C	
Year	1998 **to** 2006	**Availability** Few

				Pantone
LAB	13	-1	-21	
sRGB	17	39	68	
CMYK				

Notes   There are at least two distinct variants.

Proximity	Related Colors		Page
10.39	Earth Blue		84
20.70	Black		123
20.91	Bright Bluish Violet		96
24.68	Ultra-Dark Blue		97
24.68	Reddish Lilac		103
24.68	Light Pink		106

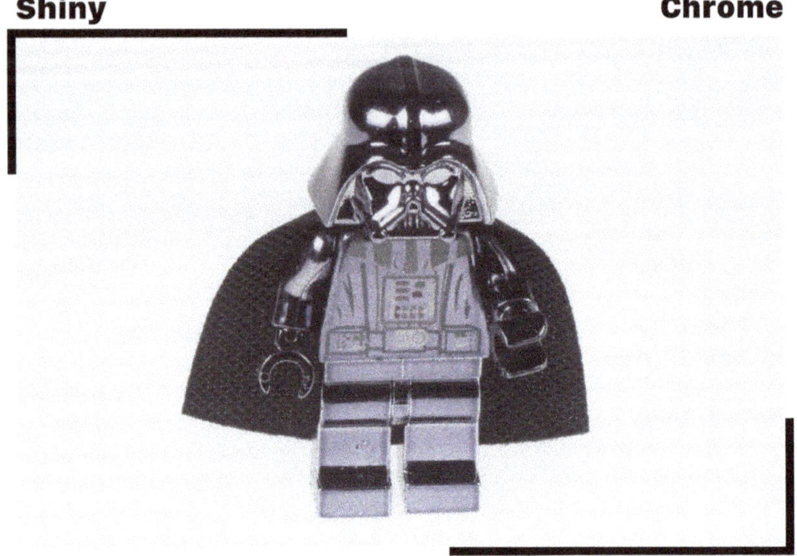

Chrome Black   116

Lego					
Bricklink	Chrome Black				122
UUID	7331E053-C703-4391-9351-A8C6EF8D3E09				
Year	2009	**to**	2009	**Availability**	Some

LAB	3	1	−1	**Pantone**
sRGB	10	10	13	
CMYK				

Notes   Used only for chrome Darth Vader.

Proximity	Related Colors		Page
2.78	Black		123
2.95	Ultra-Dark Blue		97
2.95	Reddish Lilac		103
2.95	Light Pink		106
23.40	Dark Brown		27
29.89	Earth Green		72

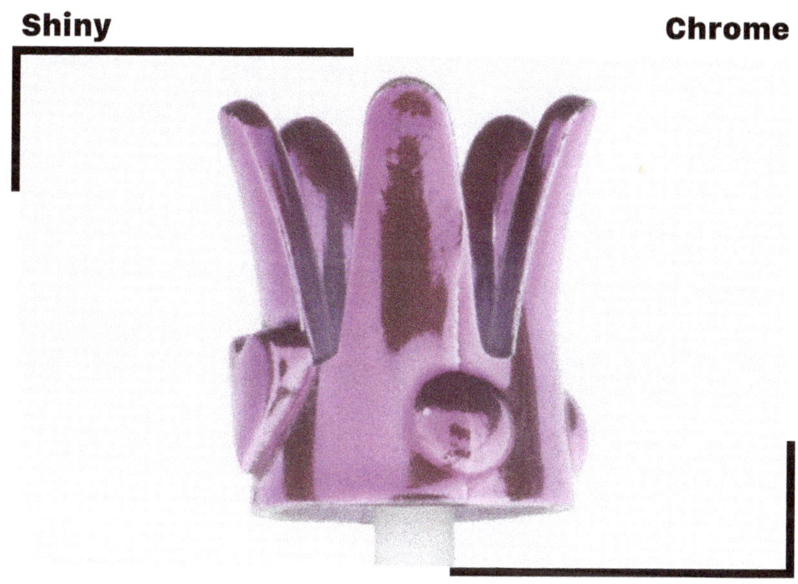

Chrome Pink   **117**

Lego				
Bricklink	Chrome Pink			82
UUID	71DCB2D5-4D58-4AB6-8F3E-3E9EF050CBA0			
Year	2001	**to**	2007	**Availability**	Few

LAB	37	43	-22	**Pantone**
sRGB	129	64	127	
CMYK				

Notes   Mainly used for Clikits.

Proximity	Related Colors		Page
10.07	Bright Reddish Lilac		105
15.38	Bright Violet		102
23.04	Medium Lavender		101
23.68	Bright Purple		109
23.68	Medium Reddish Violet		110
24.24	Medium Lilac		99

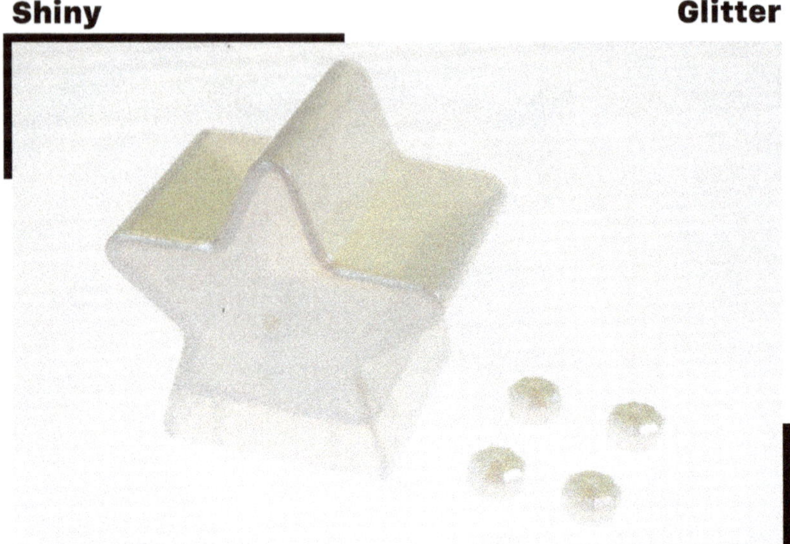

Transparent Clear Opal   118

Lego	Transparent Clear Opal	360
Bricklink	Satin White	228
UUID	A0C108B6-140C-44AF-96C0-19859DED6682	
Year	2020 **to** current	**Availability** Few

LAB				**Pantone**
sRGB	201	201	201	
CMYK				

Notes   Only in the Dots sets.

Proximity	**Related Colors**		**Page**
	Neon Orange		17
	New Dark Red		18
	Fabuland Red		19
	Light Red		20
	Medium Red		21
	Rust		22

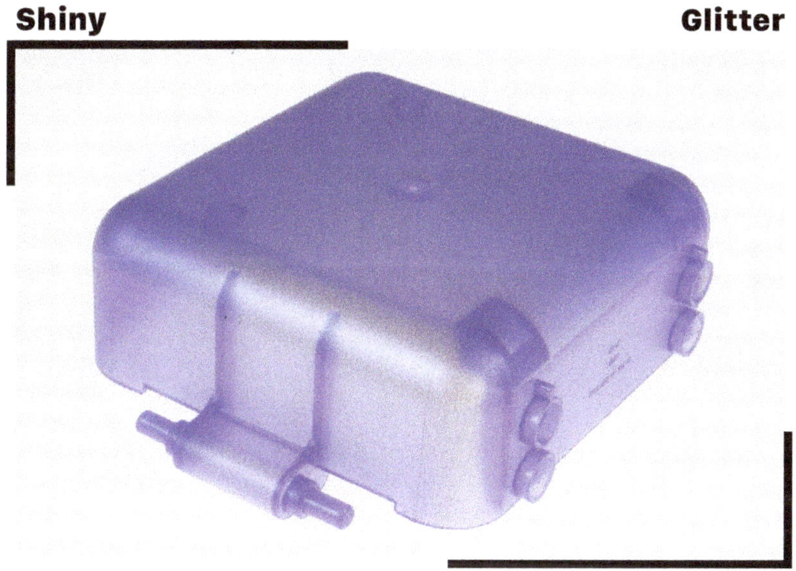

Transparent Violet Opal   187

Lego	Transparent Violet Opal	365
Bricklink	Satin Trans-Purple	230
UUID	AD57A634-E46E-4FD9-819D-FEDD9CABD71D	
Year	2020 **to** 2020	**Availability** Few

LAB   **Pantone**

sRGB

CMYK

Notes

Proximity	Related Colors		Page
	Neon Orange		17
	New Dark Red		18
	Fabuland Red		19
	Light Red		20
	Medium Red		21
	Rust		22

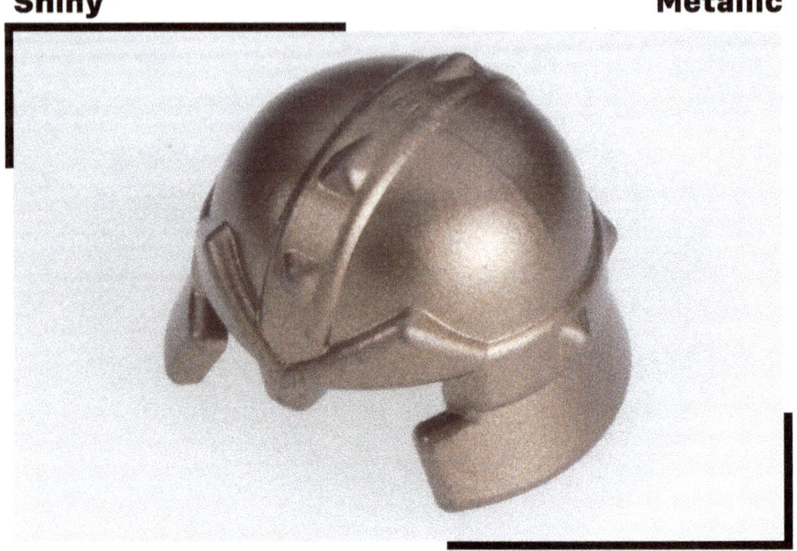

Copper, Drum Lacquered   119

Lego	Copper, Drum Lacquered				300
Bricklink					
UUID	4489A84F-CCDA-427D-B159-29F714E08F0F				
Year	2008	**to**	2012	**Availability**	Rare

				Pantone
LAB	72	18	22	
sRGB	213	160	137	
CMYK				

Notes   Not listed on Bricklink.

Proximity	Related Colors		Page
9.51	Light Nougat		37
12.91	Light Red		20
16.34	Brick Yellow		49
16.84	Light Brick Yellow		48
18.04	Rose		115
20.02	Sand Yellow		47

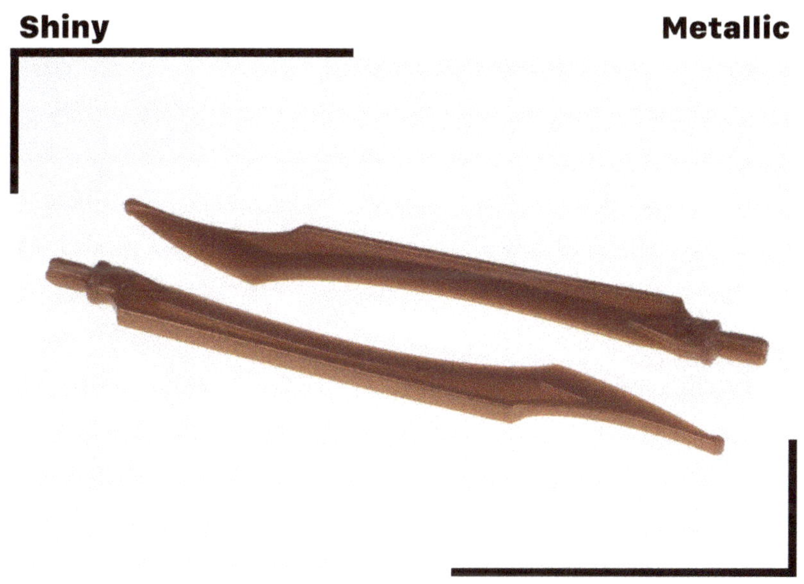

Copper Metallic   120

Lego	Copper Metallic				346
Bricklink	Copper				84
UUID	13A8458E-E289-41B9-AA4B-6280CFC68728				
Year	2017	**to**	current	**Availability**	Some

				Pantone	7517 C
LAB	36	30	40		
sRGB	130	60	19		
CMYK	31	79	100	31	

Notes   In current color palette.

Proximity	Related Colors		Page
17.42	Rust		28
17.42	Light Brown		42
17.60	Brick Red		31
17.94	Dark Orange		40
18.12	New Dark Red		18
18.12	Rust		22

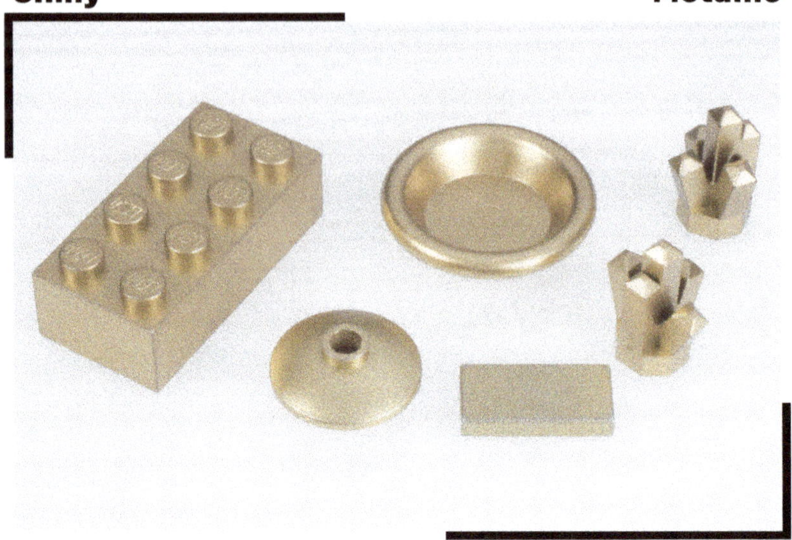

Warm Gold 121

Lego	Warm Gold			299
Bricklink	Metallic Gold			65
UUID	A8B003F4-F3FF-4F48-A57B-51855E6C7ED4			
Year	2005	**to** current	**Availability**	Several

LAB	48	7	30	**Pantone**
sRGB	135	105	60	
CMYK				

Notes Replaced Reddish Gold 189 and Sand Yellow Metallic 147 in 2006.

Proximity	Related Colors		Page
12.68	Sand Yellow		47
13.05	Olive Green		55
13.71	Light Yellowish Orange		44
13.77	Brown		34
16.13	Medium Nougat		39
16.60	Dark Army Green		57

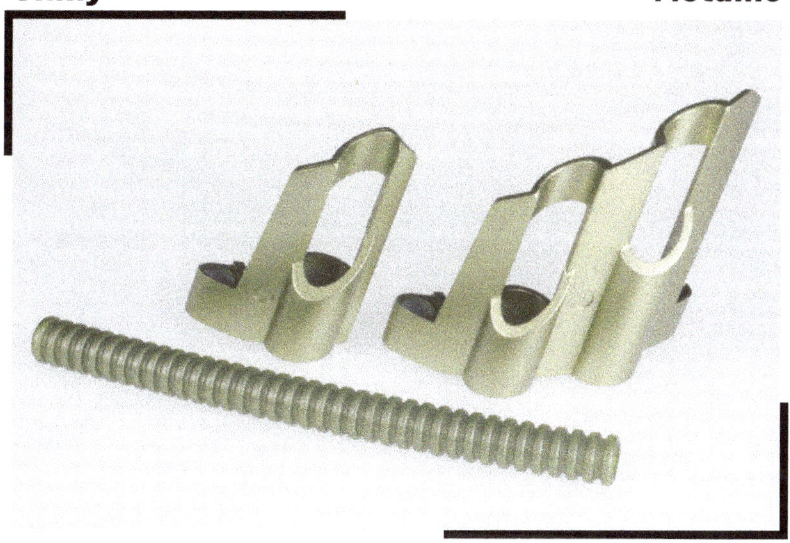

Metallic Green   122

Lego					
Bricklink	Metallic Green				70
UUID	B050C658-F5CA-4949-9F45-BBF632F98346				
Year	2001	**to**	2001	**Availability**	Some

LAB	45	-7	24	**Pantone**	
sRGB	109	107	64		
CMYK					

Notes	Used only in two sets (8465 and 8466). No official LEGO name or ID.

Proximity	**Related Colors**		**Page**
7.66	Dark Army Green		57
9.99	Olive Green		55
16.60	Sand Yellow		47
19.30	Dark Grey		118
21.14	Sand Green		68
22.42	Brown		34

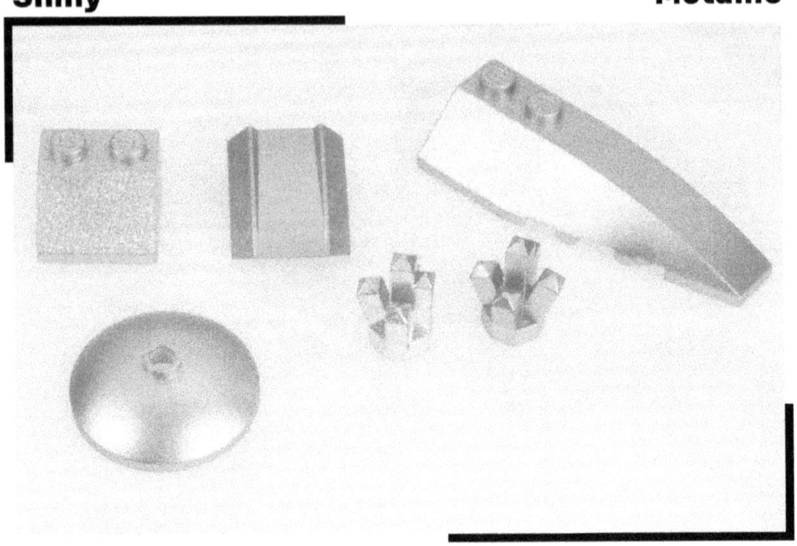

Cool Silver   **123**

Lego	Cool Silver	298
Bricklink	Metallic Silver	67
UUID	C4B846F7-A0FC-423F-B8C0-5B7FD7D81B01	

Year	2005	**to**	current	**Availability**	Several

				Pantone
LAB	56	-0	-2	
sRGB	133	136	139	
CMYK				

Notes In current color palette. Also known as Drum Lacquered.

Proximity	Related Colors		Page
9.78	Grey		119
10.37	Medium Stone Grey		122
13.34	Sand Blue		88
13.43	Sand Violet		104
14.24	Dark Stone Grey		121
17.74	Dark Grey		118

Metallic Pink   124

Lego				
Bricklink				
UUID	81A71F3D-CC83-439F-A4EE-A873D2D6503B			
Year	2006	**to**	2006	**Availability** Rare

LAB	53	42	-15	**Pantone**
sRGB	173	101	154	
CMYK				

Notes   Only used for Clikits.

Proximity	Related Colors		Page
11.10	Bright Purple		109
11.10	Medium Reddish Violet		110
16.72	Bright Reddish Lilac		105
19.75	Medium Lavender		101
20.52	Pink		113
23.72	Flamingo Pink		111

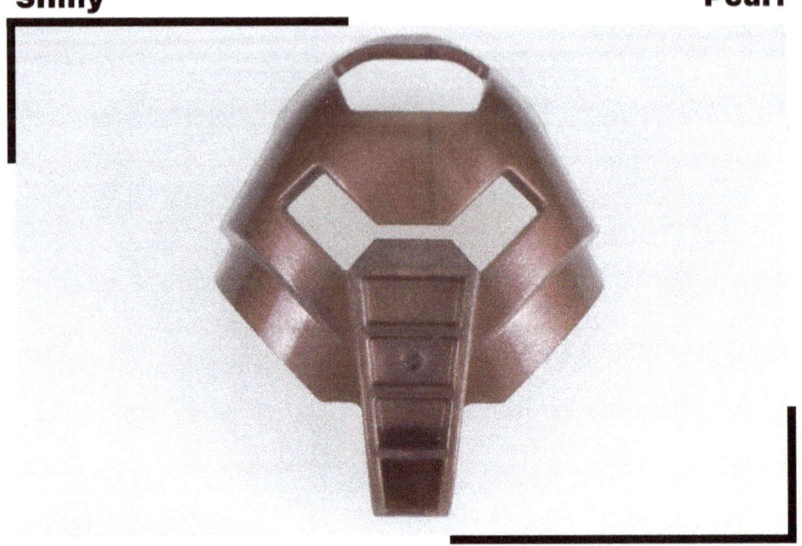

Red Flip/Flop   125

Lego	Red Flip/Flop				176

Bricklink

UUID   703C68D4-F465-4B8D-BE40-14EB933F04D8

Year	2001	to	2001	Availability	Rare

				Pantone	483 C
LAB	32	24	14		
sRGB	109	57	55		
CMYK	40	70	70	0	

Notes   Only used for Bionicle and not listed on Bricklink.

Proximity	Related Colors		Page
10.08	Reddish Brown		29
10.58	Medium Brown		32
14.63	Brown		34
15.22	Earth Orange		36
16.11	Rust		28
17.76	Dark Brown		27

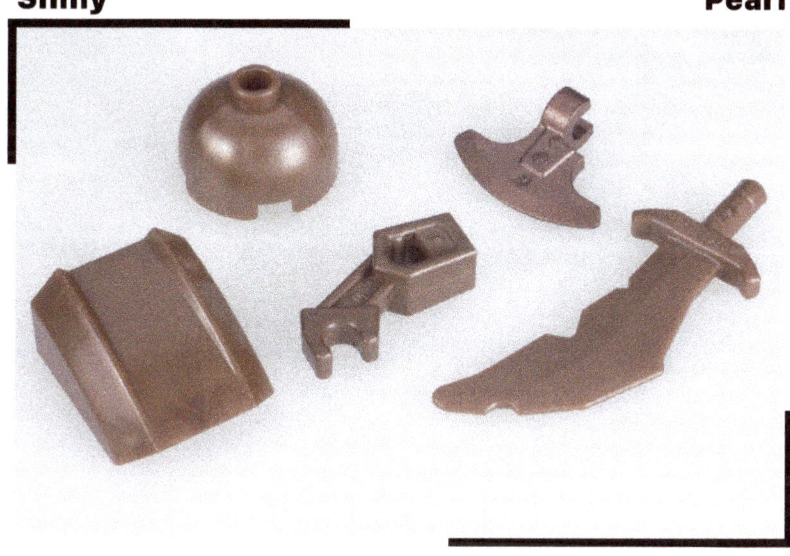

Copper   126

Lego	Copper		139
Bricklink	Copper		84
UUID	A87AC178-91DA-422A-BD2A-DADD09FB903F		
Year	2004	**to** 2020	**Availability** Some

				Pantone
LAB	29	18	18	
sRGB	96	56	42	
CMYK				

Notes   Used across several themes.

Proximity	Related Colors		Page
6.20	Medium Brown		32
7.47	Reddish Brown		29
9.16	Earth Orange		36
11.80	Brown		34
13.83	Dark Brown		27
18.06	Rust		28

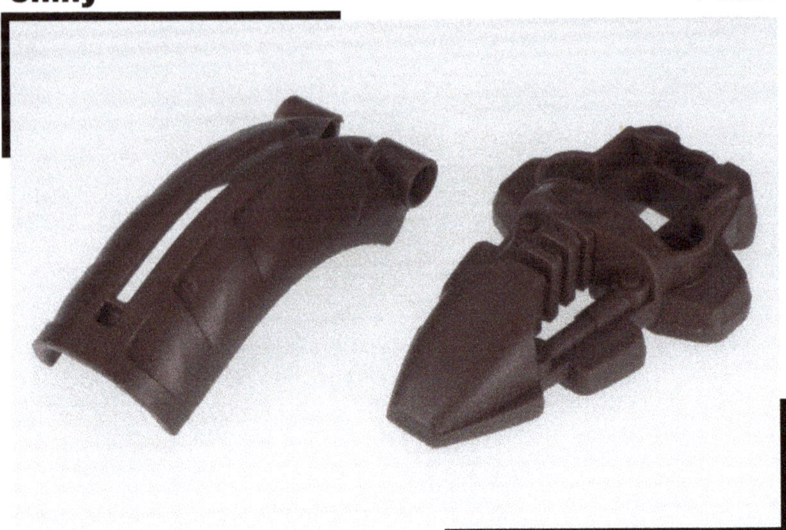

Metallic Earth Orange   127

Lego	Metallic Earth Orange				187
Bricklink					
UUID	96E1D18F-AA45-4240-B827-3DCF7ADDA69A				
Year	2003	**to**	2006	**Availability**	Rare

LAB	34	15	17	**Pantone**
sRGB	106	69	54	
CMYK				

Notes   Only used for Bionicle parts and not listed on
               Bricklink.

Proximity	Related Colors		Page
1.12	Medium Brown		32
7.70	Brown		34
10.03	Reddish Brown		29
12.26	Earth Orange		36
15.61	Dark Brown		27
16.76	Rust		28

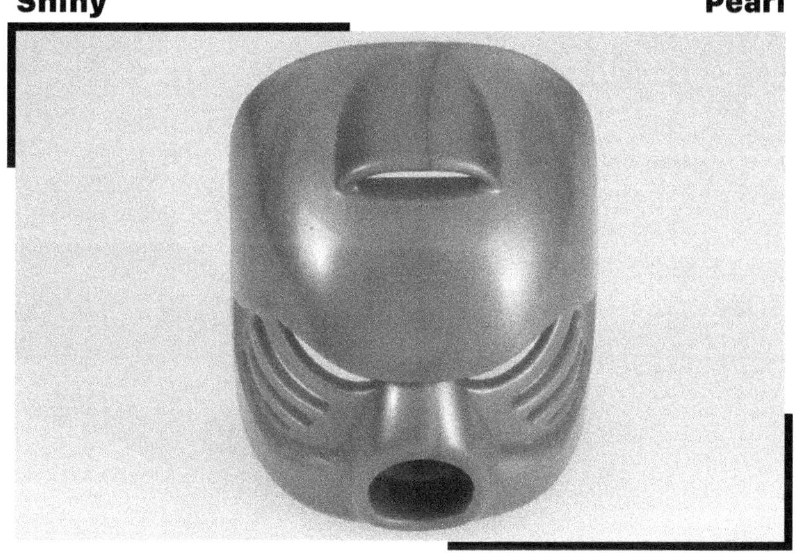

Silver Flip/Flop 128

Lego	Silver Flip/Flop				179
Bricklink	Flat Silver				95
UUID	0F720E6A-1494-4EDF-A54E-B6912AB6BCB7				
Year	2002	**to**	2002	**Availability**	Several

LAB	48	2	4	**Pantone**	410 C
sRGB	121	114	109		
CMYK	50	42	43	5	

Notes Only used for Bionicle parts and not listed on Bricklink.

Proximity	Related Colors		Page
8.34	Dark Grey		118
8.52	Dark Stone Grey		121
13.58	Sand Violet		104
15.09	Dark Army Green		57
16.72	Grey		119
18.44	Sand Red		24

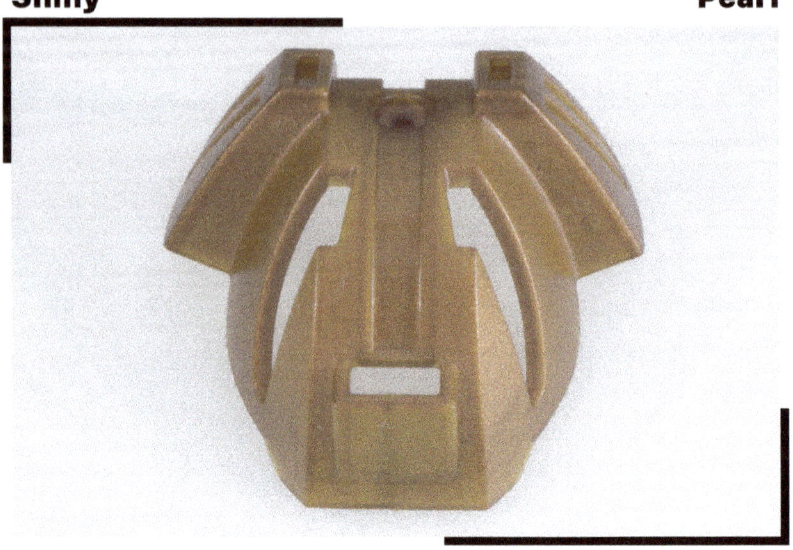

Yellow Flip/Flop   129

Lego	Yellow Flip/Flop				178

Bricklink

UUID   A5A0309F-6EF9-49F0-95C5-CC58C70D37D5

Year	2002	to	2002	Availability	Rare

LAB	38	18	32	Pantone	160 C
sRGB	123	76	36		
CMYK	25	55	80	5	

Notes   Only used for Bionicle parts. Not listed on Bricklink.

Proximity	Related Colors		Page
11.14	Brown		34
11.19	Earth Orange		36
11.49	Reddish Brown		29
12.53	Rust		28
13.32	Brick Red		31
15.30	Medium Brown		32

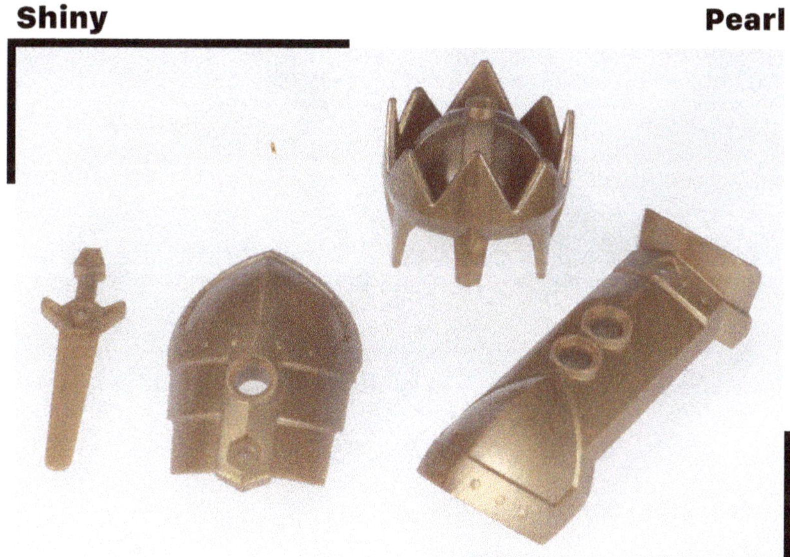

Reddish Gold / Gold Metallic   130

Lego	Reddish Gold / Gold Metallic				189
Bricklink	Reddish Gold				235
UUID	DE810724-1A9E-4F52-ADBC-A52B98EE46AF				
Year	2003	**to**	2005	**Availability**	Few

LAB	48	18	38	**Pantone**
sRGB	151	98	48	
CMYK				

Notes   Replaced by Warm Gold 297 around 2006.

Proximity	Related Colors		Page
6.80	Medium Nougat		39
6.99	Light Brown		42
9.35	Light Yellowish Orange		44
10.90	Dark Nougat		33
11.57	Brick Red		31
16.17	Rust		28

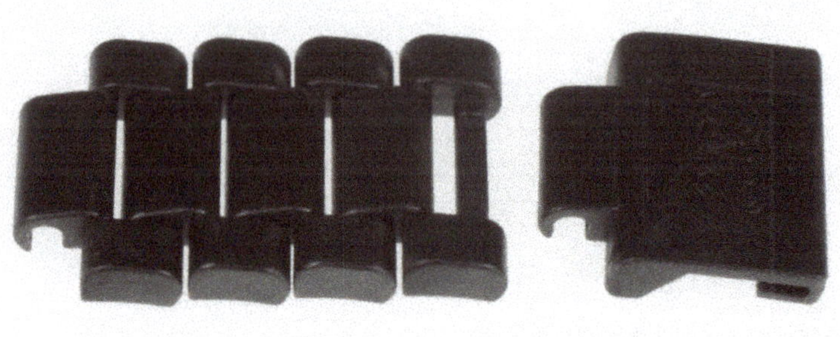

Gun Metallic   131

Lego	Gun Metallic					168
Bricklink						
UUID	858F8873-940A-497F-9183-DAEE8185BCF8					
Year	2000	**to**	2000	**Availability**		Rare

				Pantone	WarmGray
LAB					
sRGB	96	86	76		
CMYK	56	54	62	15	

Notes   Only used in the Grinder Fob watch.

Proximity	**Related Colors**		**Page**
	Neon Orange		17
	New Dark Red		18
	Fabuland Red		19
	Light Red		20
	Medium Red		21
	Rust		22

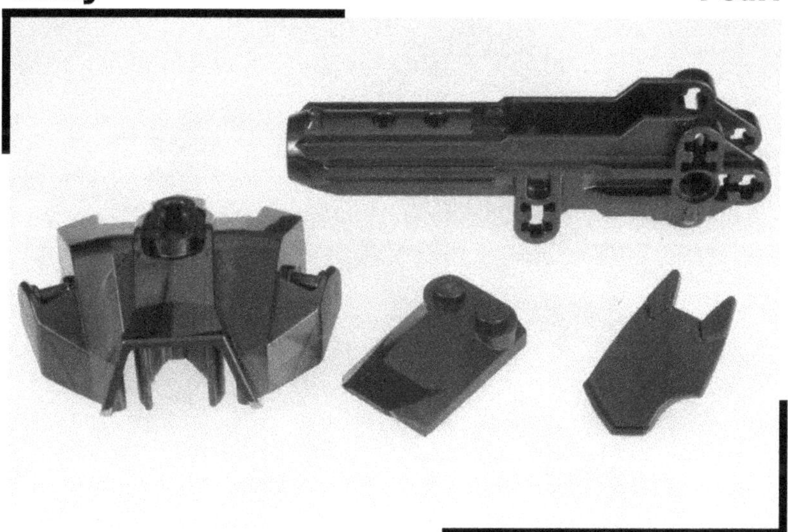

Titanium Metallic   132

Lego	Titanium Metallic			316
Bricklink	Pearl Dark Gray			77
UUID	DD191FB2-6048-4212-A083-F3888E22D768			
Year	2010	**to** current	**Availability**	Several

LAB	47	-0	2	**Pantone**
sRGB	114	112	110	
CMYK				

Notes   Replaced Metallic Dark Grey 148 in 2010.

Proximity	Related Colors		Page
6.04	Dark Stone Grey		121
8.06	Dark Grey		118
13.96	Sand Violet		104
16.36	Dark Army Green		57
17.38	Grey		119
17.62	Sand Blue		88

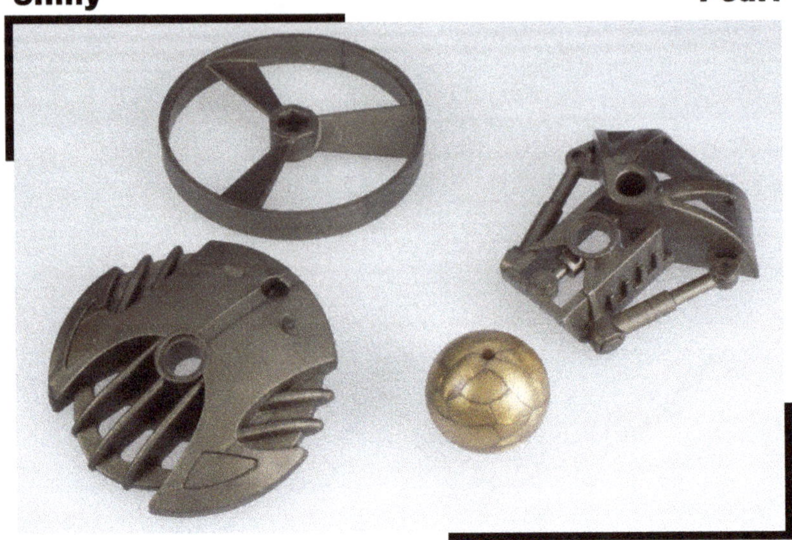

Metallic Sand Yellow   133

Lego	Metallic Sand Yellow	147
Bricklink	Flat Dark Gold	81
UUID	4BCBD64E-72F7-4CD5-93E6-7C3232B9EF0B	

Year	2003	**to**	2006	**Availability**	Some

				Pantone	873 C
LAB	44	4	19		
sRGB	119	98	71		
CMYK	45	45	70	3	

Notes   Replaced by Warm Gold 297 in 2006.

Proximity	Related Colors		Page
8.90	Dark Army Green		57
11.38	Brown		34
12.25	Sand Yellow		47
13.72	Dark Grey		118
13.73	Medium Brown		32
15.78	Olive Green		55

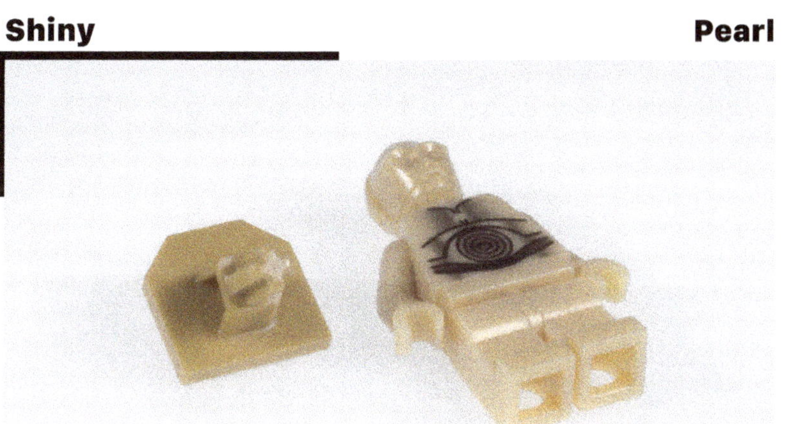

Gold   134

Lego	Gold				127
Bricklink	Pearl Light Gold				61
UUID	D5CE1315-D74D-4CAC-9B2E-E14D2DA19ADC				
Year	2000	**to**	2005	**Availability**	Some

				Pantone	156 C
LAB	48	10	45		
sRGB	171	128	55		
CMYK	10	27	60	0	

Notes   Replaced by Warm Gold 297 around 2006.

Proximity	Related Colors		Page
11.10	Light Yellowish Orange		44
13.25	Light Brown		42
15.25	Medium Nougat		39
22.02	Dark Nougat		33
22.79	Olive Green		55
23.13	Brick Red		31

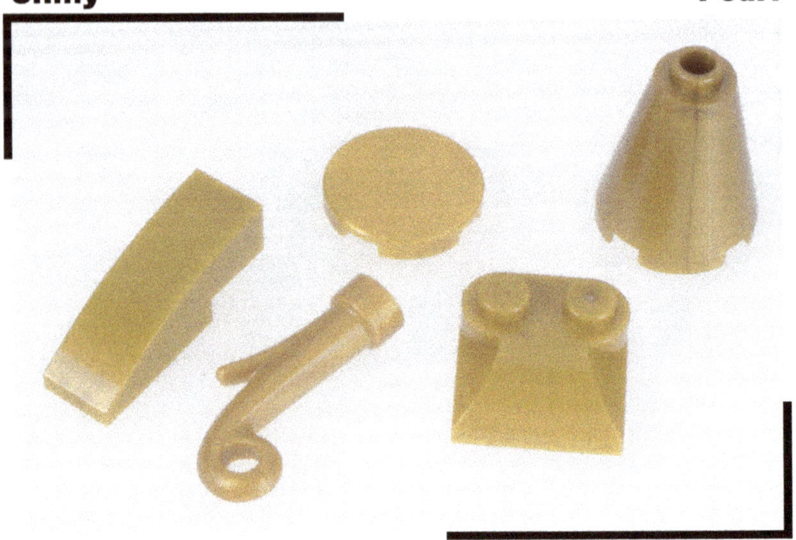

Warm Gold   135

Lego	Warm Gold	297
Bricklink	Pearl Gold	115

| **UUID** | A4AD046A-3549-4A1D-B440-FB7084FCC194 |

| **Year** | 2006 | **to** | current | **Availability** | Several |

				Pantone
LAB	58	10	52	
sRGB	172	126	39	
CMYK				

Notes   Also known as Drum Lacquered, Gold Metalized and Gold Laquered.

Proximity	Related Colors		Page
13.38	Light Yellowish Orange		44
16.36	Light Brown		42
18.49	Medium Nougat		39
18.89	Light Orange Brown		41
24.15	Nougat		35
26.44	Dark Nougat		33

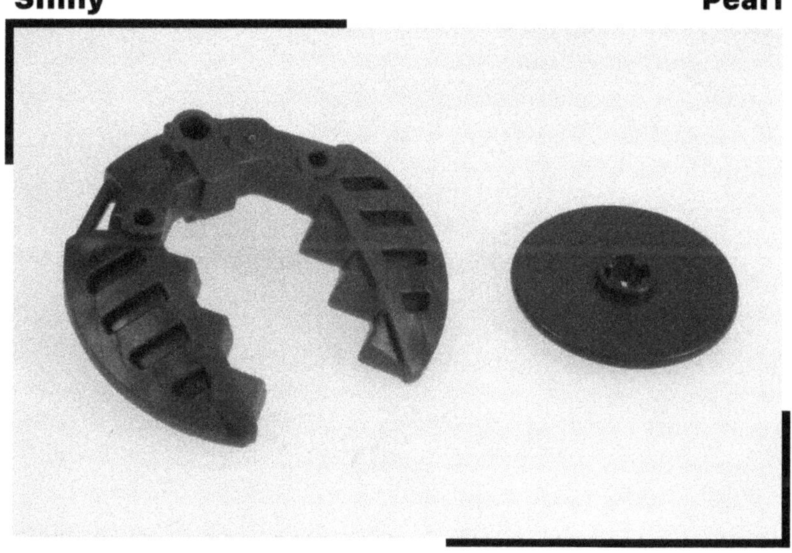

Metallic Dark Grey   136

Lego	Metallic Dark Grey	148
Bricklink	Pearl Dark Gray	77

UUID   996AAAB1-8B2C-44BA-A355-CC478A5D08A3

Year	2000	to	2010	Availability	Several

LAB	27	0	7	**Pantone**	446 C
sRGB	69	64	54		
CMYK	77	67	67	10	

Notes   Replaced by Titanium Metallic 316 in 2010.

Proximity	Related Colors		Page
11.95	Dark Brown		27
13.54	Dark Grey		118
17.08	Dark Stone Grey		121
18.92	Medium Brown		32
22.51	Earth Green		72
22.72	Dark Army Green		57

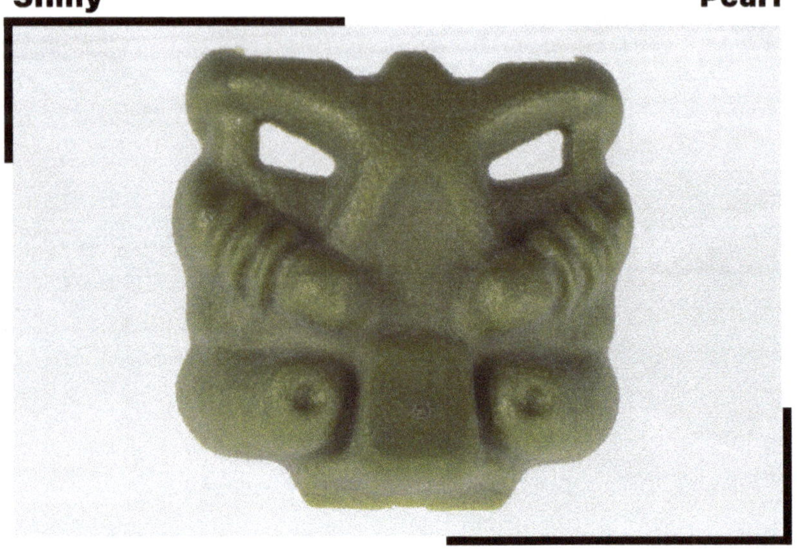

Lemon Metallic   137

Lego	Lemon Metallic					200
Bricklink	Metallic Green					70
UUID	302981FE-D1D3-4A11-ABE4-CFC4B8279D5C					
Year	2001	**to**	2003	**Availability**		Some

LAB	55	-9	29	**Pantone**	5767 C
sRGB	136	132	80		
CMYK	56	35	80	5	

Notes   Only used for a few Bionicle parts.

Proximity	Related Colors		Page
5.45	Olive Green		55
15.01	Dark Army Green		57
16.68	Sand Yellow		47
20.76	Pastel Green		62
21.37	Sand Green		68
22.73	Light Faded Green		65

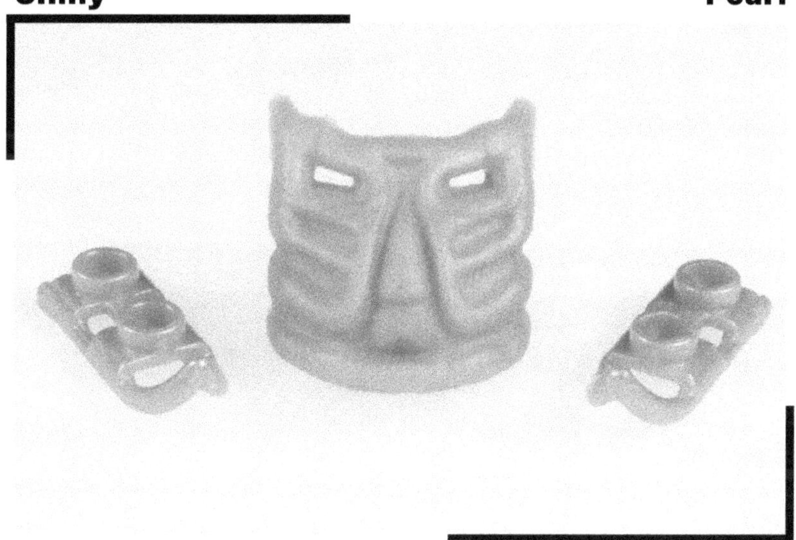

Metallic Light Grey 138

Lego	Metallic Light Grey				150
Bricklink	Pearl Very Light Gray				119
UUID	4390F3F2-0EC2-45AB-8F16-97308DFFC9B8				
Year	2002	to	2003	Availability	Some

LAB	52	-1	1	Pantone	422 C
sRGB	123	125	122		
CMYK	36	27	30	0	

Notes Used for only very few parts.

Proximity	Related Colors		Page
10.04	Dark Stone Grey		121
12.41	Dark Grey		118
12.82	Grey		119
13.98	Sand Violet		104
14.84	Medium Stone Grey		122
15.78	Sand Blue		88

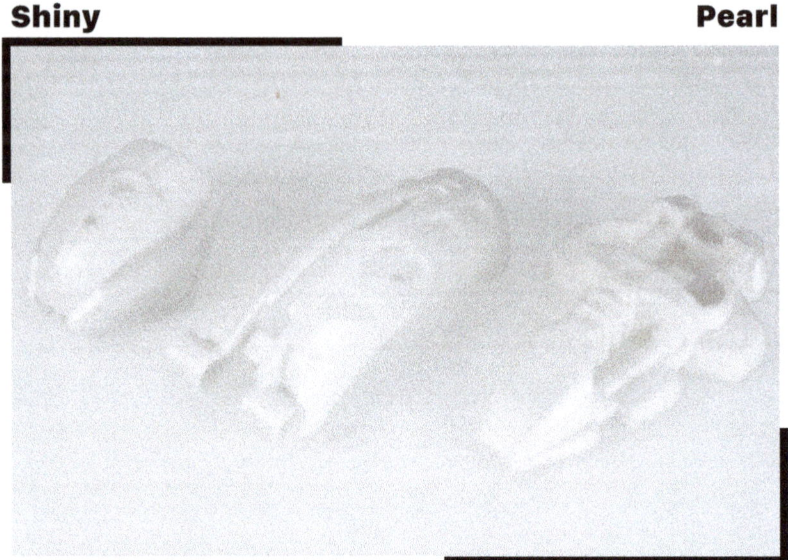

Metallic White   139

Lego	Metallic White			183
Bricklink	Pearl White			83
UUID	E1B04F6B-8CA1-4725-907B-DC28AC6D7262			
Year	2003	**to**	2006	**Availability** Few

LAB	99	-1	0	**Pantone**
sRGB	252	254	252	
CMYK				

Notes   Only used for Bionicle parts.

Proximity	Related Colors		Page
7.39	White		116
15.70	Aqua		73
20.61	Light Stone Grey		120
22.99	Light Bluish Violet		93
26.26	Light Blue		83
26.48	Light Grey		117

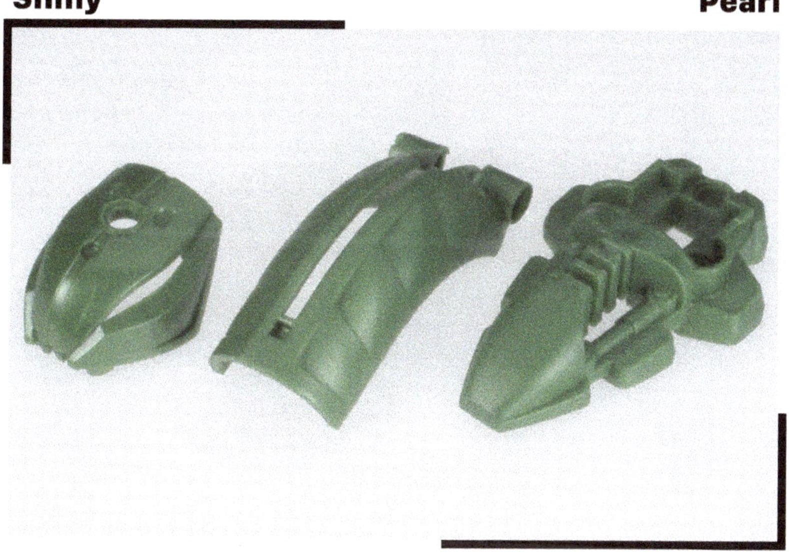

Metallic Dark Green   140

Lego	Metallic Dark Green				186
Bricklink					
UUID	4E766A6D-6C6D-4576-B327-1AB987498D8E				
Year	2003	**to**	2006	**Availability**	Rare

				Pantone	
LAB	47	-44	18		
sRGB	35	128	76		
CMYK					

Notes   Mainly used for Bionicle parts.

Proximity	Related Colors		Page
14.28	Faded Green		69
26.48	Dark Green		71
27.06	Bright Green		70
29.32	Medium Green		67
29.34	Sand Green		68
32.81	Bright Bluish Green		75

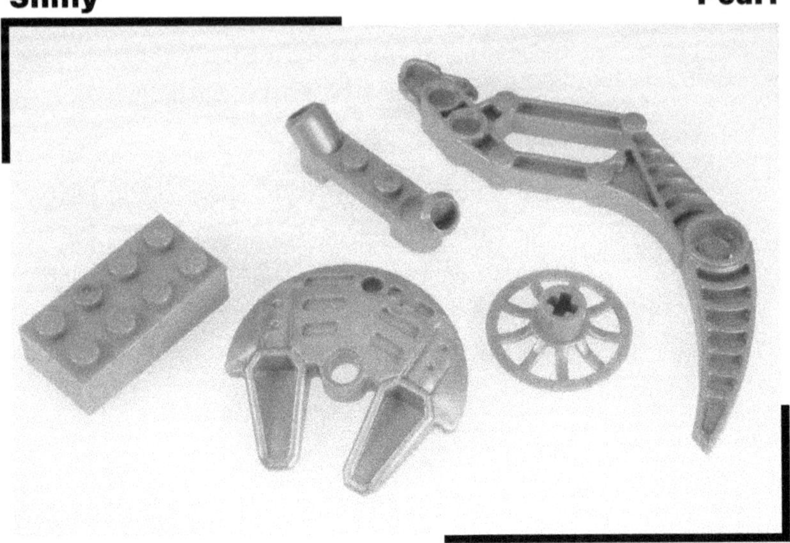

Silver   141

Lego	Silver				131
Bricklink	Pearl Light Gray				66
UUID	8F69CF1C-9D39-4AED-88C4-1FC8B540B504				
Year	1998	to	2010	Availability	Several

				Pantone	429 C
LAB	61	-2	-4		
sRGB	130	148	153		
CMYK	44	29	30	0	

Notes	Replaced by Silver Metallic 315 in 2010.

Proximity	Related Colors		Page
6.82	Medium Stone Grey		122
7.55	Grey		119
13.34	Sand Blue		88
16.51	Light Grey		117
16.96	Sand Violet		104
18.56	Light Stone Grey		120

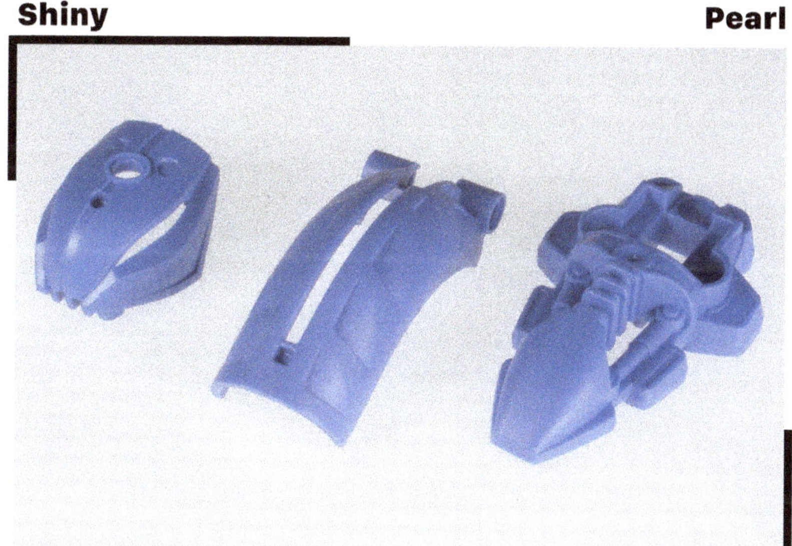

Metallic Bright Blue   142

Lego	Metallic Bright Blue				185
Bricklink					
UUID	AD520F18-5B39-4DA3-BCC4-46E7A6349136				
Year	2003	**to**	2006	**Availability**	Rare

LAB	51	-7	-42	**Pantone**	
sRGB	25	138	192		
CMYK					

Notes   Mainly used for Bionicle parts.

Proximity	Related Colors		Page
8.62	Medium Royal Blue		91
15.52	Medium Blue		85
17.76	Dark Azure		81
18.97	Lilac		94
21.25	Bright Blue		89
21.35	Royal Blue		90

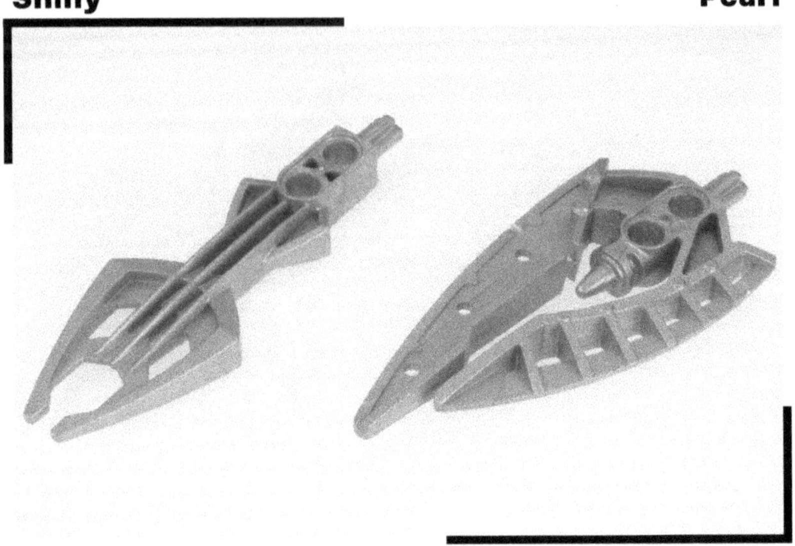

Cool Silver   143

Lego	Cool Silver	296
Bricklink	Pearl Light Gray	66

UUID   4124AC4F-EC66-4CFD-B150-2394971E465C

Year	2006	to	2006	Availability	Several

				Pantone	
LAB	48	-1	-3		
sRGB	109	115	119		
CMYK					

Notes   Similar to Silver 131.

Proximity	Related Colors		Page
5.97	Dark Stone Grey		121
12.06	Dark Grey		118
12.68	Sand Blue		88
12.83	Sand Violet		104
17.87	Grey		119
19.04	Medium Stone Grey		122

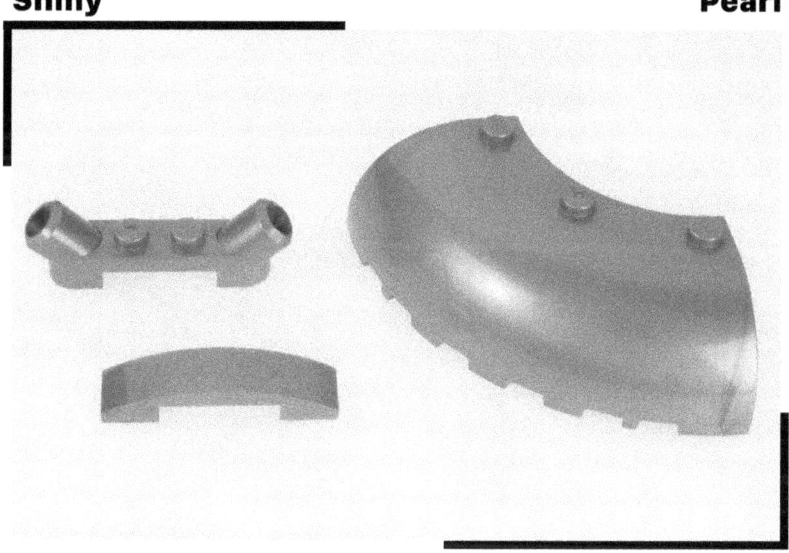

Silver Metallic   144

Lego	Silver Metallic	315
Bricklink	Flat Silver	95
UUID	38EED649-05A3-41ED-84EE-65DED1F32941	

Year	2010	**to**	current	**Availability**	Several

				Pantone	
LAB	53	-1	-3		
sRGB	122	127	131		
CMYK					

Notes   Replaced Silver 131 around 2010.

Proximity	Related Colors		Page
10.57	Dark Stone Grey		121
11.75	Sand Blue		88
12.54	Sand Violet		104
13.45	Grey		119
14.26	Medium Stone Grey		122
15.21	Dark Grey		118

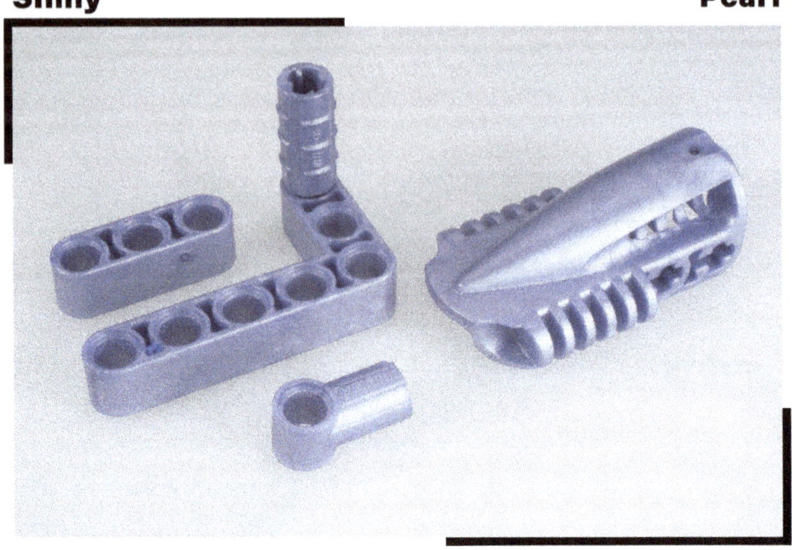

Metallic Sand Blue   145

Lego	Metallic Sand Blue	145
Bricklink	Metal Blue	78
UUID	781CBECE-2258-450E-BF98-997CE25F33DB	

Year	2002	to	2005	Availability	Some

				Pantone	652 C
LAB	41	-2	-22		
sRGB	72	104	133		
CMYK	60	38	23	4	

Notes   Mainly used for Technic and Bionicle parts.

Proximity	Related Colors		Page
14.19	Sand Blue		88
17.35	Bright Bluish Violet		96
20.86	Dark Stone Grey		121
22.32	Sand Violet		104
23.04	Medium Blue		85
23.30	Tiny-Medium Blue		82

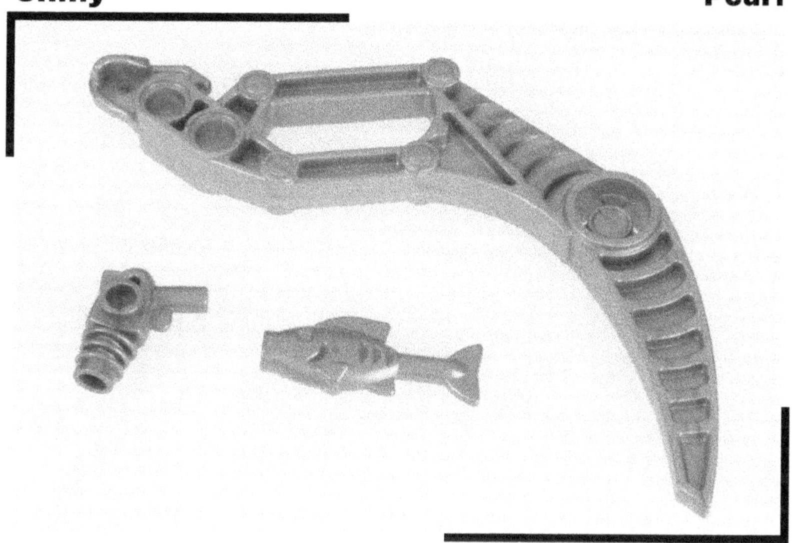

Silver   146

Lego	Silver			131
Bricklink	Flat Silver			95
UUID	0C26598F-989E-44D5-8F23-5441E911CDE9			
Year	1978	**to** current	**Availability**	Several

LAB	55	-1	-5	**Pantone**
sRGB	128	134	141	
CMYK				

Notes   New definition based on comparison between LEGO and Bricklink IDs.

Proximity	Related Colors		Page
10.62	Sand Blue		88
11.96	Medium Stone Grey		122
11.99	Grey		119
12.84	Sand Violet		104
13.53	Dark Stone Grey		121
18.24	Dark Grey		118

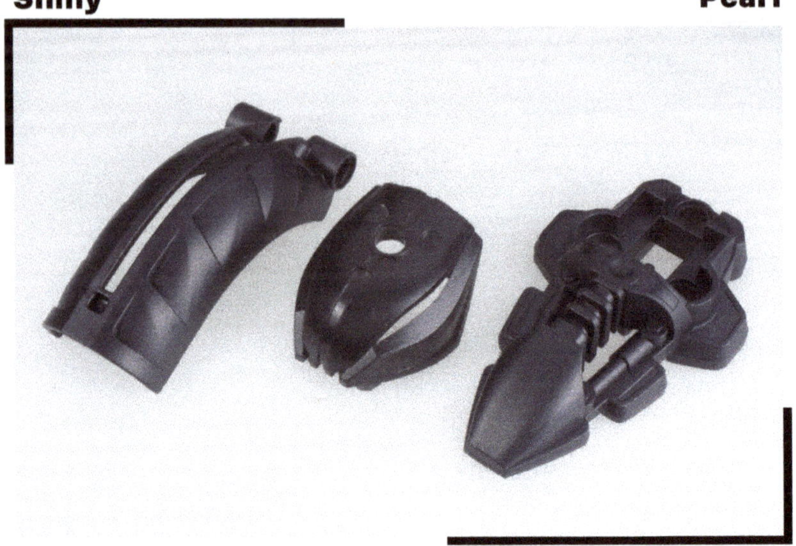

Metallic Black   147

Lego	Metallic Black				149

Bricklink

UUID	D3DB624F-F633-4AE5-B2C4-7026911F28D5

Year	2003	**to**	2006	**Availability**	Rare

LAB	19	0	-1	**Pantone**	2767 C
sRGB	47	47	49		
CMYK	100	90	55	55	

Notes   Mainly used for Bionicle parts.

Proximity	Related Colors		Page
13.94	Black		123
14.97	Dark Brown		27
19.24	Ultra-Dark Blue		97
19.24	Reddish Lilac		103
19.24	Light Pink		106
22.49	Earth Green		72

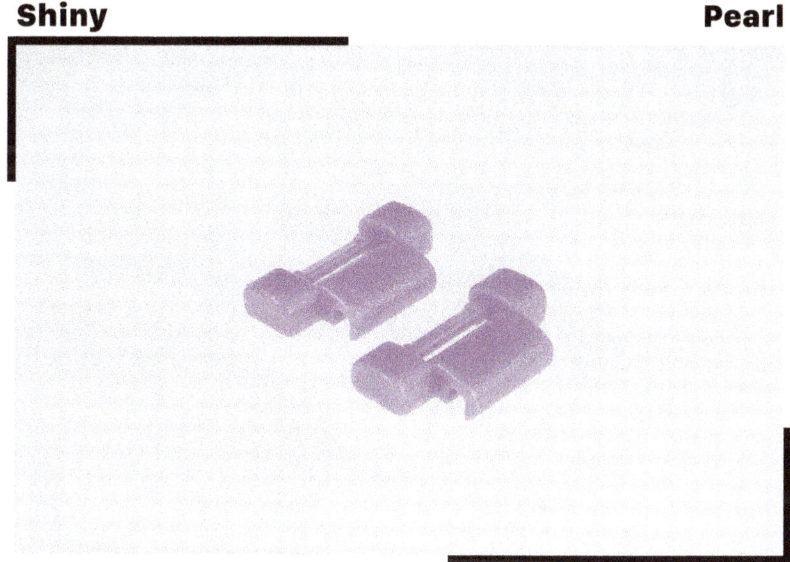

Metallic Sand Violet   148

Lego	Metallic Sand Violet			146
Bricklink				
UUID	A5BDEF5B-247A-49BC-8545-1D0EFEBBB9D9			
Year	2000	**to**	2005	**Availability** Rare

LAB				**Pantone**	5285 C
sRGB	129	117	144		
CMYK	42	42	20	5	

Notes   Misprint lid to 8794.

Proximity	Related Colors		Page
	Neon Orange		17
	New Dark Red		18
	Fabuland Red		19
	Light Red		20
	Medium Red		21
	Rust		22

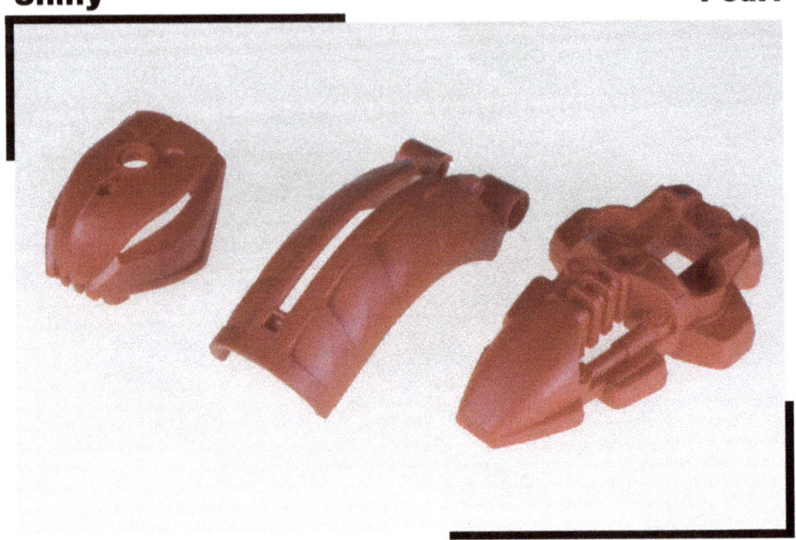

Metallic Bright Red   149

Lego	Metallic Bright Red		184
Bricklink			
UUID	54E5A0C6-708B-40F7-A66D-543811EE2DF1		
Year	2003 **to** 2006	**Availability**	Rare

LAB	55	51	17	**Pantone**
sRGB	200	93	106	
CMYK				

Notes   Mainly used for Bionicle parts.

Proximity	Related Colors		Page
19.49	Medium Red		21
24.92	Flamingo Pink		111
26.12	Rust		22
26.48	Pink		113
26.83	Red Orange		25
27.43	Bright Purple		109

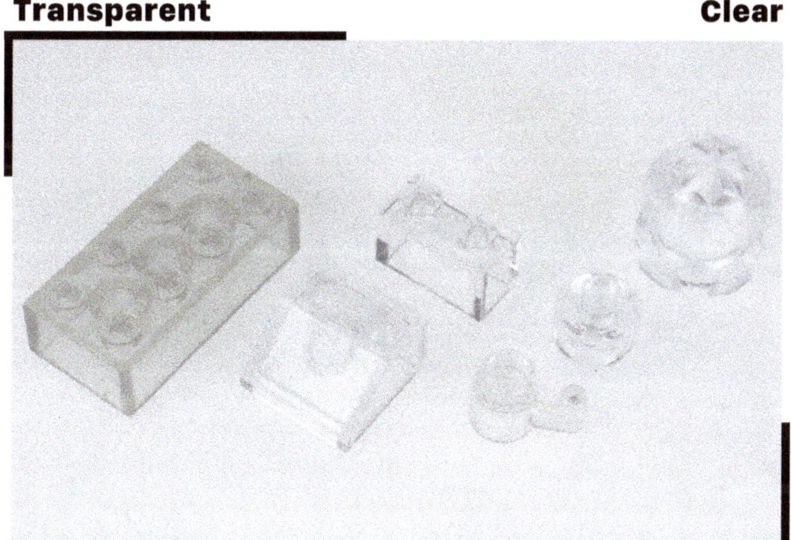

Transparent   **150**

| **Lego** | Transparent | | | 40 |
| **Bricklink** | Trans-Clear | | | 12 |

UUID   199259C4-8D8A-496C-9CB0-88E192ADA931

| **Year** | 1950 | **to** | current | **Availability** | Several |

LAB				**Pantone**	CoolGray
sRGB	238	238	238		
CMYK	0	0	0	8

Notes   In current color palette.

Proximity	**Related Colors**		**Page**
	Neon Orange		17
	New Dark Red		18
	Fabuland Red		19
	Light Red		20
	Medium Red		21
	Rust		22

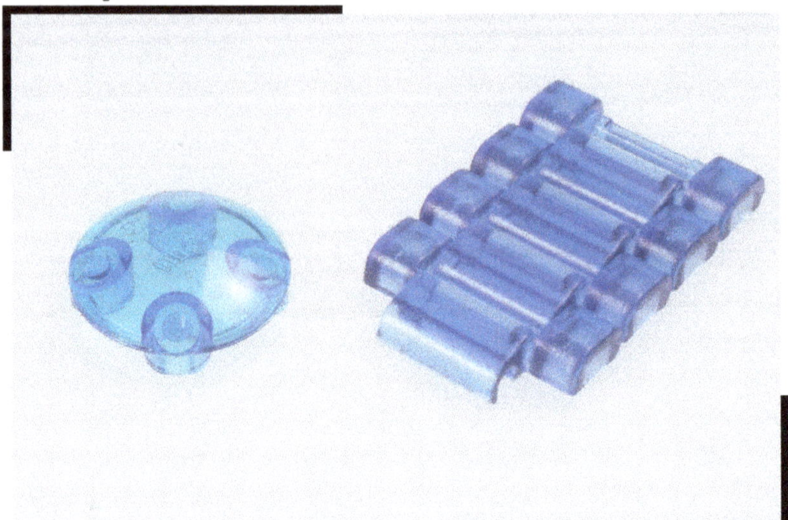

Transparent Deep Blue   151

Lego	Transparent Deep Blue				156
Bricklink					
UUID	F97E6352-7DB4-44F5-AA4C-E7CCF7CA2B46				
Year	2000	**to**	2002	**Availability**	Rare

LAB			**Pantone**	
sRGB	255	255	255	
CMYK				

Notes   Only used for two parts.

Proximity	**Related Colors**		**Page**
	Neon Orange		17
	New Dark Red		18
	Fabuland Red		19
	Light Red		20
	Medium Red		21
	Rust		22

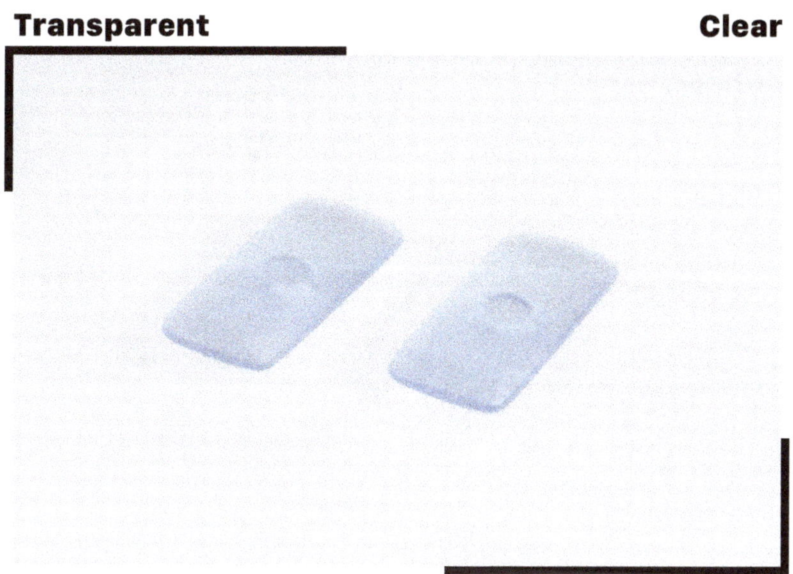

Transparent Light Royal Blue   152

Lego	Transparent Light Royal Blue	293

Bricklink

UUID	18DB53C7-0665-41DD-8DD8-6402F883DA55

Year	2005	to	2005	Availability	Rare

LAB				Pantone	
sRGB	255	255	255		
CMYK					

Notes   Only used by Clikits and not listed on Bricklink.

Proximity	Related Colors		Page
	Neon Orange		17
	New Dark Red		18
	Fabuland Red		19
	Light Red		20
	Medium Red		21
	Rust		22

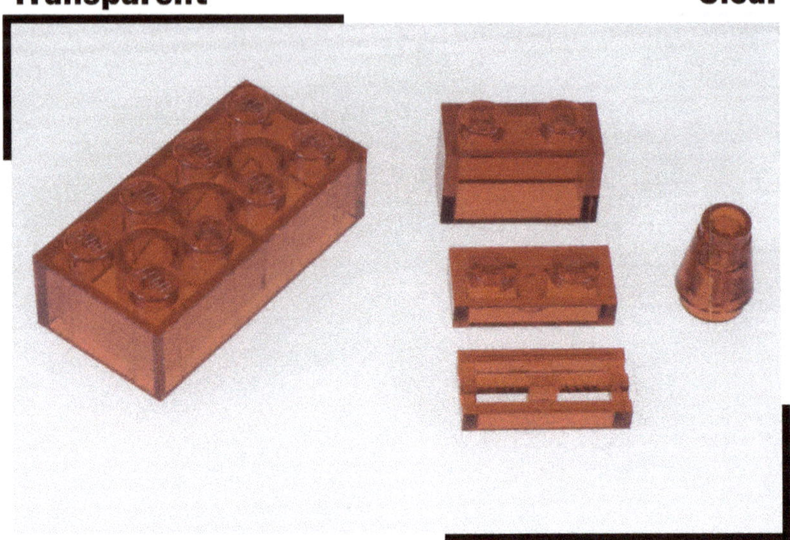

Transparent Red   153

Lego	Transparent Red	41
Bricklink	Trans-Red	17

UUID 6ADAEF61-BBCE-418F-8032-11EF425934D6

Year	1969	**to**	current	**Availability**	Several

				Pantone	185 C
LAB					
sRGB	184	39	0		
CMYK	0	85	75	0	

Notes   In current color palette.

Proximity	**Related Colors**		**Page**
	Neon Orange		17
	New Dark Red		18
	Fabuland Red		19
	Light Red		20
	Medium Red		21
	Rust		22

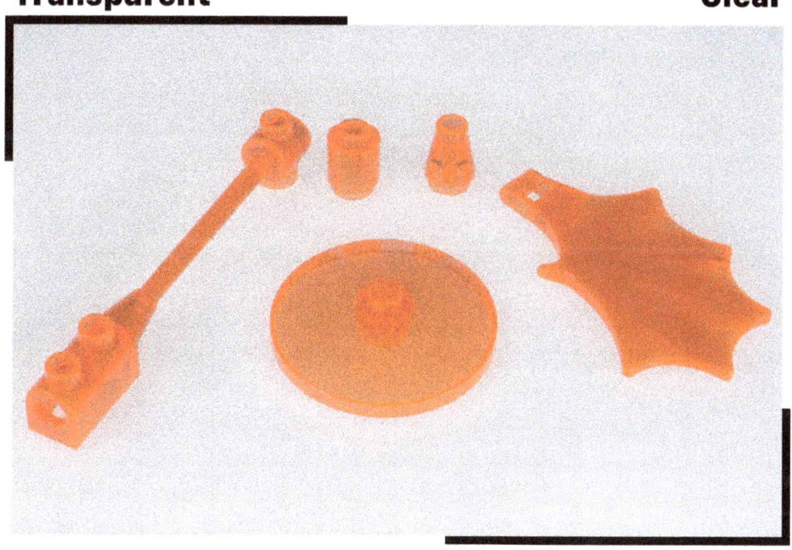

Tr. Fl. Reddish Orange   154

Lego	Tr. Fl. Reddish Orange	47
Bricklink	Trans-Neon Orange	18
UUID	5DE3C53A-B390-461E-AB23-E4039C3FF92D	
Year	1993 **to** current	**Availability** Several

LAB				**Pantone**	165 C
sRGB	208	109	79		
CMYK	0	60	60	0	

Notes Full name is Transparent Fluorescent Reddish Orange.

Proximity **Related Colors**   **Page**

Related Colors		Page
Neon Orange		17
New Dark Red		18
Fabuland Red		19
Light Red		20
Medium Red		21
Rust		22

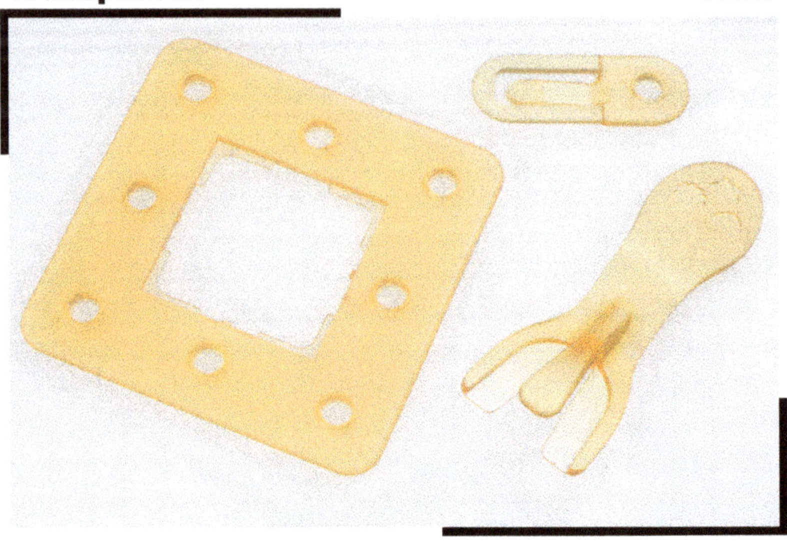

Trans. Fl. Yellowish Orange   155

Lego	Trans. Fl. Yellowish Orange	231
Bricklink	Trans-Light Orange	164
UUID	98993DB6-7084-497A-BC3A-9991BD543A52	

Year	2003	**to**	2006	**Availability**	Some

				Pantone	
LAB					
sRGB	252	183	109		
CMYK					

Notes   The full name is Transparent Flame Yellowish Orange.

Proximity	**Related Colors**		**Page**
	Neon Orange		17
	New Dark Red		18
	Fabuland Red		19
	Light Red		20
	Medium Red		21
	Rust		22

Transparent Bright Orange   156

Lego	Transparent Bright Orange	182
Bricklink	Trans-Orange	98
UUID	6C85B8FD-ADE9-4FFC-95A0-A0534E22B8B6	
Year	2003 **to** current **Availability** Several	

LAB				**Pantone**
sRGB	225	141	10	
CMYK				

Notes   In current color palette.

Proximity	**Related Colors**		**Page**
	Neon Orange		17
	New Dark Red		18
	Fabuland Red		19
	Light Red		20
	Medium Red		21
	Rust		22

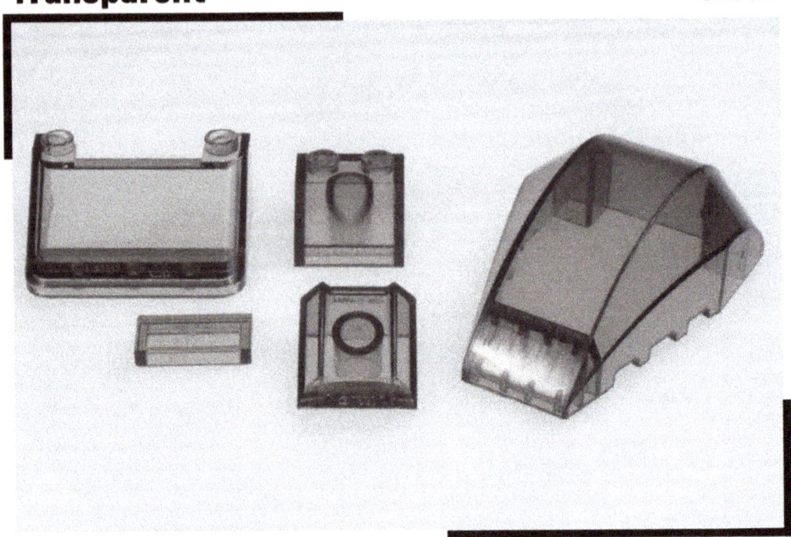

Transparent Brown   **157**

Lego	Transparent Brown	111
Bricklink	Trans-Black	13
UUID	54115950-8654-467B-B387-635FF8B2047C	
Year	1999 **to** current	**Availability** Several

				Pantone	WarmGray
LAB					
sRGB	187	178	158		
CMYK	25	25	28	0	

Notes   In current color palette.

Proximity	**Related Colors**		**Page**
	Neon Orange		17
	New Dark Red		18
	Fabuland Red		19
	Light Red		20
	Medium Red		21
	Rust		22

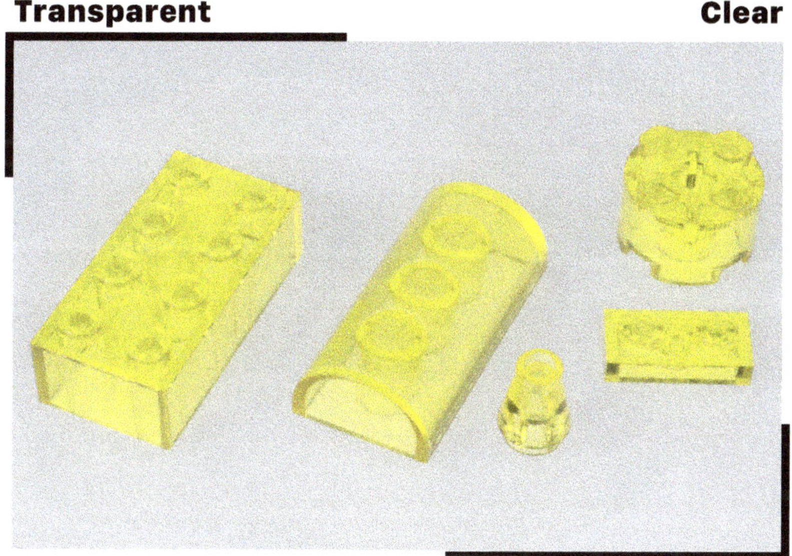

Transparent Yellow   158

Lego	Transparent Yellow	44
Bricklink	Trans-Yellow	19
UUID	64D2AD67-9BD0-4EC1-B2D3-F05DF694352E	
Year	1969 **to** current	**Availability** Several

				Pantone	393 C
LAB					
sRGB	250	241	93		
CMYK	5	0	60	0	

Notes   In current color palette.

Proximity	**Related Colors**		**Page**
	Neon Orange		17
	New Dark Red		18
	Fabuland Red		19
	Light Red		20
	Medium Red		21
	Rust		22

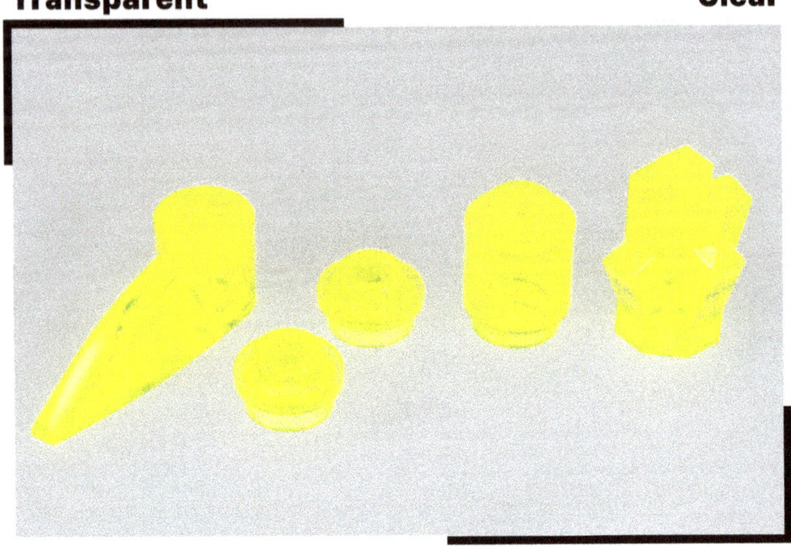

Transparent Fluorescent Green   159

Lego	Transparent Fluorescent Green	49
Bricklink	Trans-Neon Green	16
UUID	4FC407D1-4085-4E01-B340-DE621B2974D3	

Year	1990	**to**	current	**Availability**	Several

LAB				**Pantone**	387 C
sRGB	250	241	91		
CMYK	5	0	65	0	

Notes   In current color palette.

Proximity	**Related Colors**		**Page**
	Neon Orange		17
	New Dark Red		18
	Fabuland Red		19
	Light Red		20
	Medium Red		21
	Rust		22

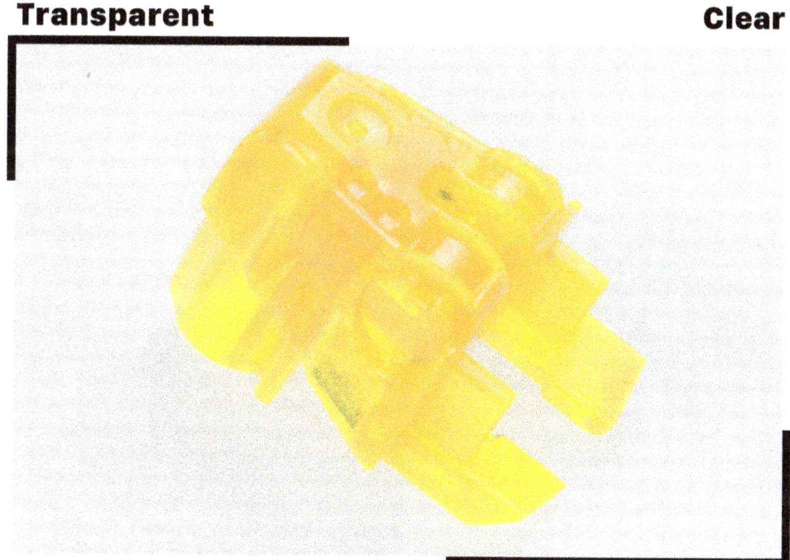

Transparent Fluorescent Yellow   160

Lego	Transparent Fluorescent Yellow	157
Bricklink	Trans-Neon Yellow	121
UUID	FAABC25F-FAC1-4431-B691-03684DDFE814	

Year	2001	**to**	2005	**Availability**	Some

				Pantone	395 C
LAB					
sRGB	255	246	92		
CMYK	0	0	70	0	

Notes   Mainly used by Clikits.

Proximity	**Related Colors**		**Page**
	Neon Orange		17
	New Dark Red		18
	Fabuland Red		19
	Light Red		20
	Medium Red		21
	Rust		22

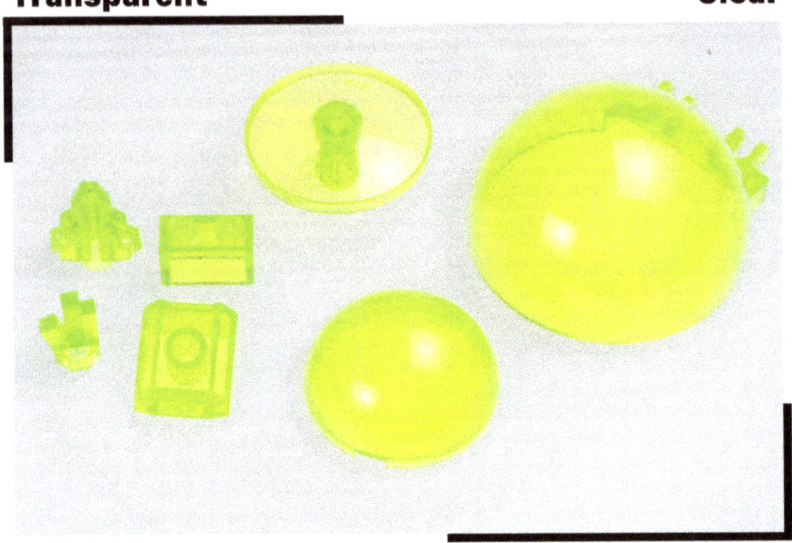

Transparent Bright Green   161

Lego	Transparent Bright Green	311
Bricklink	Trans-Bright Green	108
UUID	C32F8D78-0EC5-4A9E-B8B8-826B093F1198	
Year	2010 **to** current	**Availability** Several

LAB			**Pantone**
sRGB	175	210	70
CMYK			

Notes   In current color palette.

Proximity	**Related Colors**		**Page**
	Neon Orange		17
	New Dark Red		18
	Fabuland Red		19
	Light Red		20
	Medium Red		21
	Rust		22

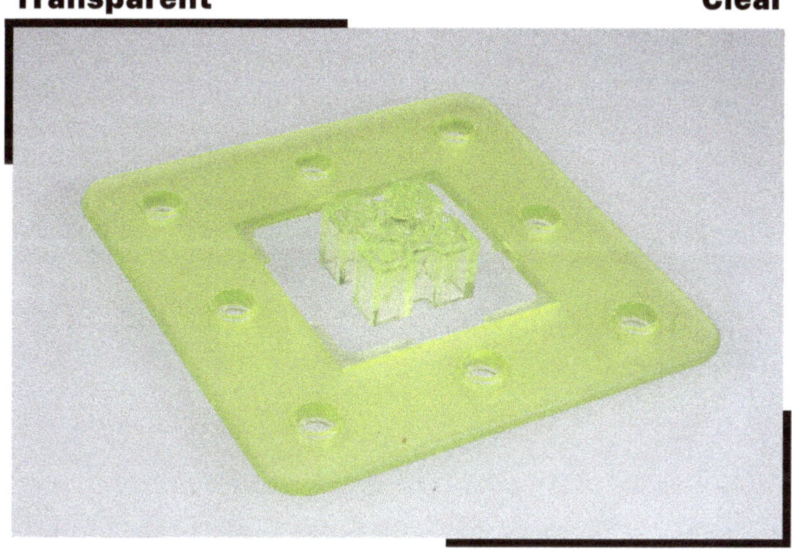

Tr. Br. Yellowish Green   162

Lego	Tr. Br. Yellowish Green		227
Bricklink	Trans-Light Bright Green		226
UUID	8753FC8F-F041-46D9-AA24-C3B0BC2EE757		
Year	2003 **to** 2006	**Availability**	Some

LAB				**Pantone**
sRGB	201	231	136	
CMYK				

Notes   Mainly used by Bionicle and Clikits parts. The full name is Transparent Bright Yellowish Green.

Proximity	Related Colors		Page
	Neon Orange		17
	New Dark Red		18
	Fabuland Red		19
	Light Red		20
	Medium Red		21
	Rust		22

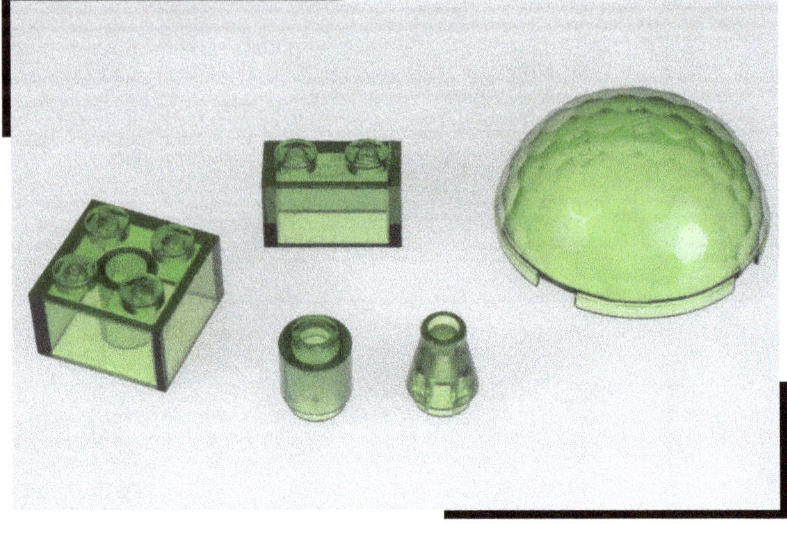

Transparent Green   163

Lego	Transparent Green			48
Bricklink	Trans-Green			20
UUID	5668D314-A610-487E-BFCC-D2BD76B71408			
Year	1969	**to** current	**Availability**	Several

				Pantone	360 C
LAB					
sRGB	115	180	100		
CMYK	60	0	60	0	

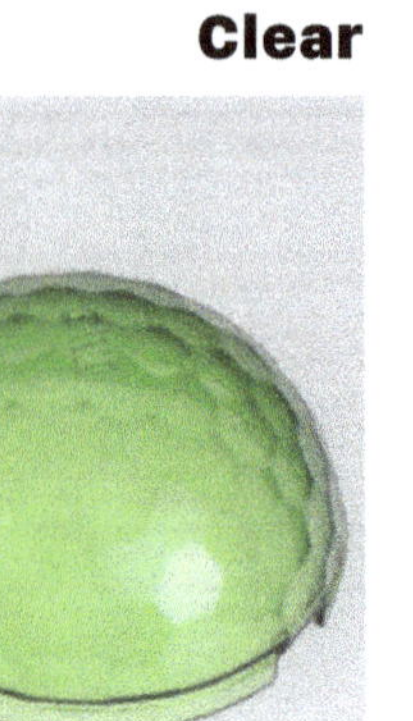

Notes   In current color palette.

Proximity	**Related Colors**		**Page**
	Neon Orange		17
	New Dark Red		18
	Fabuland Red		19
	Light Red		20
	Medium Red		21
	Rust		22

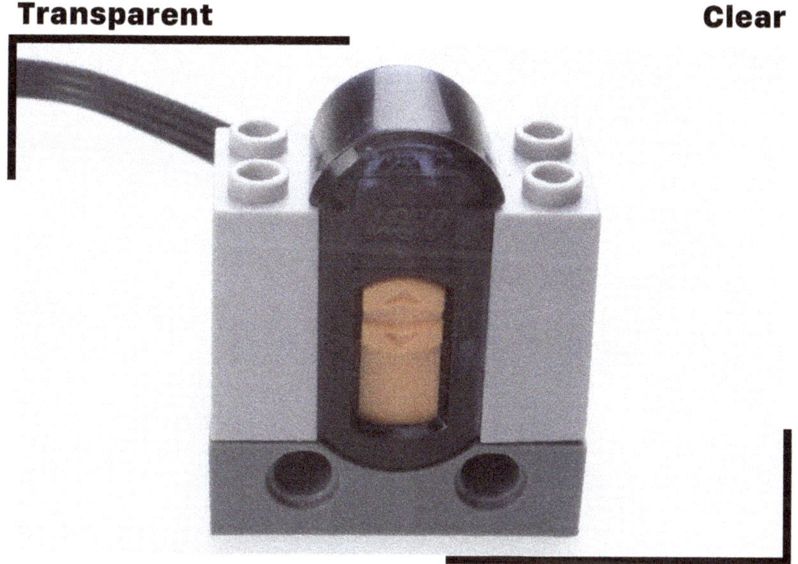

(PC) Black IR   **164**

Lego	(PC) Black IR	109
Bricklink		
UUID	5FAB9DA6-166C-4053-8954-765866258409	

Year	1998	**to**	current	**Availability**	Rare

LAB				**Pantone**
sRGB	0	20	20	
CMYK				

Notes   Since 2017 as Trans Black IR (355)

Proximity	**Related Colors**		**Page**
	Neon Orange		17
	New Dark Red		18
	Fabuland Red		19
	Light Red		20
	Medium Red		21
	Rust		22

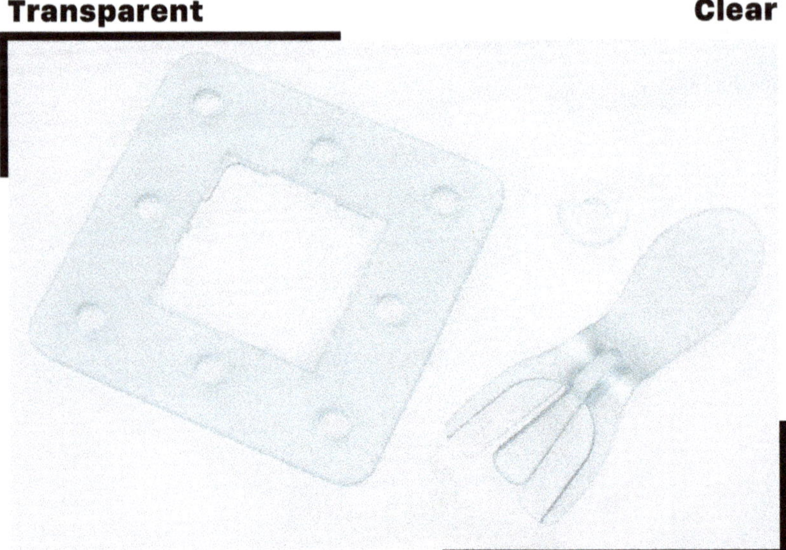

Transparent Light Bluish Green   165

Lego	Transparent Light Bluish Green	229
Bricklink	Trans-Very Lt Blue	113
UUID	EBCD4323-626A-41A8-A53B-0930FFF291A0	

Year	2003	to	2006	Availability	Some

LAB				Pantone	
sRGB	172	212	222		
CMYK					

Notes   Mainly used by Clikits parts.

Proximity	Related Colors		Page
	Neon Orange		17
	New Dark Red		18
	Fabuland Red		19
	Light Red		20
	Medium Red		21
	Rust		22

Transparent Blue   166

Lego	Transparent Blue	43
Bricklink	Trans-Dark Blue	14
UUID	F488495C-EEAA-49F7-BF55-B2AE88F57CE8	

Year	1978	**to**	current	**Availability**	Several

				Pantone	298 C
LAB					
sRGB	119	183	204		
CMYK	60	5	0	0	

Notes   In current color palette.

Proximity	**Related Colors**		**Page**
	Neon Orange		17
	New Dark Red		18
	Fabuland Red		19
	Light Red		20
	Medium Red		21
	Rust		22

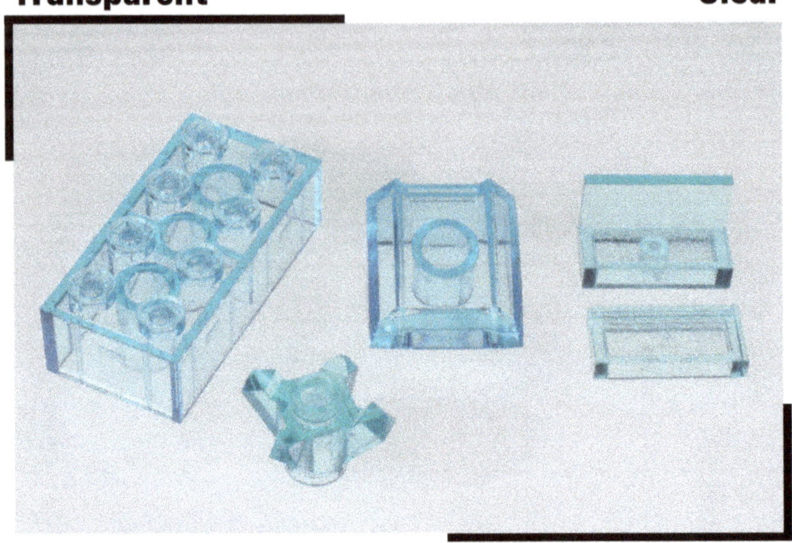

Transparent Light Blue   167

Lego	Transparent Light Blue	42
Bricklink	Trans-Light Blue	15
UUID	57111FBD-0C7F-49ED-9C48-AE854CA3B7B9	
Year	1985 **to** current	**Availability** Several

LAB				**Pantone**	304 C
sRGB	173	221	237		
CMYK	27	0	5	0	

Notes   In current color palette.

Proximity	Related Colors		Page
	Neon Orange		17
	New Dark Red		18
	Fabuland Red		19
	Light Red		20
	Medium Red		21
	Rust		22

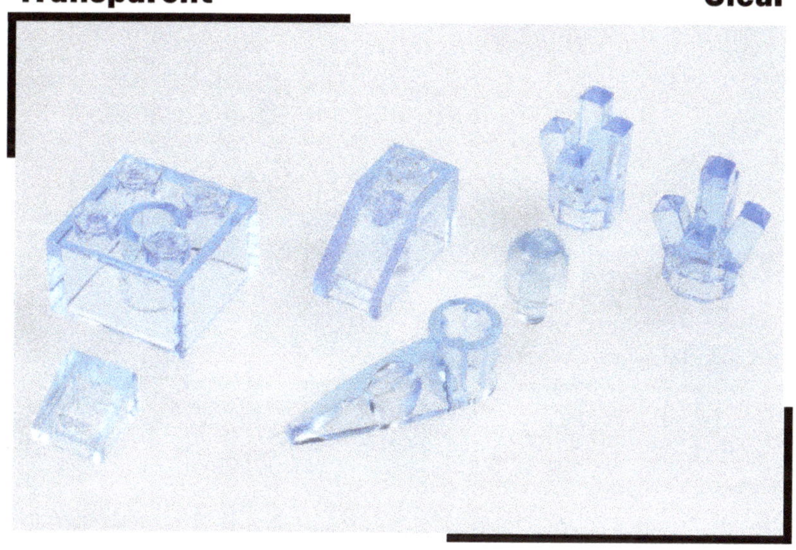

Transparent Fluorescent Blue   168

Lego	Transparent Fluorescent Blue	143
Bricklink	Trans-Medium Blue	74
UUID	1F014CA4-8DC6-4303-8CF2-F183BB53CCF7	

Year	2001	**to**	current	**Availability**	Several

				Pantone	657 C
LAB					
sRGB	208	229	255		
CMYK	20	3	0	0	

Notes   In current color palette.

Proximity	**Related Colors**		**Page**
	Neon Orange		17
	New Dark Red		18
	Fabuland Red		19
	Light Red		20
	Medium Red		21
	Rust		22

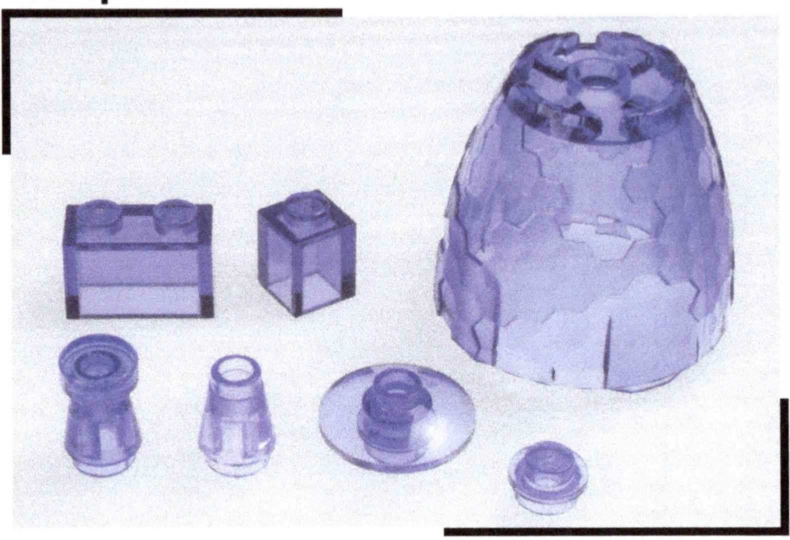

Trans. Br. Bluish Violet 169

Lego	Trans. Br. Bluish Violet	126
Bricklink	Trans-Purple	51
UUID	EB4933DC-CADE-40B2-9B01-3BEE416FC124	
Year	2000 **to** current	**Availability** Several

LAB				**Pantone**	271 C
sRGB	156	149	199		
CMYK	37	32	0	0	

Notes The full name is Transparent Bright Bluish Violet.

Proximity	**Related Colors**		**Page**
	Neon Orange		17
	New Dark Red		18
	Fabuland Red		19
	Light Red		20
	Medium Red		21
	Rust		22

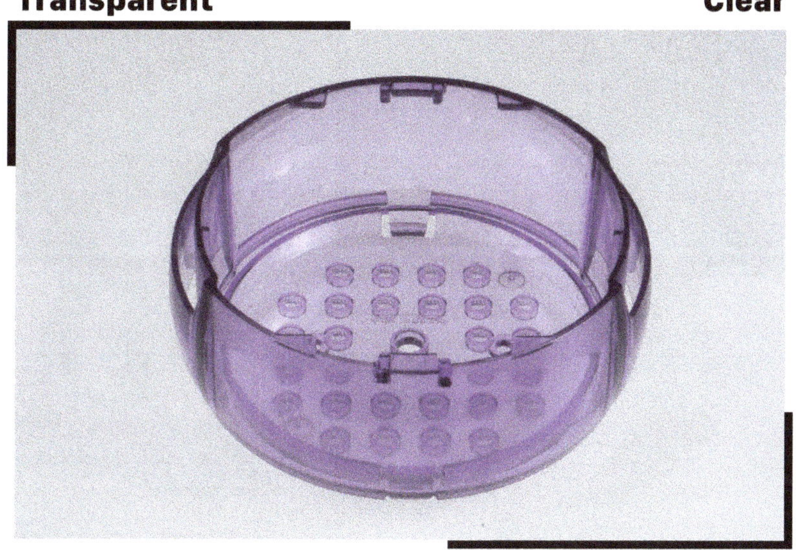

Tr. Br. Reddish Lilac   170

Lego	Tr. Br. Reddish Lilac	236
Bricklink	Trans-Medium Purple	234

UUID	BCE632CE-0974-4A97-B187-588BF4671439		
Year	2003	to	2006	Availability	Some

LAB				Pantone
sRGB	141	115	179	
CMYK				

Notes   Mainly used by Clikits parts. The full name is Transparent Bright Reddish Lilac.

Proximity	Related Colors		Page
	Neon Orange		17
	New Dark Red		18
	Fabuland Red		19
	Light Red		20
	Medium Red		21
	Rust		22

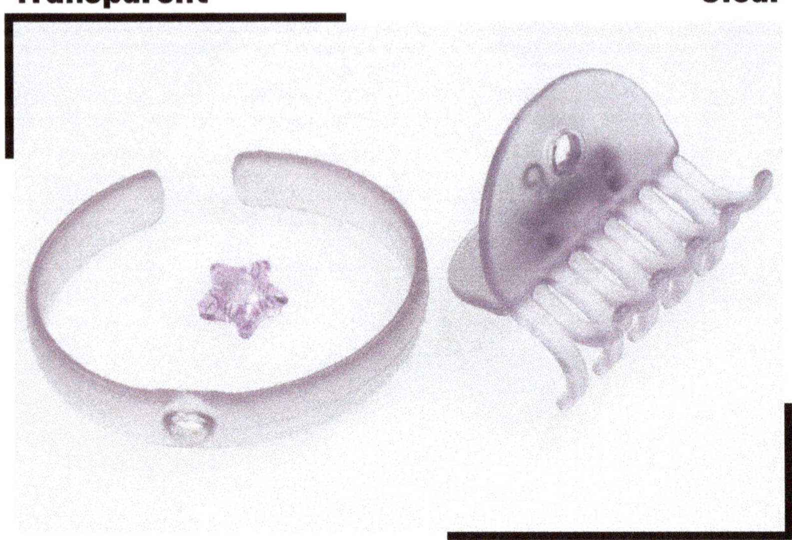

Transparent Reddish Lilac   171

Lego	Transparent Reddish Lilac	284
Bricklink	Trans-Light Purple	114
UUID	D3F615BD-4594-494A-9C08-F5A39EACEA74	

Year	2005	**to**	2005	**Availability**	Some

LAB				**Pantone**
sRGB	224	208	229	
CMYK				

Notes   Mainly used by Clikits parts.

Proximity	Related Colors		Page
	Neon Orange		17
	New Dark Red		18
	Fabuland Red		19
	Light Red		20
	Medium Red		21
	Rust		22

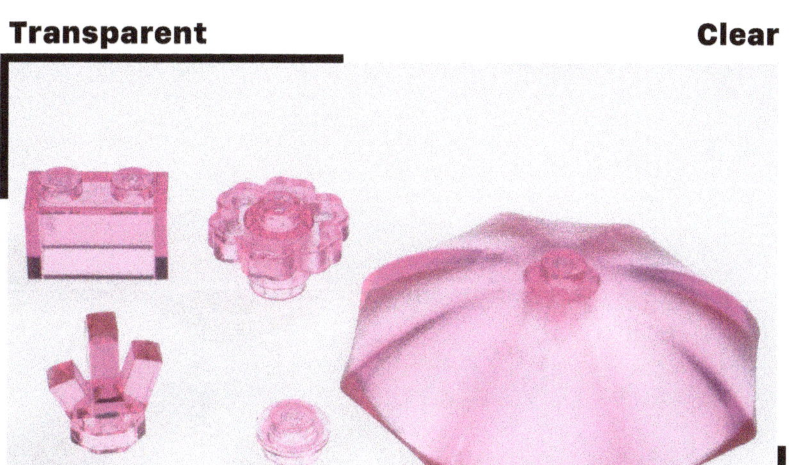

Tr. Md. Reddish Violet   172

Lego	Tr. Md. Reddish Violet	113
Bricklink	Trans-Dark Pink	50
UUID	51ED689C-A4DC-4110-BC34-2B292B5B5590	

Year	1998	**to**	current	**Availability**	Several

					Pantone	230 C
LAB						
sRGB	253	142	207			
CMYK	0	40	0	0		

Notes   The full name is Transparent Medium Reddish Violet.

Proximity	**Related Colors**		**Page**
	Neon Orange		17
	New Dark Red		18
	Fabuland Red		19
	Light Red		20
	Medium Red		21
	Rust		22

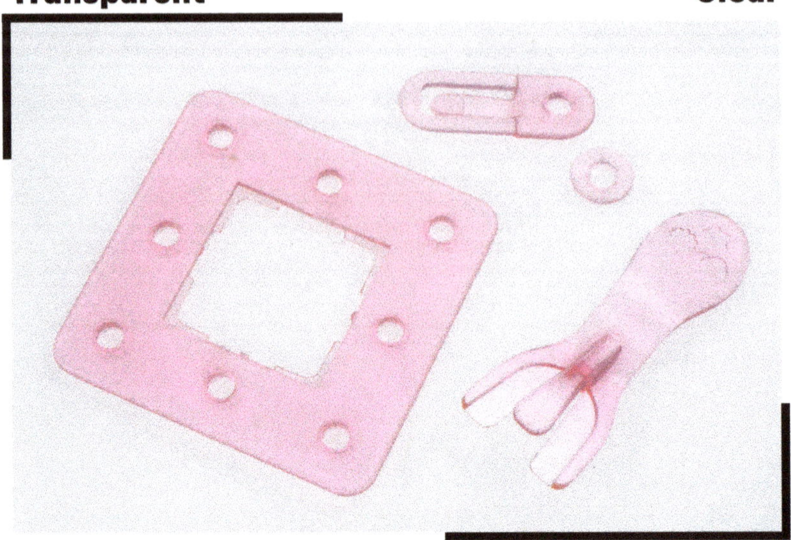

Transparent Bright Purple   173

Lego	Transparent Bright Purple	230
Bricklink	Trans-Pink	107
UUID	16F7DC77-444B-41A1-BBBE-82FC0BD45820	

Year	2003	**to**	2006	**Availability**	Some

LAB				**Pantone**	
sRGB	236	163	201		
CMYK					

Notes   Mainly used by Clikits parts.

Proximity	Related Colors		Page
	Neon Orange		17
	New Dark Red		18
	Fabuland Red		19
	Light Red		20
	Medium Red		21
	Rust		22

Transparent Fluorescent Red   174

Lego	Transparent Fluorescent Red	158
Bricklink	Trans-Dark Pink	50
UUID	6D54C591-02A5-4241-A532-A3E7A4A84CBD	
Year	2001 **to** 2002 **Availability**	Several

LAB				**Pantone**	211 C
sRGB	241	142	187		
CMYK	0	45	0	0	

Notes   Mainly used by Bionicle parts.

Proximity	Related Colors		Page
	Neon Orange		17
	New Dark Red		18
	Fabuland Red		19
	Light Red		20
	Medium Red		21
	Rust		22

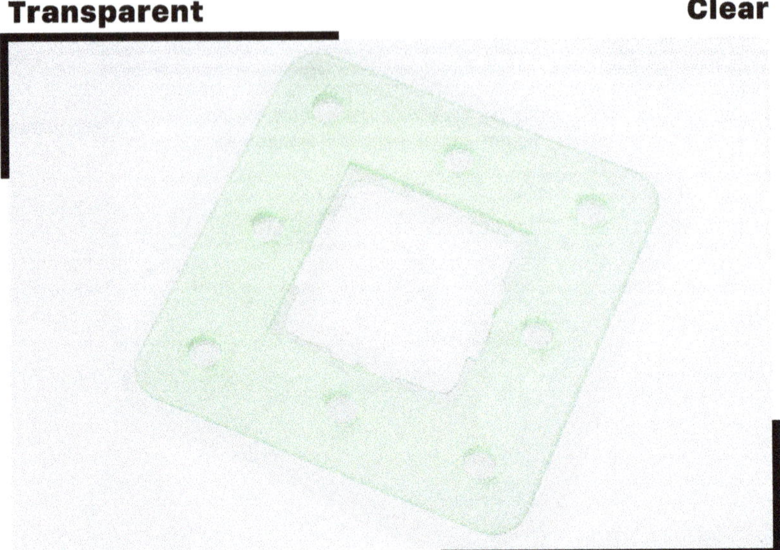

Transparent Light Green   175

Lego	Transparent Light Green	285
Bricklink	Trans-Light Green	221
UUID	2D74103A-8A5A-4853-B1BE-2F27B422ACB6	
Year	2005 **to** 2006 **Availability**	Some

LAB				**Pantone**	
sRGB	228	214	218		
CMYK					

Notes   Mainly used by Clikits parts.

Proximity **Related Colors**		**Page**
Neon Orange		17
New Dark Red		18
Fabuland Red		19
Light Red		20
Medium Red		21
Rust		22

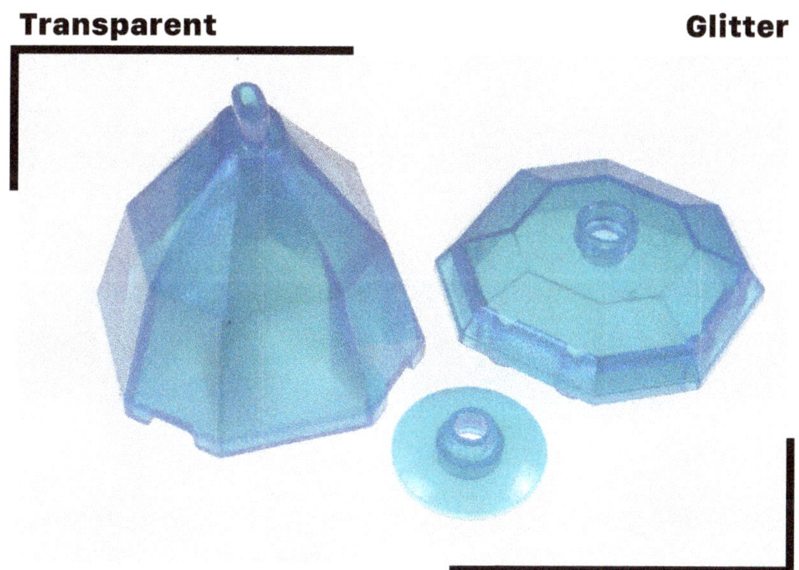

Transparent Blue Opal   184

Lego	Transparent Blue Opal	366
Bricklink	Satin Trans-Dark Blue	232
UUID	E84DF8DA-BF0D-4189-BC6A-572CA871E986	
Year	2021 **to** 2022 **Availability**	Few

LAB	**Pantone**
sRGB	
CMYK	

Notes

Proximity	**Related Colors**		**Page**
	Neon Orange		17
	New Dark Red		18
	Fabuland Red		19
	Light Red		20
	Medium Red		21
	Rust		22

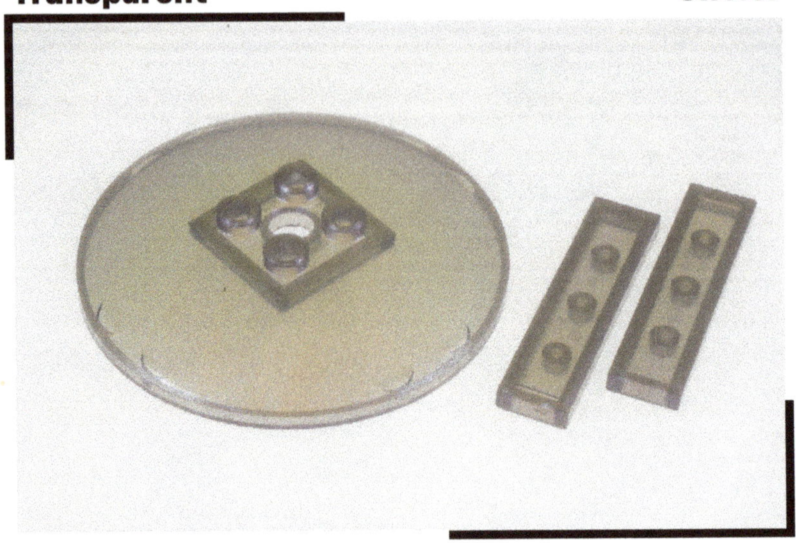

Transparent Brown Opal   185

Lego	Transparent Brown Opal	363
Bricklink	Satin Trans-Black	229
UUID	455E5C14-A664-420D-B3A5-763C1A92F37E	
Year	2020 **to** 2021 **Availability**	Few

LAB   **Pantone**

sRGB

CMYK

Notes

Proximity **Related Colors**		**Page**
Neon Orange		17
New Dark Red		18
Fabuland Red		19
Light Red		20
Medium Red		21
Rust		22

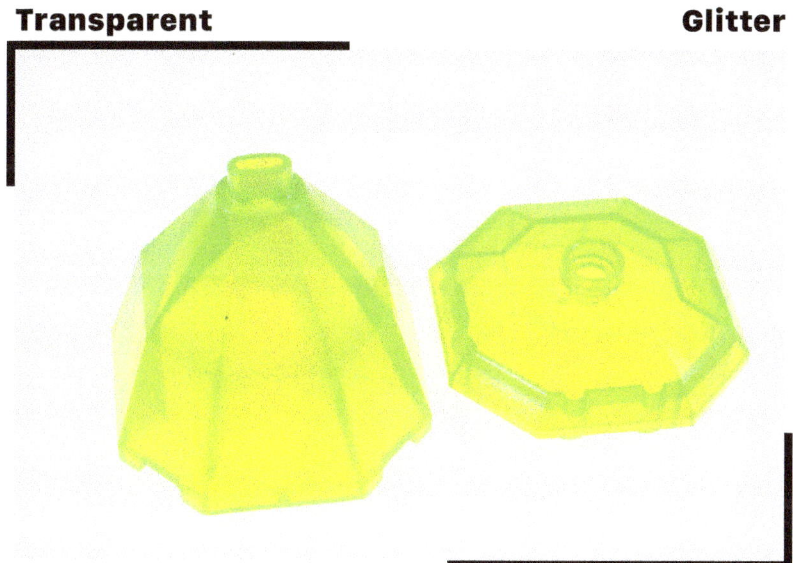

Transparent Green Opal   186

Lego	Transparent Green Opal	367
Bricklink	Satin Trans-Bright Green	233
UUID	9B7CDCA1-F7E7-43E3-B247-97A1195AB218	

Year	2021	**to**	2022	**Availability**	Few

LAB		**Pantone**	
sRGB			
CMYK			

Notes

Proximity	**Related Colors**		**Page**
	Neon Orange		17
	New Dark Red		18
	Fabuland Red		19
	Light Red		20
	Medium Red		21
	Rust		22

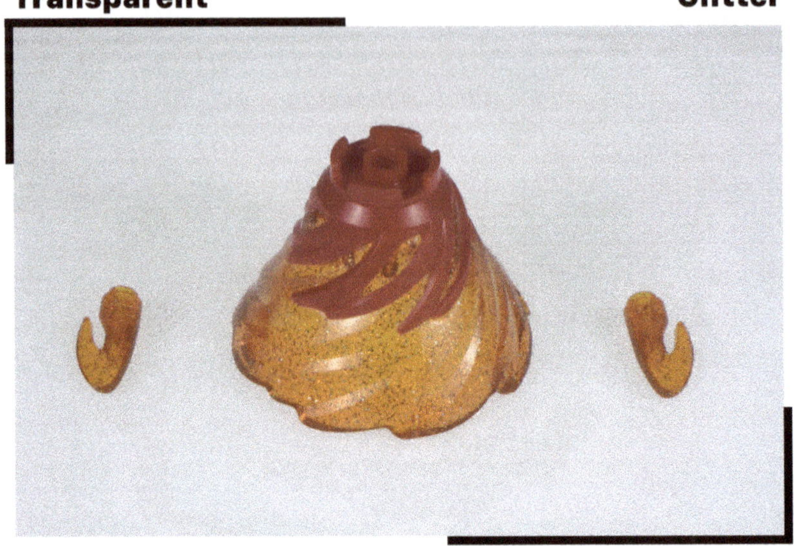

Trans. Bright Orange w. Glitter   176

Lego	Trans. Bright Orange w. Glitter	341
Bricklink	Glitter Trans-Orange	222
UUID	7AC45D43-0686-48D5-9029-05A7C2C02B9E	
Year	2020 **to** 2020	**Availability** Few

				Pantone
LAB				
sRGB	240	143	28	
CMYK	3	52	100	0

Notes	The full name is Transparent Bright Orange with Glitter.

Proximity	**Related Colors**		**Page**
	Neon Orange		17
	New Dark Red		18
	Fabuland Red		19
	Light Red		20
	Medium Red		21
	Rust		22

Trans. Bright Green w. Glitter   177

Lego	Trans. Bright Green w. Glitter	351
Bricklink		
UUID	3B624553-D43C-471C-80F0-7E4FA843D555	
Year	2020 **to** current **Availability**	Rare

LAB				**Pantone**
sRGB	86	230	70	
CMYK				

Notes   The full name is Transparent Bright Green with Glitter.

Proximity	**Related Colors**		**Page**
	Neon Orange		17
	New Dark Red		18
	Fabuland Red		19
	Light Red		20
	Medium Red		21
	Rust		22

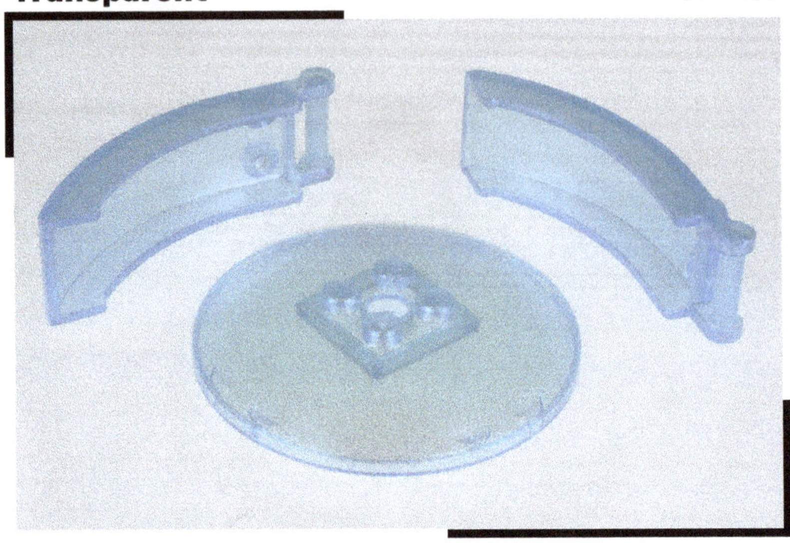

Transparent Blue Opal   178

Lego	Transparent Blue Opal	362
Bricklink	Satin Trans-Light Blue	223
UUID	199665B2-D5DD-4F22-9C92-CDCB3ED20F8E	
Year	2020 **to** current	**Availability** Some

LAB				**Pantone**
sRGB	174	233	239	
CMYK				

Notes   Has a shimmer and sparkles.

Proximity	**Related Colors**		**Page**
	Neon Orange		17
	New Dark Red		18
	Fabuland Red		19
	Light Red		20
	Medium Red		21
	Rust		22

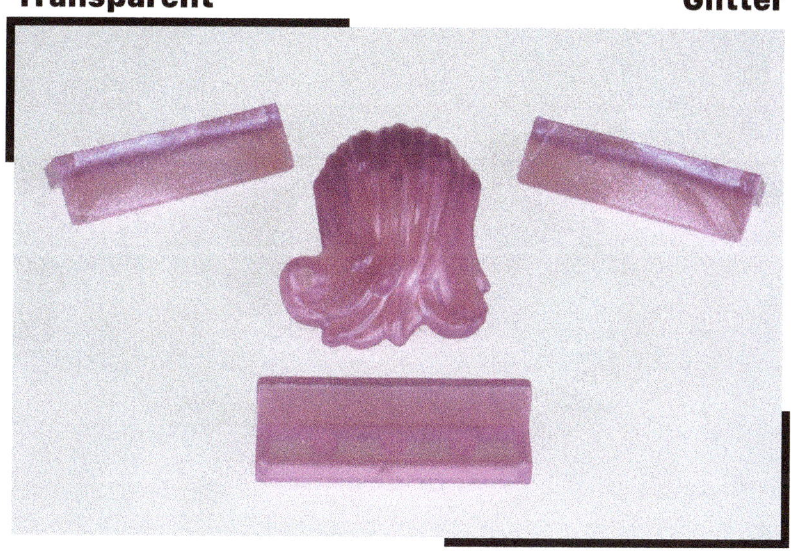

Trans. M. Red. Violet w. Opal.   183

Lego	Trans. M. Red. Violet w. Opal.	364
Bricklink	Satin Trans-Dark Pink	224
UUID	DE0A7335-681C-43E5-806F-D3FFBD47267B	
Year	2020 **to** current **Availability**	Few

LAB				**Pantone**
sRGB	223	102	149	
CMYK				

Notes   The full name is Transparent Medium Reddish Violet with Opalescence.

Proximity	**Related Colors**		**Page**
	Neon Orange		17
	New Dark Red		18
	Fabuland Red		19
	Light Red		20
	Medium Red		21
	Rust		22

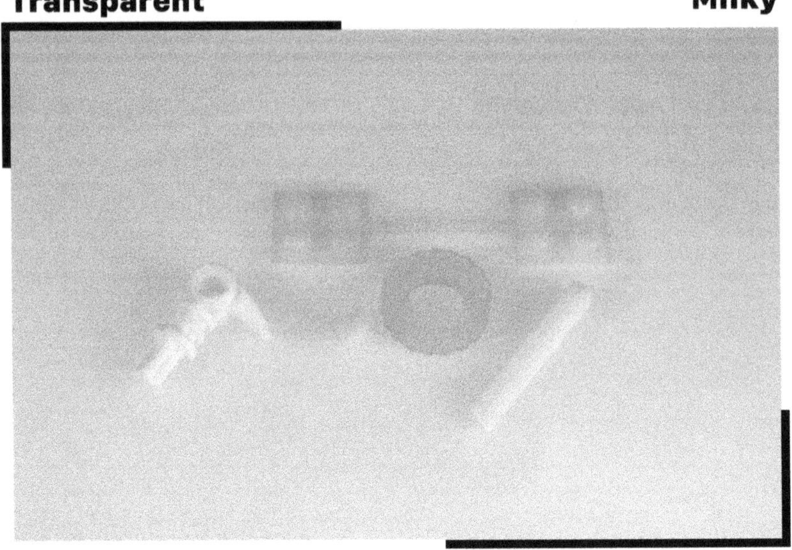

Nature   179

Lego	Nature	20
Bricklink	Milky White	60
UUID	B5EF6C21-2767-412B-AFB0-42200CA9ABD3	
Year	1963 **to** 2008	**Availability** Some

LAB	68	-1	8	**Pantone**
sRGB	168	165	150	
CMYK				

Notes   Typically pure ABS.

Proximity	Related Colors		Page
6.34	Grey		119
9.08	Light Grey		117
9.08	Medium Stone Grey		122
13.59	Light Stone Grey		120
18.81	Sand Yellow		47
19.94	Sand Green		68

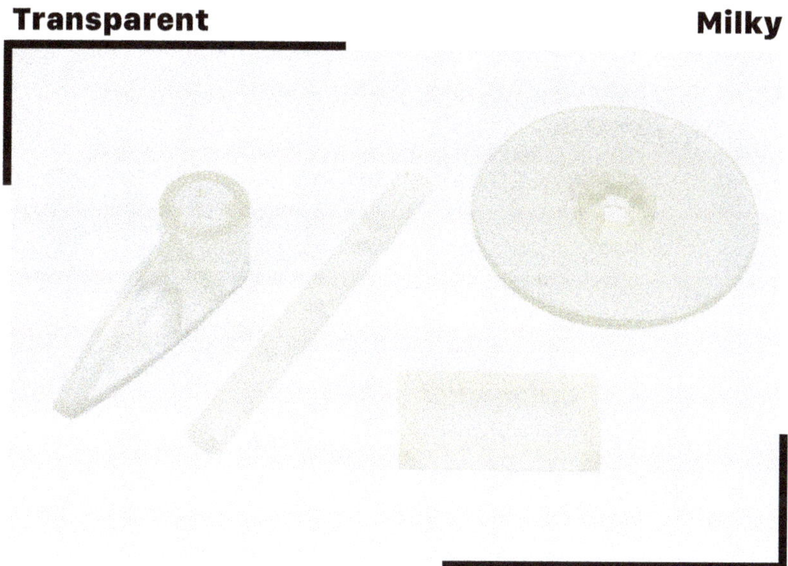

Phosphorescent Green   180

Lego	Phosphorescent Green				294
Bricklink	Glow In Dark Trans				118
UUID	481E242B-E817-4FEE-95B4-DC8497C05EEC				
Year	2005	**to**	2011	**Availability**	Some

LAB	51	-3	9	**Pantone**	
sRGB	121	122	102		
CMYK					

Notes   Replaced Phosphorescent White 50 starting in 2005, replaced by White Glow 329 in 2012.

Proximity	Related Colors		Page
9.09	Dark Army Green		57
10.21	Dark Grey		118
13.62	Dark Stone Grey		121
14.89	Sand Yellow		47
15.48	Grey		119
15.51	Sand Green		68

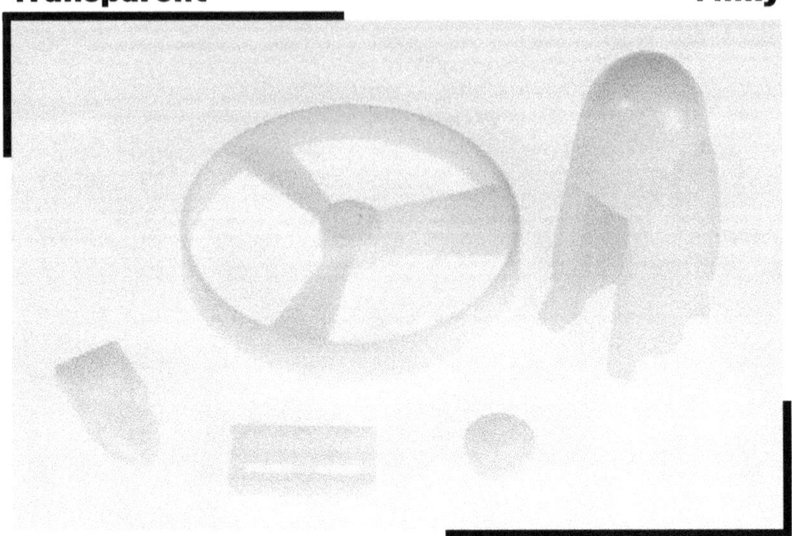

Phosphorescent White   181

Lego	Phosphorescent White	50
Bricklink	Glow In Dark Opaque	46
UUID	7AF7C690-5ABE-4087-9264-D926BEB32CFE	

Year	1990	to	2006	Availability	Some

				Pantone	
LAB	67	-3	7	**Pantone**	427 C
sRGB	163	164	149		
CMYK	7	7	12	0	

Notes   Replaced by Phosphorescent Green 294 starting in 2005.

Proximity	Related Colors		Page
5.01	Grey		119
8.38	Medium Stone Grey		122
8.62	Light Grey		117
13.92	Light Stone Grey		120
18.29	Sand Green		68
19.38	Sand Yellow		47

White Glow   182

Lego	White Glow	329
Bricklink	Glow in Dark White	159

UUID	69B78D5F-9AD8-4D8B-BCBA-78AEB106B026

Year	2012	**to**	current	**Availability**	Some

LAB	89	-2	6	**Pantone**	
sRGB	224	226	212		
CMYK					

Notes	Replaced Phosphorescent Green 294 in 2012.

Proximity	Related Colors		Page
5.68	White		116
12.05	Light Stone Grey		120
13.07	Aqua		73
16.23	Light Grey		117
19.39	Light Bluish Violet		93
23.13	Light Blue		83

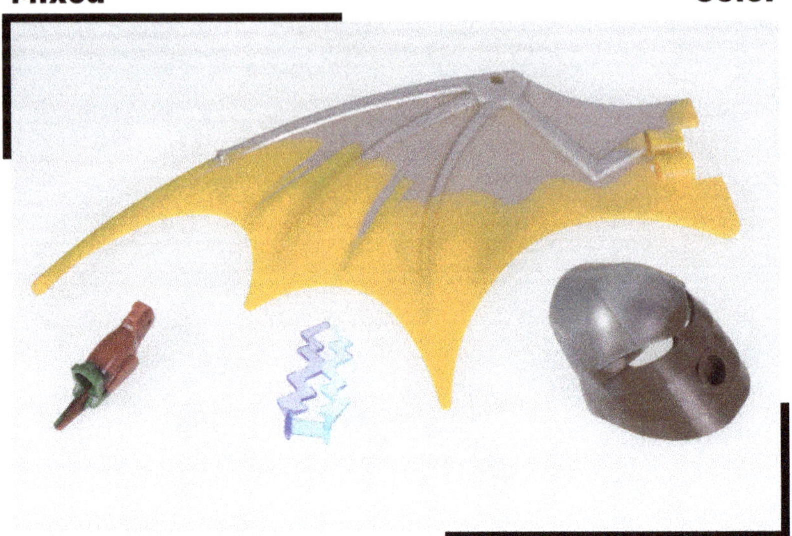

Multicombination   188

Lego	30
Bricklink	
UUID	7E043105-4963-4D92-B61B-6B5694047923
Year	? **to** current **Availability** Rare

LAB			**Pantone**	
sRGB	255	255	255	
CMYK				

Notes   Parts that have more than one plastic color in them.

Proximity	**Related Colors**		**Page**
	Neon Orange		17
	New Dark Red		18
	Fabuland Red		19
	Light Red		20
	Medium Red		21
	Rust		22

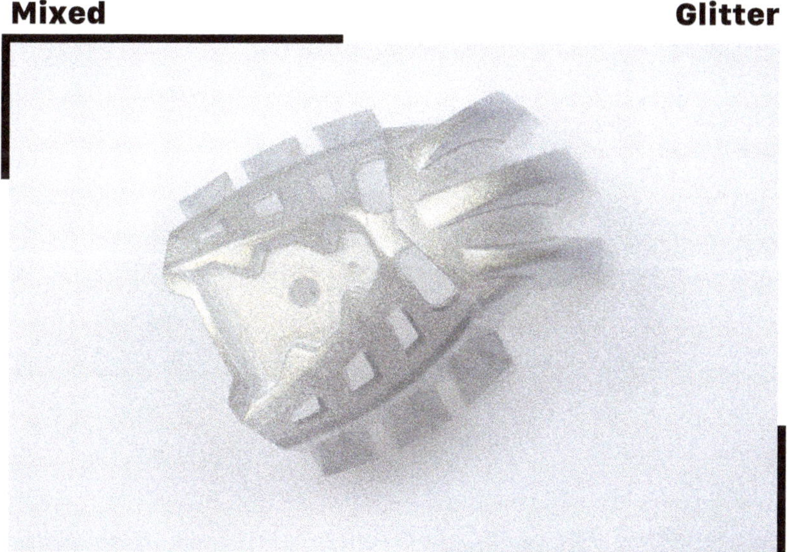

Glitter Trans-Clear   189

Lego					
Bricklink	Glitter Trans-Clear				101
UUID	5301AEC2-DE50-48E1-840A-4EB14AA29B2A				
Year	2003	**to**	2003	**Availability**	Some

LAB				**Pantone**	
sRGB	255	255	255		
CMYK					

Notes   Only used by the Avohkii mask and not listed on Bricklink.

Proximity	**Related Colors**		**Page**
	Neon Orange		17
	New Dark Red		18
	Fabuland Red		19
	Light Red		20
	Medium Red		21
	Rust		22

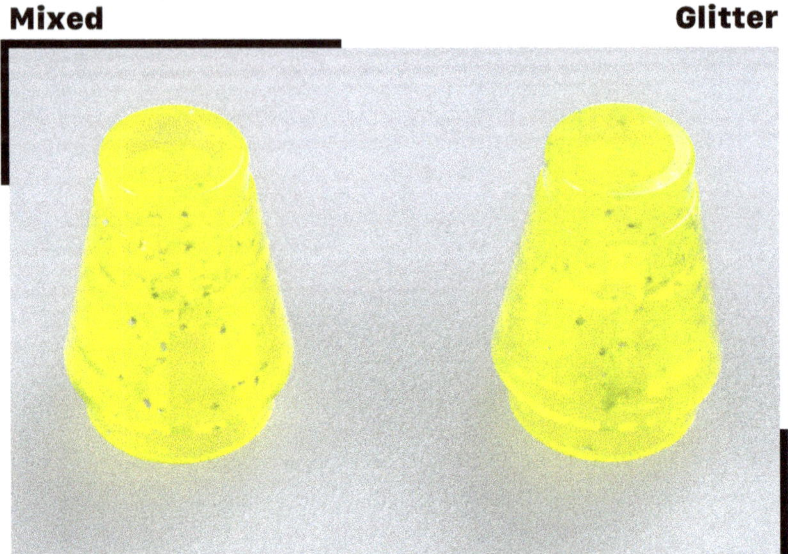

Tr. Fl. Green with Glitter   190

Lego	Tr. Fl. Green with Glitter	339
Bricklink	Glitter Trans-Neon Green	163
UUID	BA89E2B9-09D0-4BBB-8E30-8E930E9798C3	

Year	2015	**to**	current	**Availability**	Few

LAB			**Pantone**	
sRGB	255	255	255	
CMYK				

Notes The full name is Transparent Fluorescent Green with Glitter

Proximity **Related Colors**		**Page**
Neon Orange		17
New Dark Red		18
Fabuland Red		19
Light Red		20
Medium Red		21
Rust		22

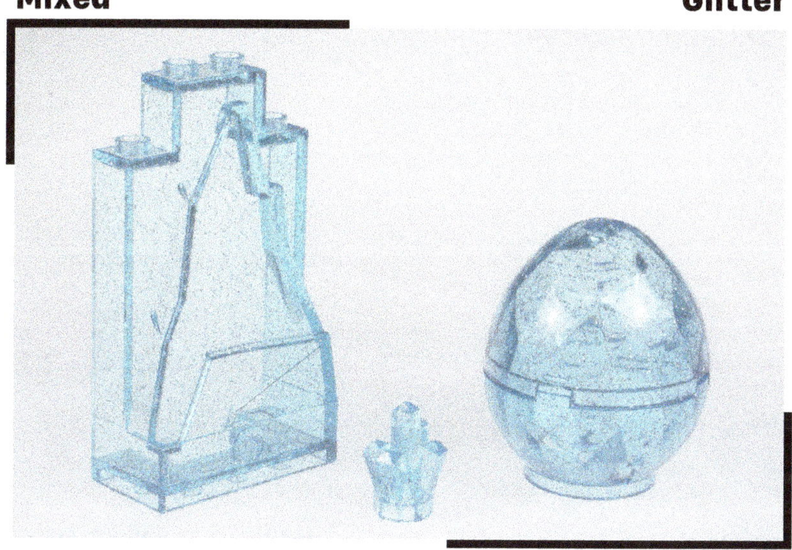

Tr. Li. Blue with Glitter   191

Lego	Tr. Li. Blue with Glitter	302
Bricklink	Glitter Trans-Light Blue	162
UUID	D3E44934-548F-4755-A4BC-199EBD75DA6C	

Year	2015	**to**	2021	**Availability**	Some

LAB				**Pantone**	
sRGB	255	255	255		
CMYK					

Notes   The full name is Transparent Light Blue with Glitter.

Proximity	**Related Colors**		**Page**
	Neon Orange		17
	New Dark Red		18
	Fabuland Red		19
	Light Red		20
	Medium Red		21
	Rust		22

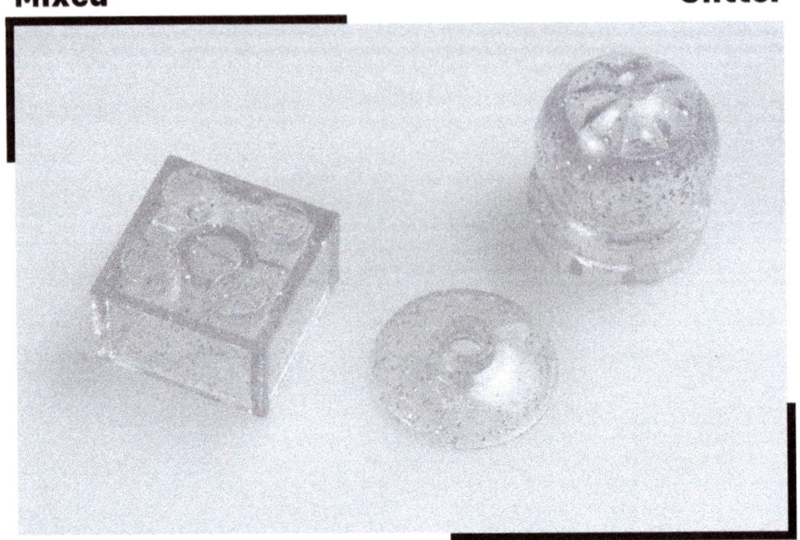

Transparent with Glitter 192

Lego	Transparent with Glitter				117
Bricklink	Glitter Trans-Clear				101
UUID	B64D5753-C98C-4D1C-AACD-86A90CC1C096				
Year	1999	**to**	2007	**Availability**	Some

LAB				**Pantone**
sRGB	247	247	247	
CMYK				

Notes No 2x4 brick available.

Proximity	**Related Colors**		**Page**
	Neon Orange		17
	New Dark Red		18
	Fabuland Red		19
	Light Red		20
	Medium Red		21
	Rust		22

Nature with Glitter   **193**

Lego	Nature with Glitter				122
Bricklink					
UUID	D9B565BE-F56C-42A1-92B2-8FE4BE67C850				
Year	1999	**to**	2005	**Availability**	Rare

				Pantone	
LAB					
sRGB	254	203	152		
CMYK					

Notes   The DUPLO spider web.

Proximity	**Related Colors**		**Page**
	Neon Orange		17
	New Dark Red		18
	Fabuland Red		19
	Light Red		20
	Medium Red		21
	Rust		22

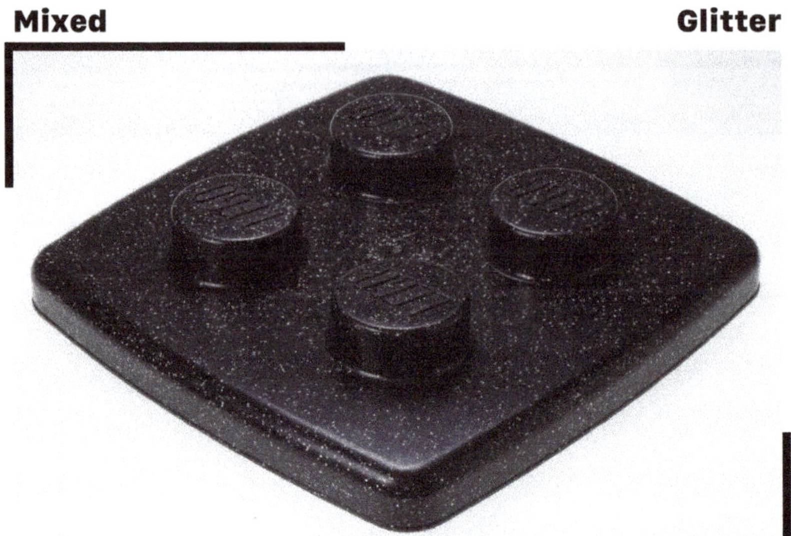

Black Glitter   194

Lego	Black Glitter				132
Bricklink					
UUID	18C9EF89-BC79-4313-9249-3AF8BE5235D7				
Year	2000	**to**	2000	**Availability**	Rare

LAB	15	0	0	**Pantone**	Hexachro
sRGB	39	39	38		
CMYK					

Notes　　Only used for a bucket.

Proximity	Related Colors		Page
10.25	Black		123
14.86	Dark Brown		27
15.30	Ultra-Dark Blue		97
15.30	Reddish Lilac		103
15.30	Light Pink		106
22.99	Earth Green		72

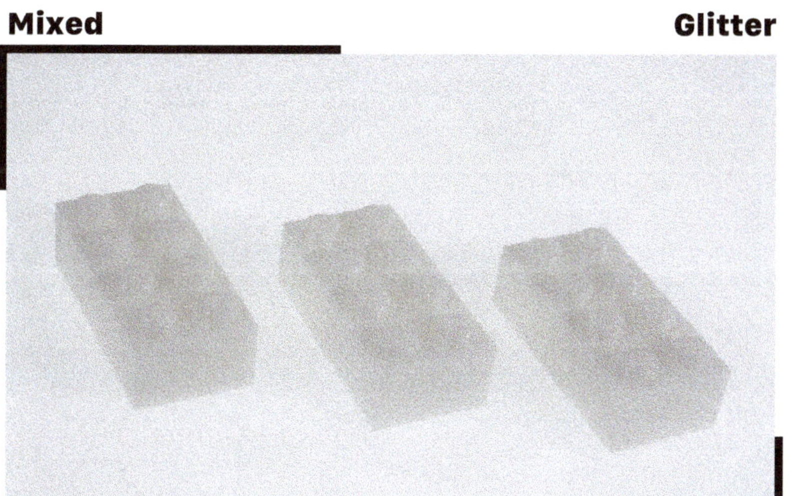

Allianz Arena   195

Lego

Bricklink

UUID	8E15611F-D154-4F0F-A766-8CEA8E6BEEF7				
Year	?	**to** current		**Availability**	Rare

				Pantone	428 C
LAB	79	-2	-1		
sRGB	192	197	196		
CMYK	10	4	4	14	

Notes   This slightly sparkly brick is available from LEGOLAND Germany.

Proximity	Related Colors		Page
0.73	Light Stone Grey		120
8.82	Light Grey		117
10.60	Light Bluish Violet		93
12.27	Medium Stone Grey		122
14.68	Grey		119
15.01	Light Blue		83

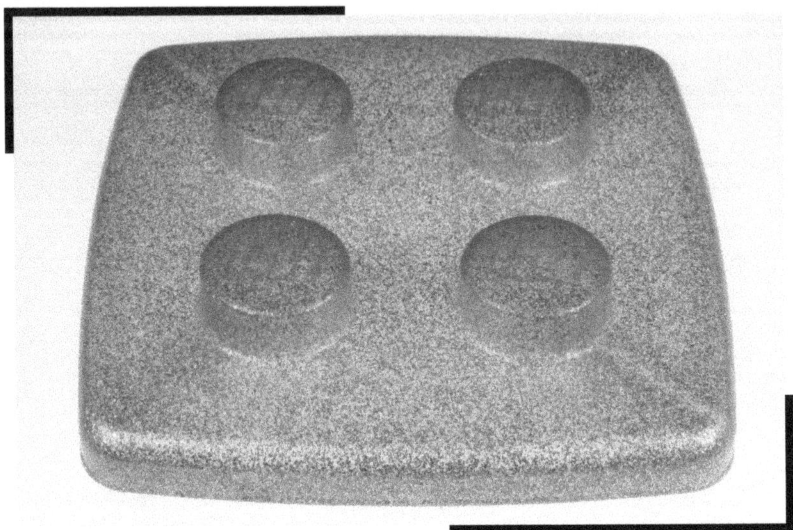

Max Glitter   196

Lego

Bricklink

UUID	D3159918-BE35-4B06-8DB1-3D15D3810E39				
Year	1998	**to**	1998	**Availability**	Rare

LAB	53	-1	-1	**Pantone**	Cool Gray
sRGB	125	128	129		
CMYK	56	46	44	10	

Notes   Only used for bucket lids.

Proximity	Related Colors		Page
11.00	Dark Stone Grey		121
12.12	Grey		119
13.17	Sand Violet		104
13.50	Medium Stone Grey		122
13.83	Sand Blue		88
14.44	Dark Grey		118

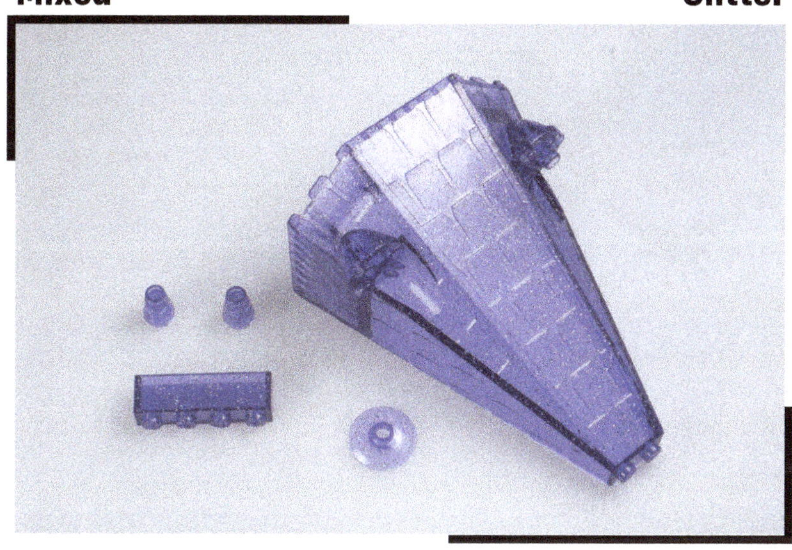

Tr. Bl. Violet (Glitter)   197

Lego	Tr. Bl. Violet (Glitter)				129
Bricklink	Glitter Trans-Purple				102
UUID	DD8E03E3-9D09-4D69-A84E-4DA55951A826				
Year	2000	**to**	current	**Availability**	Few

LAB	41	14	-39	**Pantone**	2726 C
sRGB	79	100	162		
CMYK	81	70	0	0	

Notes   The full name is Transparent Bluish Violet (Glitter).

Proximity	Related Colors		Page
6.50	Lilac		94
10.70	Medium Bluish Violet		95
14.77	Bright Lilac		98
16.68	Royal Blue		90
17.32	Medium Lilac		99
18.76	Dark Royal Blue		92

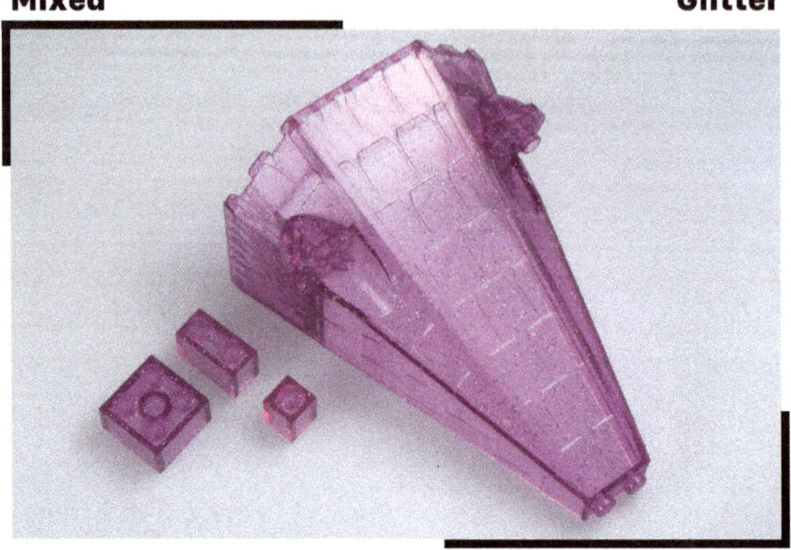

Tr. Pink Glitter   198

Lego	Tr. Pink Glitter				114
Bricklink	Glitter Trans-Dark Pink				100
UUID	935E4C9E-BFE1-465C-AEE0-B47ED645BD5D				
Year	1999	**to**	2021	**Availability**	Some

LAB	59	47	-14	**Pantone**	674 C
sRGB	197	110	171		
CMYK	16	83	0	0	

Notes The full name is Transparent Pink Glitter /
Transparent Medium Reddish Violet Glitter/
Transparent Medium Reddish Violet Glitter

Proximity	Related Colors		Page
7.06	Bright Purple		109
7.06	Medium Reddish Violet		110
17.21	Flamingo Pink		111
20.03	Bright Reddish Lilac		105
22.08	Light Purple		107
23.33	Medium Lavender		101

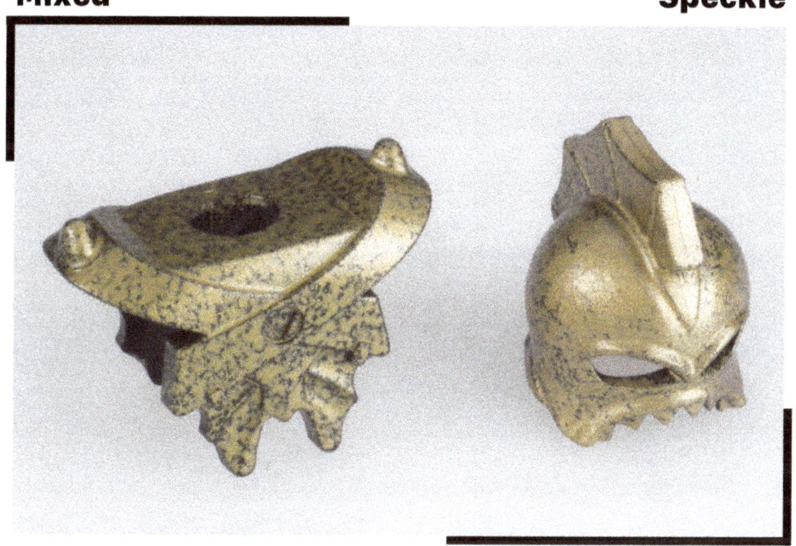

Speckle Black-Gold   199

Lego					
Bricklink	Speckle Black-Gold				151
UUID	E194960D-C141-4EE6-8A9C-10C91EC0D9F6				
Year	2010	**to**	2011	**Availability**	Few

LAB	40	1	22	**Pantone**
sRGB	105	90	57	
CMYK				

Notes   Mainly used for armory.

Proximity	Related Colors		Page
9.69	Dark Army Green		57
14.11	Brown		34
15.19	Medium Brown		32
15.30	Dark Grey		118
16.20	Olive Green		55
16.77	Sand Yellow		47

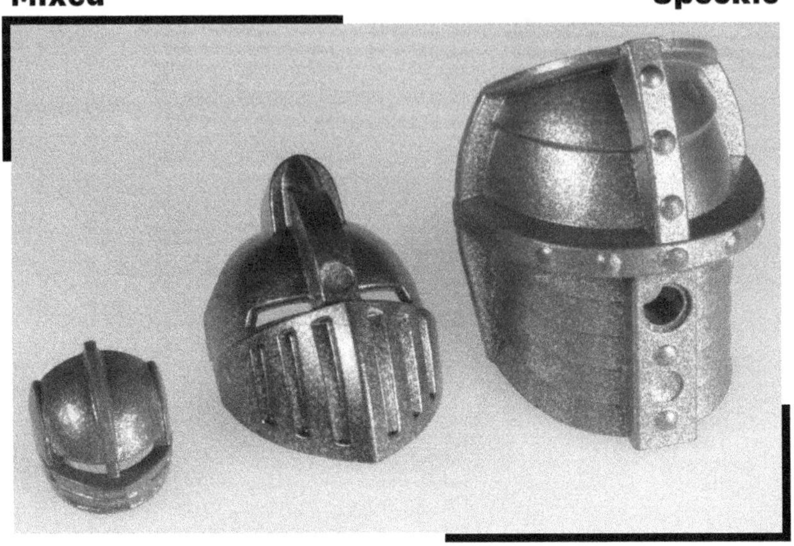

Cool Silver, Diffuse   200

Lego	Cool Silver, Diffuse	304
Bricklink	Speckle Black-Silver	117
UUID	EE900ABC-2DC6-4727-BE99-451C79D76443	

Year	2006	**to**	2006	**Availability**	Few

LAB	35	-0	1	**Pantone**	
sRGB	83	83	81		
CMYK					

Notes	Mainly used for armory. Also known as Speckle DBGray-Silver.

Proximity	**Related Colors**		**Page**
7.51	Dark Stone Grey		121
8.07	Dark Grey		118
19.55	Dark Brown		27
20.32	Sand Violet		104
20.85	Dark Army Green		57
22.39	Medium Brown		32

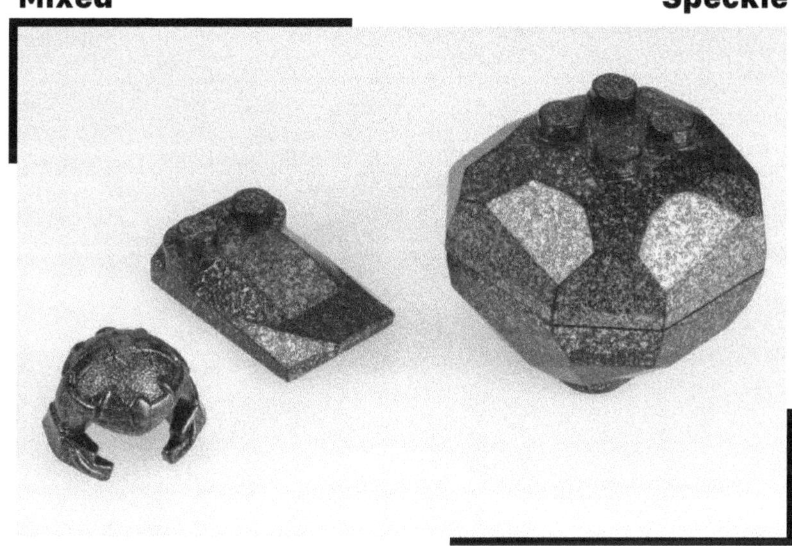

Cool Silver, Diffuse   **201**

Lego	Cool Silver, Diffuse	304
Bricklink	Speckle Black-Silver	111
UUID	53E449B7-7C3A-4A35-9A07-20A087FCEAED	

Year	2006	**to**	2006	**Availability**	Some

				Pantone
LAB	30	-0	-0	
sRGB	70	71	71	
CMYK				

Notes   Mainly used for armory. Also known as Speckle DBGray-Silver.

Proximity	Related Colors		Page
12.37	Dark Stone Grey		121
13.07	Dark Grey		118
16.84	Dark Brown		27
23.32	Earth Green		72
23.71	Medium Brown		32
23.92	Sand Violet		104

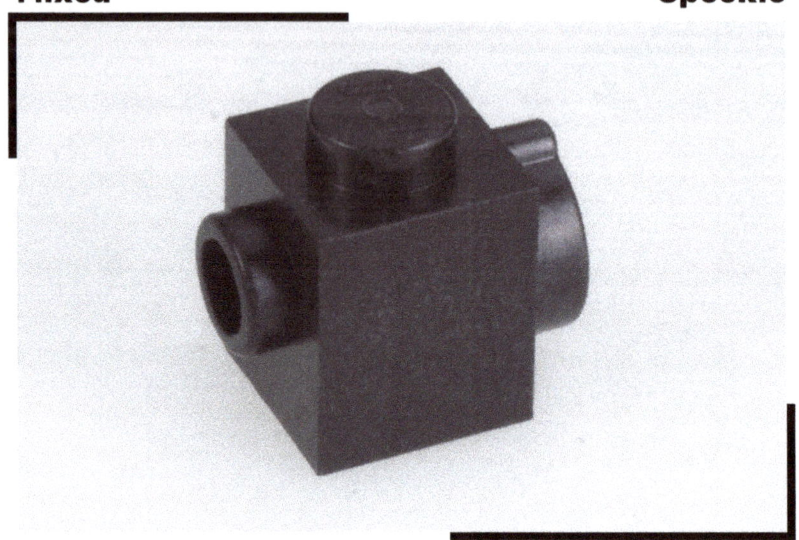

Conductive Black   202

Lego	Conductive Black	342

Bricklink

UUID   634D7EEE-5C57-4B21-ABE7-1CA3E3043001

Year	2015	**to**	2016	**Availability**	Rare

				Pantone
LAB	17	0	-0	
sRGB	42	42	43	
CMYK				

Notes   Used by one brick only.

Proximity	Related Colors		Page
11.70	Black		123
14.66	Dark Brown		27
16.91	Ultra-Dark Blue		97
16.91	Reddish Lilac		103
16.91	Light Pink		106
22.94	Earth Green		72

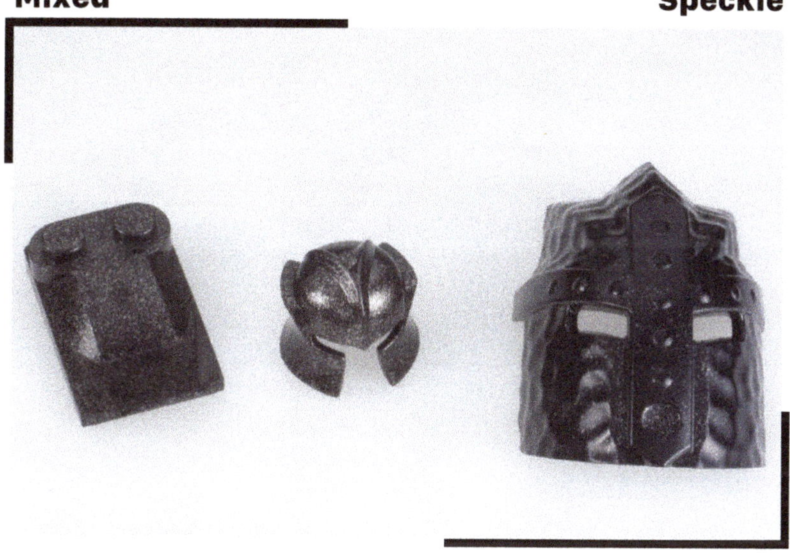

Copper, Diffuse   203

Lego	Copper, Diffuse				306
Bricklink	Speckle Black-Copper				116
UUID	07459C30-4E90-40F2-A15A-0AD36189083B				
Year	2006	**to**	2006	**Availability**	Few

LAB	14	1	-0	**Pantone**	
sRGB	37	36	37		
CMYK					

Notes   Mainly used for armory.

Proximity	Related Colors		Page
9.17	Black		123
14.31	Ultra-Dark Blue		97
14.31	Reddish Lilac		103
14.31	Light Pink		106
15.33	Dark Brown		27
23.66	Earth Green		72

113 Solid Grayscale

Shiny Chrome